EDGE OF THE NATIONAL FOREST

A social history of the village and hamlets of Yoxall

Shirley Fisher

The Magic Attic

The Magic Attic

First published in Great Britain in 2017 by

The Magic Attic
Sharpe's Pottery Museum
West Street
Swadlincote
Derbyshire
DE11 9DG

Cover design by Marvin Harding

A CIP catalogue record for this book is available from the British Library.

ISBN 978-0-9567861-7-3

Contents

Abbreviations

FACHRS   Family and Community Historical Research Society
LRO   Lichfield Record Office
NA   National Archives
RHS   Ridware History Society
SCC   Staffordshire County Council
SHC   *Staffordshire Historical Collections*
SRO   Staffordshire Record Office
SFWI   Staffordshire Federation of Women's Institutes
VCH   *Victoria County History*
WLHC   Walsall Local History Centre
WSL   William Salt Library

Author's Note

I was born in Burton upon Trent and for the last thirty two years have lived in Yoxall. Shortly after I arrived a course studying the history of the village took place, run by the Adult Education Department of Keele University. Denis Stuart, local historian and senior lecturer in history for the department was tutor and edited the resulting publication, *A Social History of Yoxall in the Sixteenth and Seventeenth Centuries*.

The knowledge and enthusiasm of Denis Stuart inspired in me the desire to continue where he had left off with the history of Yoxall. This led to several years of study, from which I obtained a BA Hons Degree in History with the Open University. While studying for my degree I also obtained Keele University's Certificate in Local History. Among the courses taken for my Open University degree was DA301 Studying Family and Community History: 19th and 20th centuries. The course led to the forming of the Family and Community Historical Research Society, of which I became a founder member, and have taken part in several of their projects. The society have kindly acknowledged that it was founded as a result of my suggestion.

Since I arrived in Yoxall the National Forest was formed, and as I return northward into Yoxall along the A515 I pass the sign which reminds me that I now live in the National Forest, and prompted the title for my book.

Denis Stuart continued to pursue his interests in history following his retirement. He attained a PhD but sadly did not live to attend his ceremony. It is thanks to his enthusiasm and support both during and after my time with Keele University, that I have now become an author of local history.

This book is dedicated to the memory of the late Dr Denis Stuart.

Shirley Fisher

Acknowledgments

I am particularly indebted to the unpublished work of Dr Gerald Armson, the last of a line of Armson doctors in the village, whose interest in Yoxall extended beyond the care of his many patients and his pivotal role within the community, to the history of the village. He researched and wrote about the past and recorded many events from his own lifetime. My thanks to his son Simon Armson who allowed me access to the unpublished text. Thanks also to Elisabeth Macfarlane, daughter of Dr Gerald and author of *120 Years a Village Doctor: the memoirs of Dr Gerald Armson*, for supplying me with photographs. On a visit to England from Australia, where she now lives, she took the time to bring the images to me on an external drive in order to preserve the quality of the images.

Special thanks also to Sarah Hodgkiss for proofreading my work, updating my software and helping me to get through the technicalities. Also to Jim and Jane Hodgkiss, who have followed the progress of my writing from start to finish and have been supportive throughout, and to Marvin Harding for the cover design.

Thanks also to Betty Housecroft for her help in transcribing early 18th century probate documents, Ray Thorpe for information on the Town Lands Trust and St Francis of Sales Catholic Church, Marny Francis, for information on Norman's Store, Elizabeth Harvey for information on Page's Shop, Hadley Street, Sarah Orson for access to information on Churchyard Cottage, Shamim Khan for information regarding Dr Arif Khan, Elizabeth Guy for information on the mill at Woodmill, and everyone who gave me access to their family archives, and allowed me to use their photographs, and the many who over the years gave me snippets of information which I was able to follow up. Photographs not acknowledged are in the public domain.

Special thanks to all at The Magic Attic, also the staff at Burton Family and History Centre, Lichfield Record Office, Staffordshire Record Office, William Salt Library, Lichfield Cathedral Library, Walsall Local History Centre and the University of Illinois.

Thank you to everyone who has helped me in any way over my years of research, this book would not be what it is without you.

Introduction

This study is the result of examining many sources, which linked together provide an insight into a bygone Yoxall community. Sources include probate documents held by Lichfield Record Office. Wills and inventories give a static picture of the testators, who in the majority of cases, evidenced by the gap between the date of will and date of probate, were near to death when making their wills. What they left could be remnants of an estate which had passed to a younger generation. For the wealthy this could be a means of escaping death duty, but for many testators who were too old or sick to work, their means of providing a living, the tools of their trade etc., had passed to those who could use them. Probate documents are therefore an unreliable source of assessing wealth, but despite their limitations, often provide a rich source of information, such as the testators' intentions regarding the distribution of their bequests and any provisos regarding inheritance. Appraisers of the often accompanying inventories described and valued the goods and chattels, giving an insight into testators' lifestyles. The last surviving inventory in the collection of Yoxall probate documents held in Lichfield was appraised in 1768.

In 1538 Thomas Cromwell created a mandate instructing that each parish was to purchase a coffer, the parson to have one key and a churchwarden another and that each baptism, marriage and burial was to be registered weekly by the minister with the churchwarden acting as witness, and the records to be kept in the chest. Often these registers were loose sheets and the survival rate is not high. An Order of Elizabeth I in 1598 required that all the loose leaf registers would be transcribed into parchment books, especially those recorded since her accession. This led to the records of many parishes surviving from 1558. Under the Order both churchwardens were to witness the entries which would be read every Sunday. Each parish was required to send a copy of the year's entries to the diocesan bishop each Easter. These are known as Bishop's Transcripts. The early registers usually have three sections, for the baptisms, marriages and burials, though sometimes they are mixed together in chronological order. Most of the early entries are single lines of brief information. The first surviving parish register in Yoxall dates from 1645 and includes baptisms and marriages. The earliest burial register dates from 1678. Occasionally more information was recorded but this was rarely so in Yoxall, additional information generally only being added when required by legislation.

During the 19th century many sources were created or increased in number, and while censuses were taken at least as far back as Domesday, the decennial population censuses from 1801 are an invaluable source of population numbers. From 1841 censuses included information regarding household members. The 1841 census does not include the relationship of those in the household to the head, and lists place of birth as either in or out of the county they were enumerated in, with exceptions such as Scotland, Ireland and other countries being listed. Occupations of heads of households were included, but otherwise the recording of occupations was sporadic, and ages were often rounded up to the nearest five year period. It is for these reasons that the censuses from 1851, which offer more information, are of greater use in studies of social history, although they remained unreliable prior to 1911 when householders first filled in the forms. Earlier enumerators recorded what they heard, or thought they heard. Often a person's place of birth differs over the censuses and in some cases this could be attributed to householders having no idea where non family members were born, or mistakenly a previous place of residence may have been given. There are also often discrepancies regarding ages.

An additional problem in rural areas is that the census is less likely to list street names. This can lead to guesswork as to where an individual household lived, unless they are found to be in or near a local public house or other place noted. This is still not a certainty as there can be several households occupying one building, also the number of houses in an area will have differed over time as some will have been demolished and others built. Despite their shortcomings they are still a good source of information on both the area and the people enumerated in it.

During the 19th century the circulation of newspapers, both national and local increased to inform and educate the growing literate population. The *Staffordshire Advertiser* covered the whole of the county but others were more localised, such as the *Lichfield Mercury*, and newspapers covering Burton upon Trent area. The *Burton Chronicle*, which was first published in 1860 included Yoxall news and was the main newspaper researched for this study. Along with reports of Yoxall local events and news items were cases heard in Burton Police Court and other courts.

With increased literacy more people wrote letters and extracts are included from letters of two women who would otherwise be only accessible to history via the official records, but can be seen through what they chose to write, giving a rare glimpse from a female perspective, of the difficult lives many people faced.

When quoting sources in this study the original spelling has been kept to give a sense of the writing of the times, except where it could make the reading inaccessible to the modern reader.

Chapter 1

From Four Ploughs

Early Years

Yoxall is an ancient Parish 7 miles north-east of Lichfield on the A515 (SK 1419). It was listed in the Domesday Book of 1086, spelt 'Locheshale' where it was stated that it had land for 4 ploughs. In early documents Yoxall had a variety of spellings, including Iokeshale and Joxhale, but by the sixteenth century the spelling became more recognisable to modern readers. The meaning of the name is uncertain, the Old English words *geoc* and *hale* from which it probably derived having several meanings, including 'yoke, yoke of oxen', 'a measure of land', and it has often been suggested that Yoxall was the area a team of two oxen could plough in a day, notionally a quarter of an acre. Horovitz suggests that *hale* could suggest 'a small valley', or 'a piece of low-lying land by a river'.[1] In 1086 Yoxall was part of the Bishop of Chester's Estate, (the bishop's seat for the diocese of Lichfield was in Chester from 1075 to 1102), and was held by Alwin and Rafwin (Alwyn and Raven), to whom the bishop appears to have sublet the manor. Their names with Ferrers, Hollys and Lovell, who were lords of the manor survive in names of roads within the village. After the conquest Tutbury became the administrative centre of a large block of territory on the Staffordshire-Derbyshire border, including Yoxall, and by the 13th century this was known as the Honour of Tutbury. Yoxall was also in Offlow, one of the hundreds of which Staffordshire had five. The Saxons had divided the country into shires and hundreds, the latter being the division of a shire for administrative, military and judicial purposes under common law.

Surrounding Yoxall and within the parish are the hamlets, listed with proximity to the village and their probable name meanings. Hadley End (1 mile north-east), the first part of the word probably taken from Old English meaning 'a heath, heather', and *leah* 'the heathy clearing'. End, generally meaning place, was often applied to squatter settlements built on common or heath land; Longcroft, (¾ mile north) a long enclosure of arable or pasture land; Morrey, (1 mile west), Old English *morgen-gifu*, literally 'morning gift', meaning 'land given by a man to his bride on the morning after their marriage'.[2] Woodhouses, (1 mile south) from Old English *wudus-hus* 'house by or in the wood'; the self explanatory Woodmill (1 ½ miles north) and Woodlane (1 mile north).

Other areas of Yoxall include Bond End, Bond derived from *bondi* or *bunde* meaning a peasant landowner,[3] although it has also been suggested as the area for serfs, who were compelled to provide a service to a master; Forestside and Luce Pool, now Luce Pool Lane at Woodhouses. Luce is an Old English word for pike, therefore most likely there was once a pool there stocked with pike, which would have been included in the diet of, presumably, the owner of the pool. Also at Woodhouses is Sich Lane, the 'sich' being a ditch. All were within the parish of Yoxall in the period covered, but the parish and manorial boundaries were not the same. Hoar Cross, a hamlet 2 ½ miles north, was a separate township in the Manor of Agardsley and part of the civil parish of Yoxall until the 20th century. The meaning of the name is generally accepted as 'grey or boundary cross' and according to the perambulations, all the wards of the forest met at Hoar Cross.[4]

Writing in 1820 Erdswick included Sale amongst the hamlets.[5] The meaning has been suggested as possibly from the Old English *salh* meaning sallow, a small willow like tree or shrub, or possibly a coppice area within a wood.[6] Shaw also mentioned 'Snelles-end' [Snail's End] and Rew-end [Reeve End] as hamlets, both were more populous at the time of his writing. Snails End could refer to a corruption of a person's name of Snell, which was not uncommon in Staffordshire,[7] or could simply refer to a particularly damp area where many snails were found. In a list of families in the Archdeaconry of Stafford compiled in 1532-3, 100 families were listed in the parish with 18 of these being at Snails End, listed as Snellis End.[8] The only remaining reminder of this name is Snails Place, a house in Victoria Street, which was formerly known more colloquially as 'Bunghole Street', which has been suggested was due to a good deal of cheese coming from that area, which if over indulged in could lead to constipation.

Reeve End Cottage, date unknown, but at the time of the photograph the property was a beerhouse.

Reeve End most likely comes from the title of reeve which was an overseer, steward or bailiff appointed by a landowner, or a churchwarden and in Yoxall was most likely appointed by the lord of the manor. One of the two oldest surviving domestic buildings is Reeve End Cottage, a medieval aisled timber-framed house, probably dating from the 14th century, of which only approximately half remains and the outer walls are now replaced with brick.

Aisle posts have been removed but arcade plates and tie-beam roof trusses remain. The following was suggested by Hislop: 'Following the conventions of late medieval planning, a bay to the north of the passage, would, in all probability, have contained service rooms, and possibly a chamber above. A southern extension of the building may have housed a parlour and possibly an upper chamber or solar'.[9] In its time, this was clearly a high status building.

Olive Green, which had the alternative name of Gallows Green has been suggested as the site of the manorial gallows, however although it appears in some documents as being in the parish of Yoxall, including White's directories of 1834 and 1851, it is now within the parish of Hamstall Ridware. It is possible that the parishes shared the use of the gallows.

When Yoxall was first settled is uncertain. In 1774 about forty vessels were found when Mr Wright of Yoxall was levelling a piece of ground. They were made of coarse, soft brown earth and were almost full of ashes and fragments of human bone. Most of the vessels were broken in taking them up but the one with the least damage was presented to Mr Greene's museum in Market Street, Lichfield, which was in existence c.1748-1793. It was described in the museum's catalogue as 'A Roman Urn, found near Yoxall, containing ashes and fragments of burnt bone'.[10]

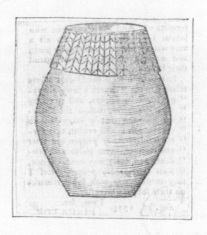

Burial Urn, woodcut engraving. Discovered half a mile from Mr Wright's home, probably Old Hall, the urn was presented to Greene's Museum 'for the inspection of the curious'. The drawing and accompanying letter were published in The Gentleman's Magazine, Vol. 44, August, 1774, p.358. (Staffordshire Views, X11.151b. Reproduced by permission of the Trustees of the William Salt Library).

The same source suggests that the site was probably a Romano-British cemetery near to which there may have been a settlement. The citing of a probable Romano-British settlement has been suggested as adjoining the cemetery at Yoxall.[11] This is the place where the vessels were discovered. However from a drawing of the collared urn the date appears to be early Bronze Age and if so, the settlement was most likely also Bronze Age. The quantity of urns discovered were unlikely to be those of a nomadic tribe, but one who for a time had settled in Yoxall, somewhere in the period 2500-1500 BCE.

Other evidence that Yoxall was occupied at an early date, includes the names of 'Barrow Moor' and 'Barrow Pingle' on the tithe apportionment of 1839.[12] Barrow monuments date from early Neolithic to the Saxons. Suggested Bronze Age ring ditches have also been recorded in Yoxall. Evidence partially due to 'intensive study' suggests potential prehistoric and Roman activity around Yoxall, concentrated within the Trent Valley, lying to the south.[13] Yoxall finds discovered by metal detecting include a Roman brooch, a late Iron Age or Early Roman linch pin, a medieval to post medieval ewer, and an early Bronze Age flat axe head, all recorded on Heritage Gateway site. Shaw wrote: 'Upon the hill, a little North-east of the ancient moat [at Moat House, Town Hill] by the mill, … is a large mound of earth, upon which formerly was a beacon, and might be a signal for Hanbury, etc'. [14] This was later listed in reference to castles in Staffordshire under the heading of 'some doubtful sites'.[15] There are numerous crop marks as well as evidence of ridge and furrow ploughing in the fields of Yoxall.

The present Yoxall parish church has its own chapter but it has long been believed that there may have been an older, Saxon church. In the Parish Magazine of July 1921 Rev. Cory wrote regarding the Wake Sunday, the anniversary of the consecration of the church 'at least 700 years ago. Probably the older floor of cobblestones, that lies below the present building, marks the site of a church, perhaps of wood, and possibly dedicated years before'.

The other oldest surviving domestic building is Pear Tree Farmhouse, in Victoria Street which dates from circa 14th century. However the crown posts have been dated as possibly the last quarter of the 13th century.[16] This timber-framed house was remodelled in the 17th century, and again circa early 18th century, in red brick. The interior retains much timber and although the hall's roof structure has been reconstructed, some of the rafters were reused. During redecorating the hall inscriptions were discovered in the plaster, these markings, known as palimpsest, include images that seem to be crudely executed pictures of medieval knights and birds, others are geometric designs precisely inscribed into the plaster, also carefully written words in gothic script, which include the words Yoxhale and Bromley.[17]

The timber-framed Old Manor House on Town Hill probably dates from the late 16th century, and features a herringbone pattern brick infill on the right-hand gable end. It is opposite the site of the medieval manor house and was possibly a gate house to it.

Although county records refer to a mill in 1341 on the site of a disused corn mill, known as The Old Mill (when listed in 1984, now The Olde Mill) on Lower Hoar Cross Road, the present building is probably 16th century in origin, but with later alterations. The main block incorporates the former dwelling of the millers. The interior has exposed timber framing and king post trusses, also much of the original machinery including drive shaft and gearing to 2 millstones, and an overshot mill wheel with two wooden buckets. The mill house extends to 2360 sq ft.

Timber-framed Thimble Hall on School Green is also probably 16th century. The interior has exposed timber frame and ceiling beams, and incorporates a timber-framed chimney.

Woodhouse Farmhouse, also known as Holly Bank Farm, is late 16th century and in 1964 the interior was described as having exposed ceiling beams to both storeys, and some 16th century panelling.

Other buildings, not as old but also of interest include Birmingham House, King Street, an early 17th century timber-frame and brick building. The Grange, formerly The Rectory, on Savey Lane, is timber-framed, brick and stone with projecting bays at each side with Dutch gables. The building was restored in the 17th century but has an earlier core.

Yoxall Rectory with Rev. Cory. Now The Grange, it remained the rectory until the 1950s, when a new rectory was built in Savey Lane.

In King Street is the Poplars, an early 19th century three-storied house with a hipped roof, deep eaves, and wood pilastered doorway with entablature.

The Rookery at Bond End dates from the 17th century. It was partly destroyed by fire and The Hollies, an 18th century three-storied 5 bay house, although described as detached, was built right up to its walls. This was once the home of Eliza Jane Arden who married Michael Thomas Bass (1799-1884) and was the mother of Michael Arthur Bass, 1st Baron Burton.[18]

Cottages dating from the 17th and 18th centuries have been updated, often during the 19th century. Many a brick exterior hides an earlier timber frame.

An old farmhouse in Yoxall, half-timbered and brick, whereabouts uncertain. Pencil drawing 1815. Anonymous [H. C. Allport], 'Yoxall June 29th' in bottom right hand corner. (Staffordshire Views, XII.155. Reproduced by permission of the Trustees of the William Salt Library).

Part of the Crown Inn was where the car park is now. The remaining older building has a Victorian addition. The Golden Cup is a later building than the original parts of the Crown, being possibly 18th century with 19th century alterations.

Old Hall, demolished in the 1960s was once a large house with many gables, but eventually only one gable was habitable. There was said to be a passage from Old Hall to the church, but it has been suggested that this was probably an entrance to the cellars.[19]

Yoxall Manor

Following the Conquest the manorial system was introduced throughout England. The medieval manor was a landed estate that involved rights and obligations. The Parish Magazine of October 1921 contained an article regarding the Yoxall Manor, which refers to the compulsory service rendered by the villagers, or villeins; feudal tenants entirely subject to the lord of the

6

manor, as payment for their cottage and croft. Through this service the lord's land was ploughed and the great barn of his hall was filled with sheaves, his sheep shorn, his grain malted, and wood hewn for his hall fires. Yoxall's lords of the manor appear to all have been absentees, and the manor house tenanted by those they chose. There was also a small rectory manor at Yoxall.

The Court Baron, regularly held at Yoxall, dealt with land transfers and regularly issued fines especially for default of fencing and failure to scour ditches.[20] Amongst the defaults in October 1645 was Widow Arden, fined 1s for default of fencing between 'Steerefield and Fumley', Thomas Buckram, fined 4d for a gap at Northcroft and Thomas Taylor fined 1s for default of a gate called 'Meglane Yate'. Another offence presented at the courts was the breaking of the assize of bread and ale. This was a 13th century statute which regulated the price, weight and quality of the bread and beer manufactured and sold.

In April 1646 The Court Baron issued the order that everyone was to remove dung heaps and tree trunks lying in the highway before the feast of Pentecost, (Whit Sunday) and that no one was to wash flax or hemp in the Swarbourn, the penalty for failure to abide by either of these orders was 3s 4d. Also all pigs were to be secured round the neck or ringed. There was a pound for stray animals sited half way between Trent Bridge and the junction with Meadow Lane.[21] In 1665 the constable, churchwardens and alehouse keeper were each fined between 1s and 2s for being in the alehouse at prayer time on the Lord's day, their fines were to be for the use of the Yoxall poor.

Lords and the Manor

Henry de Ferrers is widely believed to have come to England with William the Conqueror and fought at the Battle of Hastings in 1066 as his name appears on various versions of the Battle Abbey Rolls. He was a Domesday Commissioner and in 1086 held lordships and manors, gifts of the Conqueror. The last Ferrers to hold the manor of Yoxall was Robert, 6th Earl of Derby who rebelled against King Henry III and was imprisoned at the Tower of London and Windsor Castle, and in 1266 his lands were forfeited to Edmund Crouchback, 2nd surviving son of Henry III, who received the Earldom of Leicester and later that of Lancaster. However Robert's mother Margaret retained the manor of Yoxall until her death in 1281, when it reverted to the Earl of Lancaster.[22]

The ancient manor house is generally believed to have been on the site of Moat House, home of the Armson family, Dr Gerald Armson wrote that foundations would be struck by the spade whenever the garden was dug. He stated that a charter dated in 1262 was signed in Yoxall at the time Robert Ferrers held the manor. Also that it was 'mentioned in the Inquisition Post Mortem of the Earl of Lancaster in 1297 and again in 1322, when 'Friends of the Earl of Lancaster' razed it to the ground as a reprisal for the treachery of his servant and Fermor of the demesne lands, Robert Holland, after the battle of Burton Bridge'.[23]

However it was possibly rebuilt at some time as it has been suggested that Robert 'Ardern' who tenanted the manor may have died in the manor house in 1537.[24] It appears to have been in ruins in 1798, when Shaw wrote of the manor and referred to the 'ancient mansion' as being close to the mill with the remains of a moat that once surrounded it. The same source believed this to have been the seat of the de Yoxall family who were granted land by Earl Ferrers during the rein of Henry III (1216-1272).[25] In 1897 ruins remained in which farm animals were housed.[26] When the manor house was no longer habitable it is likely that the manor court was held at Old Manor House. Edmund Crouchback died in 1296 and his eldest son Thomas, 2nd Earl of Lancaster inherited. In the Plea Rolls of Staffordshire 1297/8, Blanche, Queen of Navarre through her first marriage to Henry I of Navarre, and later widow of Edmund Crouchback, sued Adam de Char for a third of half the manor of Yoxall excepting the forest of Needwood, Rowley Park and advowson of the Church as her dower. Adam stated that Edmund had demised half of the manor on him for life and called for Thomas of Lancaster, son and heir of Edmund Crouchback to be summoned.[27] The Manor of 'Yoxhale' was in the hands of Adam de Carru ? for the term of his life, the gift of the Lord Edmund, the brother of the King of England, rendering yearly £33 6s 8d, but the true yearly value was said to be £66 14s 4d. There were 7 burgages, rendering yearly £7 2s 0d and 25 stalls in the market rendering yearly 2s 6d. Also a rent of assize of free tenants with one bow and one sparrow hawk worth yearly £15 8s 11d. A meadow there called Wolricheseyes rendered yearly 6s 8d and a rent of assize of the free tenants was worth yearly £24 2s 6d.[28]

In 1299/1300 Thomas of Lancaster obtained from Edward I a grant of a market 'every week, on Saturday, and a fair yearly on the eve, day and morrow of St Swithin, July 15'.[29] At the time this would have been on 2 July, the anniversary of the death of St Swithin in 862, and was probably changed with the translation of dates in 1752 when 1 January became the first day of the year and 11 days were lost from the calendar. Sir Robert de Holland was a favourite of Thomas of Lancaster, from whom he acquired large plots of land including, in 1315-16, the manor of Yoxall.[30] It was that year Lancaster was beheaded for leading a rebellion against the king. Robert Holland was declared a traitor by followers of Henry, 3rd Earl of Lancaster in 1328 and was beheaded. Hollands continued as lords of Yoxall manor until 1374 when it passed to John Lovell through his marriage to Robert Holland's only daughter. The last Lovell Lord of the Manor was Francis, a favourite of Richard III, also his Chief Butler and Chamberlain of the household. He fought at Bosworth in 1485 and that year his lands were seized by the Crown.

From 1513 William Fitzwilliam (created Earl of Southampton in 1537), held the manor.[31] He had previously been chosen as a companion to the young Prince Henry, later Henry VIII. The extent of the manor of Yoxall in 1538/9 is revealed by the granting of it by Fitzwilliam to William Hollys in that year. The land listed was: 'forty messuages, twenty cottages, one water-mill, two dovecotes, forty gardens, forty orchards, 2,000 acres of land, 300 acres of meadow, 1,000 acres of pasture, 100 acres of wood, 400 acres of furze and heath, 200 acres of marsh and £10 of rents in Yoxall and the advowson of the church'. William Hollys paid £1,220 for the grant.[32] He was a London merchant, and Lord Mayor in 1539-40. A later Hollys, John, was created Earl of Clare in 1624 and the family held the manor until Henrietta, daughter of John Hollys, Duke of Newcastle, sold the manor and advowson to Henry Paget Earl of Uxbridge in 1719, who was succeeded by his son Henry.

In 1761 Lord Paget's agent William Wyatt wrote regarding the value of the Manor of Yoxall: 'The Chief Rents for the Copyholds and Freeholds are so mixed and have been for a number of Years that I think it is not in the Act of Man to distinguish them separately to any exactness'. He referred to the fact that he received the accounts for 18 years from Robert Shipton of Yoxall 'who has been himself or some of his Family Bailiffs of their Manor for a great Number of Years till about the Year 1745'. However due to being denied access to the rolls of the manor he was unable to be precise as to the profits, but concluded 'I think if your Lordship could get £2600 for the Manor it would be very well sold'. In 1764 Wyatt again wrote regarding the manor of Yoxall stating that Lord Leigh had been advised by friends that it was overpriced and hoped that it could be reduced by £50. However Wyatt considered that if Lord Leigh wanted it he must pay the asking price, and it had been agreed that he would.[33]

The following year Edward, 5th Lord Leigh of Stoneleigh held the lordship and in 1767, he lapsed into insanity and died without issue in 1786 and was succeeded by his spinster sister the reclusive Hon. Mary Leigh, who died without issue in 1806. The Rev. Thos. Leigh, Rector of Broadwell and Aldestrop, cousin of Cassandra Austen, mother of Jane Austen, was then lord of the manor, followed on his death in 1813 by his nephew James Henry Leigh, whose eldest son Chandos, created Baron Leigh of Stoneleigh in 1839, held the manor from 1824. Chandos was succeeded by his second son, William Henry, in 1850 and in 1905 Yoxall manor was held by his son Francis Dudley Leigh, 3rd Baron who was lord of the manor when manorial court business ceased in 1932.[34]

George Walton

A dispute arose regarding the keeping of the manor court rolls which led to a court case in 1564. It was claimed that it had always been the custom to keep the court rolls in the parish church in a chest with three locks, appointed for the purpose, for the use of the lord of the manor and his tenants. A key was to be kept by the bailiff of the manor, which at the time was George Walton, the other two keys were to be held by two customary tenants. However it was stated that George Walton, who had been bailiff 'for a long time' had possession of 'a great number' of the court rolls which concerned the title to parcels of land, and although he had repeatedly been asked to put the rolls in the chest he had refused. The tenants were concerned that he intended to alter entries to his own advantage. Thomas Salte of Yoxall, on behalf of himself and others petitioned Sir William Hollys, lord of the manor, to ensure that Walton deposit the rolls in the chest.

In his defence Walton claimed that by the command of Sir William Hollys he had custody of the rolls, therefore the claim should be against Sir William, not himself. He denied any knowledge of a custom of keeping the documents in the chest, adding that if there were such a custom it should be abolished, as he had heard that when court rolls were in a chest in the church, under the direction of a previous lord of the manor, the chest had been broken into by someone intending to either sell or alter the rolls.[35]

St Peter's Square, now King Street, looking down Victoria Street, when Leedhams occupied Birmingham House. Their signs advertise that they were saddlers and harness makers.

Through his son Gervais, George was the grandfather of Stafford born Isaac Walton, famous for his book 'The Compleat Angler' who was baptised in 1593. In his will of 1570/1 George requested burial in the churchyard at Yoxall and declared himself to be a yeoman, but in his inventory the appraisers stated him to be a bailiff. It is likely that both were true as he died possessed of items of husbandry, cattle and 4 oxen. It has been suggested that he lived at Birmingham House, although this is unlikely as the Grade II listed building is, according to the listing, early 17th century. Another, but more credible story regarding the house is that Joseph Green who ran a grocers shop on the premises named it Birmingham House, due to the fact that instead of obtaining his stock nearer to home he travelled to Birmingham market, believing the produce there was better and named his shop accordingly as a means of advertising the quality of the produce he sold. However if local legend is true, he would sometimes be late at the market as he is said to have set out early in his wagon and fallen asleep. His horse's reaction was to return home, this led to him being known as 'Dozy Green'. The building at one time belonged to the King family, which gave their name to the area, King Street, which was once known as St Peter's Square.

Perambulation of the Manor

The Oldest Tree in Staffordshire,
Longcroft Park.

The Raven Oak showing Longcroft Hall in the background. If it was named after Raven, tenant of the lord of the manor in 1086, it would be a contender for the oldest tree in Staffordshire. However it is likely it was favoured by ravens and was named accordingly.

In 1867 the *Burton Chronicle* reported on a perambulation of the Manor of Yoxall, Lord Leigh of Stoneleigh Abbey was at that time lord of the manor, but his property only consisted of about 100 acres, part of which was woodland, and the manor house, reported as being 'an ancient timber framed cottage occupied by John Bloore, and probably only a remnant of some large building in feudal ages'. This was the first perambulation since 1843 and after a jury had been sworn in and other business completed, the journey, undertaken by officials and many inhabitants, began at an oak tree on the border of Hamstall Ridware. It skirted the parish of Hamstall to the River Trent and down the river in a boat to a field opposite Orgreave Hall, where sandwiches, bread and cheese and a barrel of Bass was provided. This was followed by resuming the boat journey, where the route continued down to the parishes of Alrewas and Wychnor. The report continues 'To describe the incidents on the banks of the Trent and the sudden and frequent immersions would be a detail too long'. The party then passed from Wychnor to the borders of Agardsely Manor and to the Raven Oak at Longcroft. From there the party adjourned to the Crown Inn where the landlord, Mr Roobottom, provided dinner. On the following day the perambulation continued from the Raven Oak where the company was met by Major Arden of Longcroft Hall 'where nineteen good sized boys and one young man, were stowed inside the hollow of this ancient oak. Orders were then given to march'. The party proceeded, leaving Hoar Cross to the right, in a zigzag direction, through Hadley End to a field called 'The Bottoms' where they halted for lunch, supplied by Mr Hancock of the Cup Inn. This was followed by a pony race and the party reached the tree from where the perambulation had begun the previous day at about 5 o'clock in heavy rain and continued to the Cup Inn for dinner.[36]

Ward of the Forest

Needwood was actually a chase, not a forest since only the Crown could hold a forest. Under the Ferrers family of Tutbury Castle, who were also lords of the manor of Yoxall, Needwood Forest was divided into five wards for the purpose of administration, these were Tutbury, Marchington, Uttoxeter, Yoxall, and Barton (the addition of 'under Needwood' was current by the late 13th century). Robert Earl Ferrers parcelled out land to bond tenants, who were bound to work his land by ploughing, sowing, reaping and mowing and taking crops to his castle at Tutbury, or manor house at their own expense. In Yoxall Ward in 1296-97 the agistment of cattle taken there to feed was 30s. Customary tenants gave 88 hens yearly, worth 7s 4d in exchange for bark. The sale of the bark of the teil (lime or linden) tree was worth another 13s 4d. Pannage, paid for the feeding of hogs in the ward was worth 30s. Ransoms of the Wodemote (a lower forest court) were worth 6s 8d yearly. In 'Rouleye' (Roughley) Park profits in herbage and mast were annually worth £8. The sale of old wood blown down was worth 26s 8d per year. The total being £13 14s.[37] By the 15th century there was a forester and lodge for each ward. At the head of the administrative system was the chief forester, known as the wood master or master forester of Needwood, chosen by the king. Daniel Astle, a keeper of Needwood Forest died in 1775. He was buried in Yoxall church, his monument, a plaque with pillars on the north wall of the tower, records that his and his wife's remains were deposited near the monument.

A survey taken in the first year of the reign of Elizabeth I (1558-59) gives the following account: 'The forest, or chase of Needwood, is in compasse by estimation 23 miles and a half, and the nearest part thereof is distant from the castle of Tutbury but one mile. In it are 7869 yards and a halfe, and very forest-like ground, thinly set with old oakes and timber trees, well replenished with coverts of underwood and thornes, which might be copiced in divers parts thereof, for increase of wood and timber, but lately sorely decayed and spoyled. It is divided into four wards, viz. Tutbury Ward, Marchington Ward, Yoxall Ward and Barton Ward, each containing five miles or more in compasse'.[38] Uttoxeter Ward was separate from the main body of the forest.[39] At a Woodmote (forest court) held during the reign of Elizabeth I, it was stated that 'the tenants and cottagers of Yoxall have more cattle in the forest and make more spoil in the woods than any other towne in the forest'.[40] Three of the four gates into the forest were in the north of the parish, the other at Woodhouses, situated at the timber framed cottage opposite Bank House. Animals turned into the forest for grazing were branded, the Yoxall brand was two vertical lines within a circle. In 1636 a commission was appointed to partition the ward of Uttoxeter between the king and the inhabitants of Uttoxeter who claimed common rights in the ward. This partition was cited as a precedent when it was later proposed to enclose the whole of Needwood.

An Act of 1653 ordered the disafforestation and sale of forests which had belonged to the Crown eighteen years before. Needwood was one of six excluded and was reserved to provide security payment for troops who had not received money they were owed. In 1654, it was decreed that 4 of the forests were to be surveyed, enclosed, and sold, Needwood being one of them. The inhabitants of 22 towns and townships in east Staffordshire had for centuries enjoyed common rights in the forest of Needwood, where they pastured their animals and gathered firewood etc. and a petition was sent to Parliament.[41] The Grand Jury reacted strongly against the proposal for the deforestation and enclosure of Needwood due to the fact that many thousand poor people that lived by the help of the forest would be utterly impoverished by the enclosure,[42] but in 1656 commissioners were appointed to survey the forest and this was completed in 1658 when preparations were made to enclose the land. That autumn there were riots. The following is an extract from depositions made during March 1685/9 regarding a serious riot against the proposed enclosure: 'Abraham of Whorecross…did acknowledge that he was amongst them that lately rose in Needwood and threw downe the ditches and inclosures and that as long as he had life he would be there in defence of his commons, and knock down the first man of his party that should run away'.[43] Needwood was not disafforested until the early 19th century.

Sluice or Floodgate

During the fifteenth century, certain tenants at Yoxall held their lands on condition that they maintained a 'sluice or floodgate' to drain off floodwaters.[44] This suggests an early date for the construction of water meadows, which brought water from the Swarbourn to flood grassland and promote rich meadows to feed agricultural animals during dry summers. Water would be diverted from the Swarbourn, via culverts and ditches which were controlled by sluice gates, now gone, but ditches and arched brick culverts between the Swarbourn and Meadow Lane remain. During the reign of Henry VIII a case came to the Star Chamber regarding the 'sluice or floodgate' which was maintained by John Marres and had been by his family for about 30 years. It was his job to ensure that any flooding was contained by this method. It was claimed that water flooded adjoining ground of the defendant, Edmund Ward and the complainant, Robert Arden had erected a levy and set up a weir on the land of the defendant. It was affirmed that as the weir was on the defendant's land, he was to have the mease, and the land was given to Hugh, son of John Marres without any condition that he kept the sluice or floodgate.[45]

Yoxall Town Lands

Religious indulgences were bestowed by the Lichfield Diocese in connexion with architecture for periods of forty days to all who helped to build or repair bridges. Under this system Yoxall bridge was repaired in 1458.[46] Religious indulgences were phased out following the Reformation and all remaining traces were erased in the reign of Edward VI. Town Lands Trusts and the later Turnpikes became a means of financing the upkeep of roads and bridges. Beccles celebrated the 450th anniversary of their Town Lands in 1994, which dates the origin of the Town Lands back to at least 1544.

Yoxall Town Lands, a non-ecclesiastical charity, was noted in 1642 to provide income for the repair of Trent Bridge (later known as Yoxall Bridge), and Hall Bridge, over the Swarbourn, also of the church and any surplus to pay for a substitute for any soldier whom the parish was obliged to supply and other benefits to the village. Yoxall land which had originally belonged to the chantry priests of Lichfield Cathedral and before the Reformation had been charged with a payment of 20d for the maintenance of Yoxall bridge. Other land that had been given to maintain charities or lamps in Yoxall church may at least partly have remained in local hands.[47] The same source states that the feofees of the charity lands made their accounts annually on St John's day, which may indicate that the endowment was originally associated with a religious institution.

Yoxall Town Lands administered several charities founded by wealthy testators who bequeathed money and land, the income from which was to help support those in poverty. Most notably Thomas and Sarah Taylor, who by their wills bequeathed funds for the relief of the poor, including the education of poor boys in Yoxall. Care for the poor was the responsibility of the parish and charities eased the burden of these expenses.

At Woodhouses and Hadley End there were poorhouses, also known as townhouses, occupied rent free by paupers, and maintained by the Town Lands trustees. Those at Woodhouses had to be fumigated and refurbished in the mid 1820s and overseers still owned four dwellings at Woodhouses in 1841.[48] Yoxall became part of Lichfield poor law union in 1837 and in 1840 the Lichfield workhouse was opened. Almshouses were maintained in Yoxall until the 1950s. The Town Lands charities continue to date to give financial aid for the good of the village and its organisations.

Bridges

The Staffordshire Decrees extended from 1601-1732 and covered charities, schools, bridges and paving, curates, highways and almshouses. 'There are bridges too at Yoxall … which should be maintained out of trust funds and settled land'.[49]

The upkeep of bridges often featured in the Town Lands accounts. Various amounts were paid for 'the bridge'.[50] In 1732 5 shillings was paid for two years' barn room for boards and other wood used at the bridge and in 1737 a shilling was spent at the doctors meeting about the bridge gate. In 1732 a bill of £11 5s 8d was paid for three posts for the Hall Bridge at 10 foot apiece. In 1741 1s 6d was paid to the men that broke the ice at the Hall Bridge. A note in the Town Lands accounts book between 1747-48 states that Hall Bridge was rebuilt in 1753 and that 'the Brickwork which carried the Timber being Built crossway into the River it was taken down at the end towards the Town in the Year 1754 and one arch more added to the length of the Bridge and the Charge of the Bridge was Thirty Seven Pounds two Shillings and Ten Pence'. The accounts show that in 1753 Thomas Moor was paid 2s for pulling down the old bridge, name not stated, but presumably Hall Bridge as on 7th July 1753 1s was given to the workmen at Hall Bridge for drink and on the 16th 1s 6d 'Spent on the Men at Finishing the Bridge'. In 1784 5s was spent on timber and work on Falconers Bridge. In July 1791 £14 3s 6d was paid toward building Stair Bridge. This would have been rebuilt, rather than built, as in 1645 Clement Faulkener was fined 6d for not scouring his ditch at 'Steerbridge'. Stair Bridge is where Victoria Street becomes Longcroft Lane. Stuart wrote that it was 'where the old turnpike road bore left past the Bleachyard', adding 'beyond Stair Bridge is another small bridge over a cutting from the river to the mill dam, with a badly worn inscription 'This bridge belongs to Yoxall Mill 1813'. The water supply to the mill came originally from three pools on the Lynn Brook. Eventually these silted up and a cutting was made from the river Swarbourn just above Stair Bridge to the dam, the water returning to the river just below Hall Bridge'.[51] Dr Armson wrote that in 1834, at a public meeting, it was decided to pull down Stair Bridge and build a carriage bridge at or near the same place, also that steps would be taken to legally stop up the road running to the Bleach Yard.[52]

'The bridge of 'Yoxhall' was mentioned in the Perambulation of Alrewas Hay (part of the Forest of Cannock), made in the year 1300, and the Patent Rolls for 1549 record 'an exoneration' of twenty pence for the maintenance of this bridge'. In 1662 the bridge was said to be 'in peril of great decay, and the groundwork founderous, and will cost threescore and ten pounds to repair, and if speedy the reparacon be not made, the same will be utterly ruined'. Half of the necessary sum was given by the county.[53] The repairs of Yoxall Bridge cost about £200 between the years 1731 and 1754, one-third of which was paid by the inhabitants of Yoxall.[54] In 1733 an agreement was entered between Yoxall and the Quarter Sessions at Stafford, whereby Yoxall Bridge should be considered a county bridge and repaired at the county's expense, but when any further repairs were needed, a third of the rents of the charity lands should be applied for the repairs and the repair to the road over the bridge. In 1774 Yoxall Bridge was rebuilt and a temporary bridge erected while the work was in progress.[55] In 1837 the bridge was in great need of repair and the subject of a legal case which resulted in the county being liable only for the repair of 330 ft of road extending at each end of the bridge. It appeared from the case submitted that the bridge was originally built by the parish more than two centuries ago, but no one knew exactly when, certain lands were let to trustees for the repairs of bridges and the church, and for finding of armed men for the service of the king, or for any other necessary uses for the village of Yoxall as should seem expedient to the 'major part of the better sort of inhabitants'.[56]

During WW2 the U.S. army used Marchington camp as a maintenance and storage depot and regularly passed through Yoxall, their trucks practically demolishing the bridge. After the war the U.S. army authorities agreed to rebuild it, but did so in reinforced wire. It may have been around this time that workmen examining the footings said they had discovered elm timbers which had supported an earlier bridge. The present bridge was built in 1998.

Chapter 2

Continuity and Change

While Yoxall Manor continued into the 20th century and the Yoxall Town Lands still continues, other changes took place. The 19th century brought increased enclosure of land and ever increasing sources of information, due largely to the population censuses, increased circulation of local newspapers and trade directories, which has led to a greater knowledge of people from all walks of life than in any earlier period in history.

Disafforestation and Enclosure of Needwood Forest

The act for enclosing Needwood Forest was passed in 1801 and its disafforestation and enclosure was completed in 1811. At the enclosure 174 acres of land was allotted in lieu of rectorial tithes of the part of Needwood Forest that lay within the parish of Yoxall.[1] Brankley Pastures is one of the few remaining clues of what this once vast forest had been, and contains some ancient veteran trees which survived the devastation. Following its enclosure bequests of land 'being part of the late disafforested Forest or Chase of Needwood' appeared in wills and as late as 1847 George Harvey bequeathed land which was stated to be 'late part of Needwood Forest'.

Enclosure of Open Fields

In the late 14th century there were three open fields, and each had a pair of wardens to control access: Hall field, Stockyng field and the field of the bondmen. In 1381 the wardens were attached to the village 'ends' (Bond, Snelles [Snail's], and Reeve), and there were also wardens for Woodhouses, which had its own field called Brokenhill field. By 1503 there was a hayward, a single officer. This reduction suggests partial enclosure of open field land.[2] The same source states that piecemeal enclosure had taken place by the mid 17th century, the loss of commonable land compensated by access to pasture in Needwood Forest and its parks. The main areas of open arable land were then Hall field on the east side of the village, Church field on the west and Northcroft on the north-west, also open land in Bond field and Bridge field, south-west of the village where 62 acres were enclosed in 1815 by an Act of 1812. The Act also covered 62 acres of open meadow in the south of Yoxall, between the river Trent and the old course of the Swarbourn.[3]

The Yoxall Tithe Apportionment is a source of evidence for enclosed land as it includes both pre enclosure and enclosure names. Pre enclosure names include acre, flat, furlong, land and shot, the latter being a block of arable land, consisting of a number of selions of land; a medieval or open strip used for growing crops, typically one furlong (660 ft long) and one chain (66 ft wide). All strips ran in the same direction and had at either end a headland on which a plough team could turn. Enclosure names include, close, intake, park, rails and hay, which was a fenced piece of land; part of a forest enclosed for preserving game.[4]

Yoxall Tithes

The right to receive tithes was granted to English churches by King Ethelwulf in 855 and the tithe system affirmed under the Statute of Westminster in 1255. Originally tithes were payable in kind, and fell into three categories; all things arising from the ground and subject to annual increase, which included grain and vegetables; all things nourished by the ground, such as young cattle and sheep, and animal produce such as milk, eggs and wool; the produce of man's labour, particularly the profits from mills and fishing. The tithes were divided into great tithes, generally corn, grain, hay and wood which were paid to the rector, the rest were considered small tithes and paid to the vicar of the parish. The Commutation Act of 1836 substituted these payments in kind for a cash payment. Tithe maps were drawn up which show numbered plots of land and an accompanying apportionment contains the names of the numbered plots, acreage and their description, e.g. pasture, meadow, plantation, house and garden etc. Also the owner and occupier and amount chargeable.

The following figures exclude the roods and perches so fall slightly short of the total of able acreage eligible for tithes.

Yoxall Tithe Apportionment[5] estimated a total acreage of the parish as 4,813 of which 3,529 acres were subject to tithes, broken down into the following acreage: arable 852, meadow 896, pasture 1579, woodland and plantations 108, and farm homestead, farm roads, gardens and sites of building 91 acres. Land not subject to the tithes included 19 acres of glebe land belonging to the rector and churchyard which was agreed to be charged separately for tithe and 1,213 acres of allotments of the forest of Needwood which were not subject to tithes, the rector, Edward Willes, having part of the land of the forest in lieu of tithes of the allotment, for which the provisional agreement for the commutation of tithes of the parish of Yoxall included the annual sum of £294 in rent. It appears that by this time he had acquired more land than was allotted to the rector at the enclosure.

An annual payment of £10 11s was to be paid by the award made by the commissioners for the enclosure, in lieu of tithes on certain old enclosures of Yoxall Lodge, and enclosures at Thatchmore, were subject to an annual payment of 2s 6d. The total amount of this land was 50 acres. In addition a house and land amounting to 1 acre at Hoar Cross belonging to John Jackson in the occupation of Thomas Lester, was exempt from the payment of tithes by prescription.

As detailed land bequests were infrequent, the land ownership of many testators cannot be traced through probate documents. However, the Yoxall Tithe Apportionment of 1839 (the Tithe Map is dated 1841), shows a static picture of land ownership and occupiers at that time. Amongst the largest landowners listed were, John Bamford of Woodlane who was enumerated as a farmer in 1841, a joiner in 1851 and a proprietor of houses in 1861. In 1839 he owned over 600 acres. Margaret Elizabeth Arden, widow of Rev. John Arden of Longcroft Hall, owned approximately 300 acres and Mary Birch and Mary Lightwood jointly owned over 400 acres. The Bond family, owners of the tape factory owned a little over 25 acres, and maltster John Brown 46 acres.

Trade Directories

Directories from the 19th century contain far more information than the names and trades of those listed, giving background information regarding the towns and villages from earlier times to the time of publication.

The acreage of the civil parish of 1851 was 4,791.[6] In 1896 it was 5,074.[7] The same source records the soil produced crops of wheat and beans, also 'a good portion of excellent pasture and meadow land'. The increase in acreage would have been due to land acquired by the Divided Parishes Act of 1882.

In 1834 Yoxall was described as 'a large and well-built village, in a pleasant valley, near the south west border of the now enclosed forest of Needwood', which was 'anciently a market town and is a member of the honour of Tutbury'. That year the post office was 'at Michael Poyser's' and letters were received by horse post from Lichfield at 2 pm and despatched at 8 am daily, except for Sundays.[8] When the weekly market which had run from 1300 ceased is uncertain, but it was not until February 1769 that the first cattle and sheep market was held, with the intention that it should be held annually.[9] Also in 1834 it was recorded that two cattle fairs were held yearly, on 12 February and 19 October and a feast or wake on the first Sunday in July.[10] These were still in place at the time of White's 1851 directory. By 1870 Yoxall had a reading room and library and Rev. John Baker of the Rectory was entered both as librarian and curate.[11] In 1872 the principal landowners were listed as the Queen, in right of her Duchy of Lancaster, G. S. Arden Esq., Mrs Meynell Ingram and Lord Leigh.[12]

In 1860 charitable bequests amounting to 'about £75 yearly' were distributed to the poor in bread, clothes and money,[13] but by 1872 the amount was reduced to about £32,[14] and this figure continued to be recorded to at least 1924.[15] By 1936 it was raised to £50.[16] The entry for Hoar Cross in 1880 includes the entry of a Post Office, with Thomas Lester the receiver,[17] who by 1896 was sub-postmaster.[18]

Yoxall, Scropton and the Divided Parishes Act

Citing the Archaeological Papers compiled by S. A. H. Bourne, Dr Armson quoted the following: 'When Oliver Cromwell destroyed Tutbury Castle the Scropton people rang the church bells and so pleased him that he gave every freeholder in Scropton a grant of land in Needwood Forest. This would explain the existence of the enclosed part of Scropton in Yoxall, the grants of land extending in small patches over an area between the New Inn, the Six Lane Ends, and Yoxall'.[19] The same source states that evidence of this land disappearing from the parish of Yoxall was in a letter from an overseer of Scropton, which states 'We paid two visits annually to Needwood Forest collecting the rates which were paid willingly, until a School Board was formed in Scropton. Then our troubles started. Mr Bass of Rangemore, M.P. for Derby, built a number of semi-detached residences for his servants, and unknowingly built them on land rateable to Scropton. He and all the other rate payers objected to pay a School Board rate as they could not use the School, so Mr Bass prompted a bill which was passed, depriving Scropton of the outlying land'. By the Divided Parishes Act of 1882 four detached parts of Hamstall Ridware, situated at Woodlane were transferred to Yoxall, and by an order of the Derby and Stafford County Councils, a part of Foston and Scropton was amalgamated with Yoxall.[20] Forest Farm was a detached part of the parish of Foston and Scropton, prior to 1882.

Yoxall Ecclesiastical Parish Boundary

The Ecclesiastical and Civil parishes of Yoxall shared a common boundary until the building of churches at Hoar Cross and Newchurch when they each established their own ecclesiastical parishes. Yoxall ecclesiastical parish extends from Sich Lane at Woodhouses, down to Stoneyford and along to the Foresters Arms, across Dunstall Lane to part of Hadley End, 'by Tom Jackson's house', along Morrey Lane and down to the new Trent Bridge, then along the river Trent, cutting up the west side of Wychnor Estate back to Sich Lane.[21] Hoar Cross became a separate ecclesiastical parish in 1874 but remained in the civil parish of Yoxall until 1985.

Population

A list of families in the Archdeaconry of Stafford in 1532-3 totals 100.[22] This breaks down to Yoxall 35, Morrey 8, Snails End 18, Bond End 12, Woodhouses 16 and Hoar Cross 11. The fact that Snails End had the second highest population indicates that it was at that time probably the largest settlement outside of Yoxall itself. In 1891 only 2 households were enumerated at Snails End. Although an attempt has been made to estimate the population of 1532-3 using this list,[23] there can be no certainty regarding its accuracy. The number of 550 persons was arrived at after deducting the 54 names as presumed dead as they are marked with a cross or *sp'us* [spiritus] (for the soul of). Where children were included as *cum pueris* (with children) 5 were added per family.

According to Shaw, writing in 1798, the population of Yoxall was little changed over two centuries, due to there being 'no particular manufactories to influence it'.[24] The main occupations were agricultural labour and domestic service. A century earlier Celia Fiennes on her tour of 1698 passed through 'Yoxwell over Nedwood Forest' while travelling from Wolsley to Derby, but had nothing to say about the village.[25]

The population of Yoxall taken from the censuses 1801-1901 is as follows, the 1801 population is an estimate.[26]

1801	1811	1821	1831	1841	1851	1861	1871	1881	1891	1901
1300	1345	1463	1582	1535	1496	1443	1419	1301	1283	1160

A Migrant Workforce

The population of 1,419 in 1871 is likely to have been lower had not the building of Hoar Cross Hall been taking place. This was just one of the building works which over several years would most likely have boosted the population by bringing in outside workers to add to the local workforce, this would include the restoration of St Peter's in 1865-68.

In 1871 Hoar Cross Hall was nearing completion, with an architectural modeller, a man working on the modelling on the plaster and 10 plasterers. In 1861 there were no stonemasons enumerated in Yoxall but in 1871 there were 6. In 1861, 2 plumbers were enumerated and in 1871, 4 plus a plumber/glazier. Also in 1871 there was a coppersmith, 2 gas fitters, a clerk of the new works, 3 whitesmiths (silversmiths), and a 'Jeweller etc', none of which occupations were enumerated in 1861. Places of birth of these extra workers covered many counties of England, and from as far apart as Devon and Scotland. Clergymen in Newborough and Yoxall arranged services in Hoar Cross school room for the benefit of these workers.[27]

Hugo Francis Meynell Ingram died before the new hall was completed and in 1872 work began on The Church of the Holy Angels which his widow Emily Charlotte had built at Hoar Cross in memory of him, designed by G. F. Bodley, and commissioned for £40,000.[28] Although Hoar Cross became a separate ecclesiastical parish in 1874 the building of the church was not completed until 1876, when the body of Hugo was removed from St Peter's and laid to rest in the Chantry Chapel where his widow was also laid in 1904.

Emily's building projects included the Meynell Ingram Cottage Hospital at Yoxall, and the adaptation of the Old Hall buildings at Hoar Cross to accommodate a children's home for orphaned boys, which became The Home of the Good Shepherd. In 1891 there was a Sister in Charge and a Mission Sister, both enumerated as Sisters of Charity, with a domestic servant who was both cook and laundress. The orphanage was home to 14 boys, with ages ranging from 5 to 12. Thomas Taswell was the only Yoxall born orphan boy, the rest came from other counties. Later the orphanage became known as St Michael's and was home to approximately 18 children, both girls and boys. In the grounds were underground tunnels said to lead to The Church of the Holy Angels. In 1982 the orphanage was closed and the building is currently a nursing home.

Hoar Cross Hall, built by the Meynell Ingram family and completed in 1871.

Hoar Cross Old Hall, adapted as an orphanage for young boys in 1888.

A Declining Population

Reasons for the declining population are not apparent except for the removal of the Morrey tape factory between the censuses of 1841 and 1851. That it was likely have some impact on the diminishing population is evidenced by the Yoxall born tape workers in Alrewas in 1851.

It is possible that some chose to leave Yoxall for greater occupational opportunities. In 1881, 51 people were enumerated in Barton whose birthplace was Yoxall,[29] these included 'large numbers' of domestic servants.[30] The occupations of Yoxall born men enumerated in Burton in 1891 included labourers who were probably general labourers but also a brewer's labourer and cooper, which were particularly in demand in Burton. The Yoxall born railway engine driver, Post Office sorting clerk and telegraphist, reflect a growing industrial town with increasing lines of communication, attracting immigrants from the nearby locality.

A search of the towns of Rugeley and Tamworth in the 1891 census reveals little evidence of migration from Yoxall. In the village of Branston 11 Yoxall born persons were enumerated, including two railway workers and a brewer's labourer. During the period 1851 to 1891 there was a marked interchange of people between Hamstall Ridware, Kings Bromley and Yoxall. By 1891 more people were moving to Yoxall from farther afield, especially those born over 30 miles from Yoxall, the total of which in 1851 was 85 and by 1891 was 194. Given the continued decline in population it seems that those born in Yoxall were leaving in ever greater numbers.

William Winter Riddell

The number of people who left Yoxall to seek their fortunes in Birmingham is not within the scope of this study, but one man was instrumental in the creation of a department store that continues to date. William Winter Riddell, the son of Edward and Hannah Riddell of Whitemere was baptised at Christchurch, Newchurch in 1827. He did not follow his father into the occupation of farmer, but in 1851 opened a retail drapery shop at 78 Bull Street Birmingham with Henry Wilkinson. Due to its success a wholesale branch was also established in Temple Row. John Rackham and William Matthew were apprenticed to the company in 1861 and 8 years later both were floor walkers. By 1878 both had become buyers and in 1881 the management of the retail side of the business was transferred to them, but shortly afterwards Wilkins withdrew from the company. Although his name does not grace the store, Rackham's of Birmingham had been founded in part by a Yoxall born entrepreneur. In 1875 William Riddell bought Blakeley Hall and Bromford Colliery in an auction for £17,200. He was the leading figure in a group of businessmen prepared to continue working the colliery but in 1877, as sole owner, he sold his leases of the Bromford and Blakely Hall mines.

A Young Community

Yoxall was a fairly young community with approximately a third of the population in both 1851 and 1891 censuses being under the age of 15, and more than half the population, nearly 59 per cent, below the age of 30. A similar pattern was evident in Abbots Bromley in 1851.[31]

In Yoxall the 1891 census shows a decline in the number of children below the age of 5 which may suggest evidence of family planning in Yoxall, or reflect the migration of young women, either for employment, or marriage. An analysis of marital status, those aged 16 and over, shows a tendency towards later marriage. In 1851 only 2 people, both men, were married under the age of 20 and none in 1891. In the age group 20-24 in 1851 there were 54 males and 73 females, 13 males and females of that age group were married. In 1891 the same age group comprised 48 males and 55 females out of which 17 females were married but only 5 males.

One possible explanation for the lack of early marriages is the number of servants 'living in'. Of the 133 servants enumerated in 1851 only 5 were married and in 1891, of 103 servants 6 were married, a clear indication that marriage amongst servants was strongly discouraged by employers.

Joseph and Jane Pott

The following case was revealed through a study of the censuses, Yoxall parish registers and registration of deaths. In 1851 Joseph, the son of John and Mary Pott of Wood Lane, was a labourer and brewer aged 37. His sister, Jane, was also in the household. In 1857 Jane married William Taswell, an agricultural labourer and in 1861 was living at Woodmill. Joseph remained at Woodlane with his now widowed mother and was enumerated as 'formerly agricultural labourer blind 15 years'. By 1881 Joseph was head of his household, which included his sister Jane, enumerated as married and also blind, and Jane's daughter, 19 year old Elizabeth Taswell, who died in 1888. In 1891 Elizabeth was enumerated with her brother, as a widow, her seemingly estranged husband having died in 1885. Joseph died the following year and in 1901 Jane was enumerated alone in Victoria Street. She died in 1912 aged 78.

Yoxall Parish Council

In November 1894 a preliminary meeting of the rate payers of the parish was held with regard to forming a parish council. It was agreed that there should be no religious or political bias and that all should work together for the good of the whole parish. It was also agreed that nine members should be elected, and these were Father Parker, Dr Armson, Messrs Symonds, Beard, Bloore, Brown, Green, Watts and Shipton. Dr Armson was appointed chairman, a position he retained for many years.[32] The number has since been increased to 11 members. Prior to the building of Yoxall Parish Hall meetings were held in the girls' school room, the library, and occasionally at the rectory.

In 1895 it was proposed and carried that a safe be provided for the use of the Council, and that two additional lamps be put up in the main street of the village.[33] In 1896 negotiations were taking place regarding separating the ecclesiastical and parochial charities. At the same meeting a copy of the will of Richard Cross was received and it was found that property left by him in the Yoxall Meadow, called Big Carr, was for 6 widows of deceased ministers, and not has had been thought by many in the parish, to widows of deceased parishioners.[34]

In 1897 the Parish Council met to discuss a new scheme for the division of the Town Lands charities. The property held by the charity was copyhold of the Manor of Yoxall. It was understood that the County Council intended to apply for power to elect two of the representative trustees, as they were interested in half of the non-ecclesiastical funds. Although the Parish Council did not object to the election, they thought the representatives from the County Council should reside in or near Yoxall, and the Parish Council should elect four representative trustees, who should be annually elected.[35]

Earlier that year Mr J. Green had asked if in future the council meetings would be open to parishioners. Rev. Cory said the law directed that meetings should be open, unless the council had private business transactions, and that he would like the public to be present, to which all agreed. Mr Barlow asked if members were agreeable for the parochial documents to be kept in the council safe instead of the church box, to which they were unanimous. Mr Barlow also asked if they were in favour of the Boys' Old School being converted into a parish room. A gentleman of the parish [John Siward Arden] had offered liberally towards fitting the room up. This was followed by a discussion as to whom the room belonged to, but they were in favour of converting it into a parish room or hall.[36] The following year it was unanimously agreed to postpone the Public Hall scheme until the next meeting.[37] It was not to be until the turn of the century that Yoxall had a Parish Hall.

In 1899 it was proposed and seconded that a pillar box should be put up at Hadley End, also a Sunday delivery of post to Morrey, and it was decided to write to the Post Office authorities in reference to this. At the same meeting J. Rowles was reappointed overseer and clerk to the Parish Council, and W. Brown and J. Barlow were reappointed trustees in place of church wardens. It was also agreed that the trustees of the Town Lands should pay the bill for the new street lamps and the lighting of them.[38] In October it was reported that there was only one tender for the lighting of the village lamps, that of Mr H. Crisp, who agreed to undertake the work up to Christmas 1899 for the sum of 8s per week, and he was to find his own materials.[39]

In 1900 the clerk's salary was raised to £1 per annum. Mr Bull applied to the parish council for a new lamp to be placed next to the post office, and Mr Roobottom for one in Victoria Street. The chairman promised to bring the matter before the parish council later in the year.[40]

Yoxall Parish Council 1904. Left to right,hand facing, back row: Mr Pott, farmer of Morrey; -?; Harry Wright, builder; -? Front row: Joseph Barlow, rates collector and farmer of Hadley End; Rev. Alex Cory, rector; Dr Frank Greasley Armson; Father Parker, priest of Woodlane; David Causer, farmer of Hadley End.

Victoria Street was not named in the population census until 1901. It seems likely that it was named at the time of the Diamond Jubilee in 1897. In 1914 a letter from the Rural District Council was read at a parish council meeting intimating that the Council had delegated its powers for one year to number the houses and name the streets in the districts of the parish councils, and questioning whether the Parish Council would proceed in the matter. It was also pointed out that the cost of providing the numbers of the houses would fall upon occupiers, and naming the streets on the District Council. As the numbering and naming seemed unnecessary it was resolved that no action be taken. A further letter was read from the District Council requesting to know for the information of the Local Government Board, the number of new houses which may be required in the district to provide necessary accommodation for the working classes, and involving the Council to consider the question in respect of the parish.[41]

Yoxall Turnpike

Turnpike Trusts were set up by Acts of Parliament to collect road tolls for maintaining principle roads in Britain. The Yoxall Bridge-Ashbourne Turnpike Road 1766-1889 was the subject of an essay published by the University of Keele in 1979, from which the following information is extracted. The total length of the road was 19 miles, and a tollhouse stood on the Yoxall side of the River Trent. The Turnpike Trust Act laid down the following maximum tolls:

Horse, pair of oxen, a bullock or other beast drawing a carriage 3d.
Pack horse or other beast not drawing a carriage 1d.
Drove of oxen or cattle 10d a score.
Drove of calves, swine, sheep or lambs 5d a score.

By an Act of 1809 the tolls had increased:

Horse, pair of oxen, bullock or other beast drawing a carriage with wheels less than six inches in breadth 6d.
As above, with wheels more than six inches 4 ½d.
Horse or other beast not drawing a carriage 1 ½d.
The charge for droves remained unchanged but tolls were double on Sundays. Extra exemptions from tolls were made for ploughs or plough animals going to and from a blacksmith or farrier, and the carriage of vagrants. Additional penalties were imposed for fraud £5, also riding on footpaths, letting animals roam on the road, damaging the surface of the road and obstructing collectors or surveyors all of which had a penalty of 40s.

The present A515 follows the original alignment of the turnpike road, except in three places where alterations were made to the turnpike road in order to avoid flooding. Near Yoxall Bridge the turnpike road used to run diagonally across the Mill Holmes and Mickle Meadow to the beginning of Meadow Lane. The original line of the road at the north end of the village was up Victoria Street and Longcroft Lane, and ran more or less parallel to the Swarbourn to join the Sudbury road at Northcroft Cottage. In 1813, due to flooding, the course of the Swarbourn was altered at Hall Bridge to move it further away from the turnpike road and the length down to Bond End was straightened. Hall Bridge must have been rebuilt at this time as the worn date stone was inscribed '1813'.[42] In 1834 a new route was taken which swung the road left away from Victoria Street and proximity to the river. The third deviation was made in the mid 1920s at Woodlane Bridge.[43] There is a cast iron milepost at Woodlane, one of the few remaining traces of the turnpike road, but no remains of the Yoxall tollhouse.

Dr Charles Greasley Armson held a season ticket for the turnpike as he used it regularly to visit his patients. He told his grandson Dr Gerald that one evening a smart carriage and pair brought a young girl in the last stages of labour to the tollhouse, the unknown woman with her left a bag of one hundred sovereigns and told the tollhouse keeper that she would return in the morning and the wife was to do what was necessary. A baby girl was born during the night and at dawn the carriage returned for the young girl and the baby was left for the keeper's wife to bring up.[44]

Turnpike roads would have been unpopular with many who had to pay for the privilege of using them. An extract from 'A Common Place Book' dated 1869, belonging to E. R. Cottingham includes its author's opinion of them while describing Yoxall: 'This antiquated village lies at the heart of the picturesque valley of the Trent. As you enter it by the Turnpike Road (for it boasts of such an abomination) on your way from Lichfield to, towering above, looking grand and solemn stands what is called the 'Town Hill' surrounded by its few huts and hovels - in old folk lore this is generally supposed to have been where Noah and his family in the Ark cast anchor, hence the name 'Woodhouses' - judging from the inhabitants of this bright little dell one would be almost inclined to believe there is some truth in such Legend, thus disputing that it was on Mount Ararat that the old ship came to anchor. The village has nothing very particular in an architectural sense to boast save and except the Noble Church lately rebuilt and this has some very good specimens of facsimile Gothic architecture about it'.[45]

Roads, Weighbridge and Sewerage

In 1838 the Town Lands paid £186 for making a new road from Mill Bridge (Hall Bridge) towards Woodhouses and the following year £20 towards completing the 'new Road at Town Hill'. In 1850 they paid Mr J. Brown £70 towards purchasing and erecting a weighing machine and in 1851 paid him a further £34, the remaining expenses of erecting the weighing machine. It became known as the 'machine house' and in 1852 Stephen Leedham was paid 2s for 'Paint & Oil etc at Machine House'.[46] This was opposite the Crown Inn, situated on the triangular road island.

In 1877 a report was read from the Inspector of Nuisances at a meeting of the Lichfield Board of Guardians regarding the drainage at Yoxall, which was said to be very bad. The sewage was conveyed by open ditches into streams from which cattle had to drink. It was agreed to refer the report to the Guardians of the Parish of Yoxall.[47]

In 1890 a letter to the editor of the *Burton Chronicle* was published regarding the state of the road in Yoxall from the Crown Inn to Bond End. This was signed 'an old inhabitant', who stated: 'It is only a short time back that one of the ladies of the village one evening walked into a pit lying beside the road, and was rescued from what might have proved a very serious incident. Surely the owner of the field or local authority will take immediate steps to have the spot fenced round and made safe'.[48]

A Railway for Yoxall

There were several attempts to run railways through Yoxall and its surrounding areas. In 1845 a scheme was proposed by the Stafford and Uttoxeter Railway to run from Castle Church in Staffordshire to Sawley in Derbyshire. It was intended that this would run through Yoxall, Hadley End and Hoar Cross but this was abandoned.

In 1895 a deputation from Lichfield, Uttoxeter and Abbots Bromley petitioned the LNWR for a railway from Lichfield to Uttoxeter, suggesting that this would make possible a large milk trade with London by opening up pasture lands round Abbots Bromley, Newborough, Hoar Cross, Yoxall, Kings Bromley and Hamstall Ridware.[49] It was also suggested that it would aid the developing industry in Uttoxeter. By 1898 it became apparent that local support for the line had waned and the scheme was dropped.[50] Barton and Walton Station, built in 1840, was as near as rail access ever came to Yoxall.

Chapter 3

Yoxall Gentry

The Welles of Hoar Cross Hall and the Ardens of Longcroft Hall are two of the Yoxall families who were entitled to bear heraldic arms. The Meynell Ingram family of Hoar Cross Hall were also armigerous and their history and that of their Staffordshire home have been covered elsewhere, notably by Gareth Evans, *Hoar Cross Hall, Staffordshire: Portrait of a Victorian Country House*. The wills and inventories of the Welles and early Ardens featured in *A social history of Yoxall in the sixteenth and seventeenth centuries,* edited by Denis Stuart.

Welles of Hoar Cross Hall

The family, whose name had anciently been Yoxall, moved to Lichfield and lived near a well in Bacon Street. They took the name Attewell, which they later changed to Welles and acquired the manor of Hoar Cross in 1426-7, when John Welles married Alice, daughter and heiress of Richard Aston.[1] During the reign of Henry VIII the estate consisted of 200 acres of arable land, 200 of pasture, 40 of meadow, and 50 of wood.[2] Shaw quotes Dr Wilkes' description of Hoar Cross Hall as '…a large house, built at several times, as appears by the several sorts of building. It stands upon a hill, and is encompassed with a moat, over which is a draw-bridge'. He added that 'Welles that married Aston seems to have built most of the old buildings and the porter's lodge because their arms are in almost every part to be met with'. In the house was a small chapel dedicated to Our Lady, with an inscription within the roof 'Pray for the soul of Thomas Wellys esq'. The old house was pulled down about 1740 and a new mansion built by the then owner, believed to be Mr Webb.[3] In 1794 this was also destroyed and later rebuilt by Lord Scarsdale as a hunting seat. Neither of the halls were built on the site of the present hall, which was completed in 1871 by the Meynell Ingrams.

Humphrey Welles

It seems likely that Humphrey, born in 1502, probably at Hoar Cross, was the great grandson of John and Alice by their son Thomas and grandson John Welles and his wife Anne, a daughter of John Fitzherbert of Norbury, Derbyshire. Much of Humphrey's career is uncertain as both an uncle and a nephew bore the same name. He may have been one of the two esquires who acknowledged receipt of an inventory of the property of Burton College, formerly Burton Abbey, in their role as deputies to Sir William Paget, Henry VIII's chief secretary. What is more certain is that he was an escheator (an official concerned with the crown's claim to property) from 1543-4, a member of parliament for Newcastle under Lyme from 1545-47, sheriff of the county 1559-60 and a justice of the peace from 1538 until his death. It seems fairly certain that he was also a clerk of the Mint at the Tower: "Welles, Humphrey (d.1569) clerk of the mint (clerk of the irons), Tower, 24 Mar. 1557 £13 6s 8d. P.a. 1557-1569". The office was filled with fees, due since the death of its holder. In fact Humphrey died in 1565 ending a highly successful career. In 1564 he was described by the Bishop to the Privy Council as "meet to continue office [as J.P.]; accounted of good men an adversary to religion and no favourer thereof, neither in word nor deed, but better learned than the rest".[4]

A collection of poetry formerly known as MS. Rawlinson C. 813 has been the subject of a thorough investigation and the conclusion was formed that Humphrey Welles was the owner and compiler of the collection, and probably the author of many of the lyrics. The work is clearly that of someone well acquainted with the Tudor court. The work is now known as 'The Welles Anthology'.[5] Humphrey married Mary, daughter of William Chetwynd of Ingestre, Staffordshire, but died without issue. In his will of 1564 Humphrey left numerous legacies to relatives, bequests to the poor of Yoxall, Newborough, Abbots Bromley and Tutbury and money for the upkeep of local bridges. He bequeathed lands in various other places, including Hamstall Ridware, Pipe Ridware, Blymhill and Wheatley Aston, also the chantry of Yoxall. Following his death the inventory of 1565 records his goods and chattels, room by room plus his farm and stock and implements for both his manor at Hoar Cross and his property at Tamhorne in Whittington.

Humphrey was very specific in his instructions regarding his tomb. His will states that should he die in Staffordshire, or any other county within thirty miles of the parish church of Yoxall he would be buried in the church and that 'the uppermost forms next beneath our Lady chapel be taken up & that my body be buried where the said forms stood between the two pillars that stand betwixt the body of the church & our Lady chapel And I will that a comely & decent tomb of alabaster set upon me with two pictures of alabaster the one for me and the other for my wife laid aloft upon the same tomb with our arms and cognisances set in divers places of the same & with the scriptures about the said tomb of the days and years of our several deaths & then I will that the said 3 forms be cut shorter & so set to the side of the said tomb or else that there be a comely pew made up and set betwixt the tomb and the body of the church'. If he died over thirty miles from the parish church he instructed that the memorial within the church in which he would be buried would be only a gravestone. The tomb was described as being under the two arches that divide the middle aisle and north aisle.[6] It is likely that it was the work of one of the Royley family, tomb makers of Burton.

Monument of Humphrey and Mary Welles, sepia, drawing 1839 by J. Buckler who expressed his indignation at its removal to a darkened corner. (Staffordshire Views, XII.154. Reproduced by permission of the Trustees of the William Salt Library).

Detail of monument of Humphrey and Mary Welles. (Photo by author).

Although Humphrey Welles was buried in the place of his choosing, his tomb chest was not to remain over his body, and may have first been moved during the substantial alterations to the church in 1819. Although an artist who signed himself only as 'B' but was most likely J. Buckler, wrote beneath his drawing in 1839 'This fine monument was most barbarously removed from the East end of the North aisle about 12 years ago, into a dark corner at the West end of the church - and pewed or boarded so closely, that it can scarcely now be seen!'

Humphrey's brother Robert, second son of John Welles succeeded to the Hoar Cross estate. He also left no surviving children and died in 1594. The estate then passed to Humphrey, the son of Richard, the third son of John Welles.

Despite the fact that the Welles family were listed as Catholic recusants from 1607-1657, James I visited Hoar Cross Hall in 1617.[7] It is perhaps surprising that James visited the family, especially following the Gunpowder Plot of 1605 and the accompanying wave of anti-Catholicism. (The plotters were apprehended at Holbeach House, Himley, which was then also within the county of Staffordshire). James would surely have been informed that the son and heir of his host had been excommunicated for Catholicism, yet he chose the hospitality of the Welles, rather than a family which demonstrated more loyalty to the King James Bible, published in 1611.

Ardens of Longcroft Hall

Few families can be traced back as far as the Ardens who according to Burke's Landed Gentry descend from Guy de Warwick, who is said to have died in 929. They can with more certainty be traced back to the Saxon Aelfwine, Sheriff of Warwickshire, whose son Thurkill of Warwick, in the time of Edward the Confessor, was said to have assumed a Norman surname, taken from the Forest of Arden. The Ardens of Longcroft descend from the Warwickshire Ardens whose main seat was at Park Hall, Castle Bromwich, Warwickshire.[8]

While the main purpose of the following is to trace the Arden succession to Longcroft Hall, some family members who did not inherit have been included, often because they had other links to the area, some by marriage, some by being commemorated on memorials in St Peter's and others for general interest. However they all have in common descent from the line of the Arden family of Longcroft Hall.

Early painting of Longcroft Hall. (Reproduced by permission of Elisabeth Macfarlane).

The first record of the name Longcroft appeared during the reign of Henry III when William Ferrers, Earl of Derby and Lord of the Manor of Yoxall, granted two pastures called Longcroft and other land to Roger de Yoxhall, rector of Yoxall.[9] Its line of descent is unknown between Roger de Yoxall and Richard Marres, gentleman, who in his will of 1558 left the occupancy of 'all that my capital cheffe house at longcroftees & all suche grounds as by noue in myne occupancy(i)on lying to the same house as well suche as I purchased of Clemande Agarde' to this widow Joyce, 'so that she may better bring up my children'. She was to pay the Lord of the Manor 12s 4d in rent and the queen the chief rent. His son and heir, Richard to have all other lands immediately after his decease. He named the overseer of his will as his kinsman, Humphrey Welles.

The gate house to Longcroft Hall overlooking Yoxall village, painted in 1731. The image of a horse and groom in a landscape became popular with many landowners, among the most famous examples is Tristram Shandy, a Bay Racehorse held by a Groom in an Extensive Landscape, painted by George Stubbs, circa 1760. (Reproduced by permission of Elisabeth Macfarlane).

The Ardens had held land in Yoxall from at least before the death of Robert Arden in 1537.[10] The land came into the possession of his cousin and heir Thomas, (second son of Thomas Arden of Park Hall, Warwickshire), who then held '2 messuages, a garden, a croft and divers lands, meadows and pastures in Yoxall' and '33 acres of arable land, and 13 acres of meadow called Milne Holmes, containing divers parcels of pasture near the water of Trent, in Yoxall and divers other messuages in Yoxall'.[11] Thomas died in 1563 and in 1568 his son Simon rented the land from William Hollys, Lord of the Manor, for 24s 3 ½ d.[12] This may have been the estate of Longcroft or it may have been established when Simon purchased unnamed land in Yoxall during the reign of Elizabeth I, providing her with one light horse and payment £1 6s 8d for his lands in Yoxall.[13] In 1573 Simon Arden was described as 'armiger of Longcroft Hall, Yoxall', but was allegedly over 80 years old when he moved to Yoxall.[14] He died in 1602 aged 100 years.[15] Shakespeare's mother, Mary Arden was related to Simon Arden, through a shared ancestor, Walter Arden of Park Hall, Warwickshire, who died in 1502. Shakespeare's father unsuccessfully applied to impale the coat of arms of the Warwickshire Ardens on his own. He was eventually granted the arms of a Cheshire branch of the Arden family.

The simplified chart below shows the connection between Simon Arden, above and William Shakespeare:

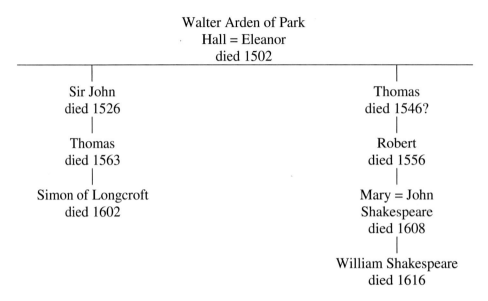

Walter Arden of Park
Hall = Eleanor
died 1502

Sir John
died 1526

Thomas
died 1563

Simon of Longcroft
died 1602

Thomas
died 1546?

Robert
died 1556

Mary = John
Shakespeare
died 1608

William Shakespeare
died 1616

Ambrose Arden (d.1624) of Longcroft Hall. Only known son of Simon Arden. In his will of that year Ambrose requested burial in Yoxall parish church and a gravestone of alabaster, which has not survived. His inventory gives some idea of the interior of Longcroft Hall as it lists the rooms as follows: best chamber, green chamber, seeled (panelled) chamber, his own chamber, the porch chamber, little chamber at the stair head, high building chamber, yellow chamber, little chamber at the kitchen, maid's chamber, little parlour, dining parlour, hall, buttery and kitchen.

Humphrey Arden (d.1634) of Longcroft Hall. Eldest son of Ambrose (d.1624). The only rooms recorded by his appraisers are the yellow, sealed, green and high building chambers and the parlour. Humphrey was succeeded by his eldest son Henry.

Henry Arden (c.1625-76) of Longcroft Hall. Eldest son of Humphrey Arden (d.1634) and his first wife Elizabeth. He inherited Longcroft Hall at the death of his father, and came of age about 1646. He died without issue and with his younger full brother John (c.1625-1709) being a citizen of London, Longcroft Hall passed to his half-brother Humphrey Arden. An alabaster slab on the floor of St Peter's commemorates Henry, his brother John, also Henry Arden Esq., of Longcroft who died in 1772 aged 63 and for whom no further information has been discovered.

Humphrey Arden (c.1631-1705) of Longcroft Hall. Only son of Humphrey (d.1634) by his second wife Jane Rowbotham. His half brother John (c.1625-1709), who died without issue, appears to have left London and spent his final years at Longcroft. In his will of 1704 he refers to himself as 'John Arden of Longcrofts'. Amongst the many bequests in his will he bequeathed to his nephew Henry Arden one hundred pounds, 'towards the building of the other part of the house'. If the house referred to is Longcroft Hall, it suggests extensive work was being carried out at that time. For how long the widowed Katherine Watson occupied Longcroft Hall is uncertain, but her will of 1691 states she was of Longcroft, and the inventory of the same year lists the rooms of a substantial house including the yellow and green chambers and high building which appear in previous inventories of Longcroft Hall. She also named her godson Henry Arden as her executor.

Henry Arden (1665-1728) of Longcroft Hall. Only son of Humphrey (d.1705) and nephew of John (d.1709). In his will he left five pounds to the poor of the parish of Yoxall to be distributed by the overseers of the poor 'on the day next after my funeral at their own houses (provided they the said poore doe not come to the house to be troublesome there on my funeral day & such as doe soe shall be excluded of their share therein)'. He requested burial in the chancel of Yoxall parish church as near to his wife and sisters 'as with conveniency it can be done'. He is commemorated on a marble plaque at St Peter's as 'of the Ancient and Worthy Family of ye Ardens in Warwickshire'. His wife Anne and twin sister Catherine are also recorded on the plaque which was erected to their memory by his son John Arden who succeeded his father.

John Arden (1693-1734) of Longcroft Hall. Only son of Henry (d.1728). In 1713 he married his first wife Anna Catherina (1697-1727), eldest daughter of John Newton of Kings Bromley. In 1728 he married his second wife, Ann, daughter of Rev. John Spateman, rector of Yoxall. The same year he inherited Longcroft Hall on the death of his father. John was High Sheriff of Staffordshire in 1730.

Henry Arden (1724-82) of Longcroft Hall. Only son of John (d.1734) and Anna Catherine, he inherited Longcroft Hall on his father's death and came of age in 1745. He married Alethea, daughter of Robert Cotton of Worcester. Their memorial is one of three marble plaques high on the west wall in St Peter's church. It also names their seven children, the eldest son being John who succeeded him. Others include Henry who died in the West Indies; Humphrey (1758-1809), an officer in the 34th Regiment, who married Maria, daughter of Dr Walter Landor of Ipsley Court, Warwickshire, and half sister to the poet Walter Savage Landor; Samuel (1760-1824), who served in the Royal Navy and was Lieut. in 1781 when he lost an arm in action against an American frigate on the Newfoundland banks. He was a captain from 1783 and is buried in the Royal Naval Hospital burial ground at Greenwich.

Rev. John Arden (1752-1803) of Longcroft Hall. Eldest son of Henry (d.1782), he was educated at Repton and St John's College, Cambridge. He was ordained deacon in 1774 and priest in 1776 and was a curate in Leicestershire and Warwickshire, also rector in Norfolk before becoming minister of Kings Bromley by 1786, and JP for Staffordshire. In 1775 he married Margaret Elizabeth, only child of Rear Admiral Joseph Hamar. His monument and that of his wife are so high on the south wall that they easily escape notice, so presumably they are amongst the Arden memorials re-sited during the restoration of the church. The inscription on John Arden's monument notes that they had 17 children and names the 12 who survived him as well as the five who died. His widow continued to live at Longcroft Hall for the rest of her life. Despite bearing so many children, she survived to the age of 88, dying in 1842. Her nearby monument records 'for upwards of 40 years she lived a widow at the head of a numerous family…'. It is most likely that the couple were buried with many other Ardens, in the family vault beneath the chancel floor.

Below are some of the children of Rev. John and Margaret Elizabeth:

John Arden (1776-1809). The first born, John was a Major in King's Own/3rd Light Dragoons.

Henry Arden (1780-1814), fourth child, Lieutenant in 61st Foot, was wounded in action at Toulouse in 1814, during the Peninsula Campaign and died shortly afterwards of his wounds.

Samuel Arden (1782-1822), the sixth child, Major in East India Co.'s 27th Regiment of Bengal Native Infantry. In 1812 he married Jane Hannah, daughter of James Franklyn, Mayor of Bristol. The couple had three sons and two daughters and died at Saugor, India, in 1822 of bilious fever. It is not known where their children lived following their deaths but it is likely that they lived at Longcroft Hall with their grandfather The Rev. John Arden. It is certain though that at least one of the children visited Longcroft Hall in adulthood. Samuel and Jane were the parents of Eliza Jane Arden, baptised at St Peter's in 1813, where she married Burton brewer Michael Thomas Bass in 1835. They were the parents of Michael Arthur Bass, 1st Baron Burton.

The second son of Major Samuel and Jane Hannah, George Arden, emigrated to Australia in 1838 at the age of 18. In Melbourne the same year, with Thomas Strode as a printer-partner, they launched the weekly *Port Phillip Gazette*. Together they produced Victoria's first pamphlet, *Articles and Rules for the…Melbourne Union Benefit Society.* Amongst their output, they published in 1840 Arden's *Latest Information with Regard to Australia Felix,* which was the first book published in Melbourne. This was published shortly afterwards in London under a modified title.

Although George was a competent writer, his promising future was not to be. His indiscretions led to legal proceedings which undermined his character and career. Strode had already left the *Gazette,* when in 1842 George lost the publication. He attempted others but without success, the *Port Phillip Herald* ran only two issues of his articles. In 1844 he came to England, returning to Melbourne in 1846 with a wife he had married on his passage out. Again his literary career was troubled. In an undated letter from Longcroft he apologised to his agent for his 'fooleries and devilries'. In 1854 he died childless at Bakery Hill, Ballarat.[16] Arden Street in Melbourne was named after him.

William Arden (1785-1860), was the eighth child of Rev. John and Margaret Elizabeth. He was an 'Esquire' living with wife Letitia in Yoxall at Swarbourne House in 1827 when their son John Siward Arden was baptised at St Peter's. William became an army captain and in 1841 was enumerated at Fullbrook House, Barton-under-Needwood. The house still stands and is in Captain's Lane, which was named after him. Nearby is Arden Road, another tribute to the Arden family. William was buried at Yoxall. John Siward Arden was still living at Fullbrook House in 1881 and married Mary Hodgetts in 1888. In 1891 the couple were living at Hadley End, Hamstall Ridware. In 1897 he started a fund to raise money for a public hall in Yoxall and initially gave £200. However no progress was made and he later gave a further £100. It was not until 1904 that a foundation stone was laid and the following year the parish hall was opened.

George Arden (1793-1819), thirteenth child, was a Lieutenant in the Royal Navy. He died at sea in the West Indies.

FROM AN OLD SKETCH OF YOXALL BY THE REV. T. ARDEN

Thomas Arden possibly drew this c.1834-46, during his curacy at Yoxall. (Reproduced by permission of Elisabeth Macfarlane, © Blurb).

Rev. Thomas Arden (1796-1860), fifteenth child, was educated at Rugby and Trinity and Queen's College, Cambridge. (The first example of the College being named as Queens' was in 1823, in a printed version of the form of service for the Commemoration of Benefactors, therefore after Thomas attended). He was ordained deacon in 1819 and priest in 1820 he was a curate in Gloucester and Warwickshire, and became rector of Bassingham, Norfolk, 1832-42, followed by a stipendiary curacy at Yoxall, c.1834-46. In 1834 he married Isabella Mary, daughter of the Rev. Edward Cooper, deceased who had been rector of Hamstall Ridware and Yoxall. During Thomas's time as curate at Yoxall the couple lived at Longcroft and four of their children were baptised at St Peter's. Thomas became chaplain to the Magdalen Asylum in Birmingham, 1850-53, and rector of Walton upon Trent 1858-1860.

The seventeenth and final child of Rev. John and Margaret Elizabeth was Mary Jane (1801-62). In 1825 she married at Yoxall George Woodroffe Franklyn (c.1801-70), a tobacco and snuff manufacturer and MP for Poole. The couple had two sons and four daughters. The marriage forged a link between the Ardens and the Franklyn family who would eventually become the owners of Longcroft Hall.

The second son of the Rev. John and Margaret Elizabeth appears below the rest for reasons of clarity, as the line of descent of the Ardens of Longcroft Hall follows on from him.

Rev. Francis Edward Arden (1777-1855) of Longcroft Hall. Second of the seventeen children of Rev. John Arden and Margaret Elizabeth. He was a curate in Norfolk and later rector in Norfolk and Cambridgeshire. In 1803 he married Rachael, daughter of John Pinckard of Towcaster, Northants. He inherited Longcroft Hall from his mother in 1842, and following his death it passed to his second son Rev. Henry Cotton Arden (q.v.). A brass strip in St Chad's corner of St Peter's was erected to his memory by his son William 'late of the King's Hussars'.

Rev. Francis Edward (1809-53), eldest son of Rev. Francis Edward Arden and his wife Rachael was sometimes referred to as Edward Francis. He was a chaplain and companion to Lord Ferrers in 1842-46 and perpetual curate at Staunton Harold, Leicestershire. He was a witness in a breach of promise case against the Earl and was described as going out at night with the Earl in disguise 'for frolics of a kind unbecoming to his calling'.[17] He was unbeneficed in 1851 and became dependent on his father for financial support. He died unmarried and without issue.

Rev. Henry Cotton Arden (1810-65) of Longcroft Hall. The second son of Rev. Francis and Rachael and eldest surviving son when he inherited Longcroft Hall from his father in 1855. He was a rector in Norfolk and let the Longcroft Estate to Benjamin Haigh Allen, who was enumerated there in 1851 as a landed proprietor, and in 1861 as a magistrate and deputy Lieutenant for the county of Stafford. At the time of his death Henry Cotton Arden was at Longcroft Hall. He was buried at Yoxall and Longcroft passed to his younger brother, George Pinckard Arden.

George Pinckard Arden (1813-86), third son of Rev. Francis Edward and Rachel, was a solicitor and insurance agent in a private practice, he lived for most of his life in Essex. He inherited Longcroft Hall from his eldest brother, Henry Cotton Arden in 1865 but never lived there and the house was occupied by his brother William to whom he sold the estate in c.1878. He was buried under the altar at St Peter's and is commemorated on a brass plaque. Three of his twelve children lived in the area, the eldest of these was his first child, Caroline Louise (1843-1941), who lived at Bond End, Yoxall and died unmarried; the second born was Emma Fanny (1845-1921) who in 1871 married her cousin Rev. Edward Thomas Arden (1837-77), vicar of Rangemore; Harriet Maria (1849-1940) the fifth child, who also lived at Bond End and died unmarried.

Rev. William Henry Percival Arden (1863-1956), was the twelfth and final child of George Pinckard Arden. In 1889 he married Emily Beatrice, the daughter of Rev. J.B. Lowe, rector of Yoxall, and was vicar of Whiteparish 1915-1925. The Calvary which stands in the Churchyard of St Peter's is dedicated to his son, Lieut. Humphrey Arden who was killed in action during WW1. WHP Arden died in February 1956 at Torquay and his wife died the following month. Their ashes were interred at the south side of the Calvary Memorial.

William Arden (1817-80) of Longcroft Hall. The seventh child of Rev. Francis Edward and Rachael, and younger brother of George Pinckard. He served as a surgeon in the Army 1841-66, and became Surgeon-Major and retired as Lieutenant-Colonel. He later held a commission in King's Own 1st Staffordshire Militia and was a JP for Staffordshire. He purchased Longcroft from his brother c.1878. He died unmarried and without issue. The east window in the chancel of St Peter's, by Messrs. Burlison & Grylls of London, is dedicated to him, also a brass plaque on the south wall, erected in his memory by his niece C. L. Arden (Caroline Louisa).

Alwyne Hills Arden (1859-1915) of Longcroft Hall. Eleventh child and second son of George Pinckard Arden and his wife Caroline. He served in the Army prior to his marriage in 1882, and the same year he purchased a brewery at Stafford. He had inherited Longcroft Hall from his uncle, William Arden in 1880. That year he employed builders Thomas Lowe and Sons of Burton to restore Longcroft Hall. When work began it was soon discovered that various additional work was necessary and a dispute arose between Alwyne and the builders. The parties failed to agree on whether the initial estimate formed the basis of a contract. Also whether the builders were liable for damage to the work by frost, the repair of glass broken by workmen, and the methods of cleaning and renovating the old oak work. The *Burton Chronicle* reported in June 1883 that the case went to arbitration and cost £3,000 but did not divulge the outcome. It seems likely that this was not in favour of Alwyne as by 1884 he was bankrupt and sold it to his older brother, George Edward Arden that year. He emigrated to South Africa and served with South African forces during WW1.

George Edward Arden (1853-1921) of Longcroft Hall. Eldest son of George
Pinckard Arden and Caroline. In 1878 he married Alice, daughter of Dr.
Edward Hemmings Snoad, surgeon of Yoxall. He farmed at Warwickshire and
Sussex and later lived in the suburbs of London. In 1884 he purchased the
Longcroft Hall estate from his brother Alwyne Hills Arden but sold it to his
kinsman, Holland Franklyn in 1890.

Rev. Thomas Ward Franklyn (1801-76) was the brother of George Woodroffe
Franklyn (c.1800-70) who married Mary Jane Arden, seventeenth child of the
Rev. John and Margaret Elizabeth.

Holland Franklyn (1835-1919) of Longcroft Hall, was a barrister and youngest
son of Rev. Thomas Ward Franklyn. Holland's daughter, Hilda Alethea
Franklyn died in British Columbia in 1988 aged 102. Apart from purchasing
Longcroft Hall in 1890 Holland also had a house in Lowndes Square, London.

Alwyne Holland Franklyn (1886-1965), only son of Holland Franklyn and his
second wife, Lottie Alves. Alwyne was 2nd Lieutenant, Staffordshire Yeomanry
in 1911. He inherited Longcroft Hall from his father in 1919 and was living
there in 1938, prior to the house being requisitioned in World War 2. He
emigrated to Metchosin, Vancouver Island, British Columbia and became a
Canadian citizen about 1940.

Longcroft Hall retained the once fashionable E shape, which suggests it was
built, or rebuilt, in the late sixteenth century. Shaw noted that the house had
been modernised but still had an appearance of antiquity, as it was surrounded
by a moat, but that in 1796 the moat was filled in. Various sources have
claimed that George Humphrey Arden (1790-1816), the eleventh child of Rev.
John and Margaret Elizabeth drowned in the moat having shortly before saved
one of his brothers from the same fate. In fact Thomas Hamar Arden (1786-91),
the ninth child was buried at Yoxall and the entry has the additional note
'drowned in the moat'. The delay of five years between the death of the child
and the filling of the moat suggests this was not the reason. In 1795 Thomas
Arden, the fourteenth child was buried at the age of 7 months. It seems unlikely
that one so young also drowned. Whether it was filled as part of the
modernisation, or as a precautionary measure, childbirth being a regular event
for the couple, can only be speculated on.

Included in Shaw's extracts from the catalogues of Greene's Museum at
Lichfield was an altar piece five feet nine inches by three feet, in oil colours,
painted on oak board, containing ten biblical scenes. This is described as an
ancient painting which had belonged to the Arden family for many years and
had been donated to the museum by the late Mrs Arden, widow of Henry Arden
Esquire of Longcroft.[18] The museum was in existence c.1748-93, the date of the
gift of the altar piece would therefore have been between 1782 when Henry
Arden of Longcroft died and the death of his widow Althea the following year.

Altarpiece from Longcroft Hall.
(Reproduced in Shaw, Staffs. I, 1798, Pl.XXXII).

Longcroft Hall, date unknown. (Reproduced by permission of the Magic Attic).

Amongst the trees which sheltered the house from the north and east winds and made the scene picturesque was 'a remarkable old oak'.[19] This may have been the Raven Oak which became one of the oldest trees in Staffordshire. How many renovations Longcroft Hall received is uncertain but the will of John Arden in 1704 suggests that work was in progress, or at least planned at that time. From the legislation which took place in 1880 when Longcroft Hall was in the ownership of Alwyne Hills Arden it is clear that large scale restoration had begun but not clear as to whether it was completed. In 1881 the census recorded two farms in the hamlet of Longcroft with a total acreage of 282 acres, these were most likely part of the Longcroft Estate. During World War II Longcroft Hall was requisitioned by the War Office and used as a training centre for the Home Guard, due to neglect and vandalism it was demolished in 1955.

For many years a beer house was known as the Arden Arms. This later became Arden Cottage, but is now known as Buttercup Cottage and is situated in Victoria Street, which leads to Longcroft Lane and the area known as Longcroft.

The Arms of the Ardens of Longcroft are: Ermine, a fess chequy or and az. [Ermine with a chequered band in gold and blue]. Crest: on a chapeau purpure, turned up erm., a wild boar passant, or. [a purple velvet cap with turned up ermine affixed to the helmet, a wild boar walking with right paw raised, gold]. Motto: Quo me cunque vocat patrai. [Wherever my country calls]. At the top of the memorial to Rev. John Arden is a boar, also depicted on a badge on the Calvary.

During the restoration of St Peter's many memorials were lost, including some commemorating the Arden family, which had been in the floor of the chancel, one was discovered in a blacksmith's shop. Lieut. Col. William Arden of Longcroft placed the remaining memorials to his family in the chancel. He also carved two pews which face north and these were used by the Arden family until they sold Longcroft.[20]

Daniel Astle, father of Thomas Astle (q.v), Rector John Spateman and Thomas Swinnerton are amongst the men of Yoxall who were armigerious.

High Hall Hill

A 14th century manuscript depicts a medieval house at Woodhouses, which is possibly the original High Hall Hill.[21]

High Hall Hill, also known as the manor of High Wall Hill is in the hamlet of Woodhouses. It appears that at various times it was occupied by tenants. In 1543 a case was heard between Stephen Warde a gentleman in possession of High Wall Hill and William Yoxsell of London. Yoxsell and others were said

Medieval House at Woodhouses, Yoxall. (Early 14th century marginal drawing in The British Library, © The British Library Board, Egerton MS. 3041, f.26v). The house was possibly on the site of the present High Hall Hill.

to have assembled at High Wall Hill and 'with weapons offensive and invasive' assaulted the tenant Richard Wood, and drove him, his wife and children from the property, a claim that was denied.[22] In 1553 Andrew Vavasour granted the manor of High Wall Hill and land in Yoxall, Hoar Cross, Morrey, Woodhouses, Barton and Edingale to Ellen Warde, widow, for her life.[23]

In the 1660s High Hall Hill was the home of Thomas Illsely, who died in 1698. His daughter Sarah was co heir of her father's estate and the wife of Thomas Swinnerton who died in 1713. Shaw recorded a flat stone at St Peter's with a Latin inscription for Thomas Swinnerton of Highwall-hill, gent., second son of Thomas Swinnerton of Butterton, gent of Staffordshire. The Arms were a cross flewry, [flory, a cross terminating in *fleurs-di-li*] over all a bend [band], impaling a chevron between 3 Cornish coughs. Crest a boar.[24] The monument has not survived.

Sarah continued to live at High Hall Hill until her death in 1717. By 1741 it had become a farm when Richard Miles bequeathed his estate to his wife Mary in his will of that year. By 1745 it was the home of Edwin Elkin a joiner and farmer. In 1760 Mary Miles a widow of High Hall Hill made her will and wished to be 'Decently Buried in an handsome manner as all my Friends heretofore have been, that is to say, with Scarfs, Hatbands and Gloves to the Ministers and Bearers'. The present building known as High Hall Hill is a farm in what is now known as Meadow Lane in Woodhouses.

Chapter 4

Yoxall Parish Church

The Early Church

Central to the village is the parish church which is believed to be of Saxon origin, although no documents have been found to substantiate this claim and there is no mention of it in the Domesday Survey of 1086. The Parish Magazine of November 1921 records that the curfew bell had been rung from Yoxall Parish Church for 900 years. If this is correct, Yoxall has had a parish church at least from 1021. The curfew was a law which imposed a duty for people to put out or cover their fire when the curfew bell rang, usually at about eight o'clock. This served the purpose of protecting people from unattended fires. It also guided travellers through the Needwood Forest and at Longcroft Hall and Yoxall Lodge a bell was rung on foggy nights. In later times curfew bells were rung to maintain the tradition and at Yoxall Parish Church it rang nightly between Michaelmas and Lady Day until 1938 when the bell and frame became unsafe.[1] The earliest surviving feature of the church is the south doorway. Its leaf capital and moulded round arch date it to c.1200. The five-bay arcade is of the decorative period (c.1290 to c.1350) and the west tower is perpendicular, (c.1335-50 to c.1530), but Pevsner noted it has also been assigned to the seventeenth century and that little is ancient.[2] In the late eighteenth century the church was described as 'a handsome old Gothic fabric of stone, having a square tower, a spacious nave, side aisles, and chancel'.[3]

In 1219 following an alleged riot in Needwood Forest, Michael Brasbrygge, who claimed to have killed someone, took sanctuary in the church at Yoxall, having stated that he had been assaulted in Needwood Forest and boasted that "he had ridd oon and toke the church ther". He remained in the church while the Court of Star Chamber awaited knowledge as to whether anyone had been murdered.[4] The outcome has not been discovered.

In the Papal Return of 1294 Yoxall tithes were valued at £13 6s.[5] In 1297 the advowson of Yoxall church was £33 6s 8d.[6]

Yoxall was amongst the parishes that marched with banners to Lichfield Cathedral to make offerings at Whitsun. The Register of Roger de Norbury, Bishop of Lichfield and Coventry from 1322-58, stated that as other bands had noisily interrupted them an order was to be written to the parishes that they were to go quietly with a simple cross and no banners.[7] The same source also noted that the rector of Yoxall was commissioned to take care of empty houses and goods.[8]

St Swithin's

The church was dedicated to St Swithin in the late middle ages and St Swithin's well was mentioned in 1505.[9] Yoxall wake was held around St Swithin's Day (2nd or 15th July) until as late as 1851.[10] In 1533 the church ornaments included 1 silver chalice with paten; copes and vestments including 2 pairs of vestments for deacon and sub-deacons; 1 latten (brass alloy) cross; 1 brass holy water stock; 2 sacring bells; 1 hand bell; 1 little sanctus bell; 3 bells one of which was a clock bell which they (the parishioners?) owed for.[11] This was probably the bell which chimed the hour and was specifically named the clock bell.[12] Two of the bells are in the current peal of six and are probably the 2nd, cast in the early fifteenth century and recast in 1868 by Taylor of Loughborough, and 3rd, cast about 1450, and inscribed *Martiris Christoferi Cantet Campana Sauve*. The 4th bell was cast by Henry Oldfield of Nottingham and inscribed with the names of the churchwardens *Richard Aneley Christopher Shakleton 1613*. The tenor, was

Inscriptions on bells 3 & 4. (Lynman, Church Bells of the County of Stafford, 1889).

cast by William Clibury of Wellington, Salop and inscribed *Gloria in Excelcis Deo 1662 WC*. The 5th bell, cast in 1706 was recast in 1951. The treble is early eighteenth century. The will of John Warner, in 1542 bequeathed 40s to John, his bastard son, but if he was dead, the money to go to the churchwardens to help buy bells. In 1607 Joan Wase bequeathed 6s 8d for mending the church bells.

The Chantry

Chantries were first founded in the twelfth century and were established for priests to sing masses, usually for the soul of their founder but also for the souls of others. At Yoxall a chantry was established in 1475 by Robert Rouse and the south aisle may have been used for the altar.[13] Some Yoxall testators requested a trental (set of thirty) or half trental of masses to be said for them. In 1546 the chantry was certified and it was recorded that it possessed 6oz. of partley gilt plate and other goods and its income was £4 0s 6 ¾ d, which was paid as a salary to the priest after the deduction of 8s 0 ¾ d.[14] Following the Reformation an Act was passed in 1545 which defined chantries as representing misapplied funds and misappropriated lands, and stated that all chantries and their properties would belong to the king. In the two remaining years of the life of Henry VIII few were closed or transferred to him, but his son, Edward VI signed a new Act in 1547 suppressing chantries. Thomas Mason received a pension of 16s 2d in 1548 which was paid up to about 1560.[15]

When Henry VIII broke with Rome, he maintained an orthodox doctrine, but during the first year of the reign of his staunchly Protestant son Edward VI, the Churchwarden's Accounts of 1547-8 record evidence of the change in religion:

'It(em)the costes at the taking downe the Immages xiijd'.[16]

This was reversed by the equally staunch Catholic, Mary I, the accounts record in 1554-5:

'It(em) payd for the rode and the ymages and to the clerke for setting them uppe ixs vd'.[17]

Between 1558 and 1562 eight wills reveal Yoxall testators who requested burial in the church or churchyard of St Swithin. Seven of the eight were witnessed by curate Ralph Parker.

St Peter's

By 1571 the name of the church had changed as a chalice of that date was inscribed 'St Peter's Church, Yoxall'. No wills have been discovered naming the church as St Peter's.

With the ascension of Elizabeth I to the throne the Protestant faith was again reinstated but not everyone attended church. In 1586 Ralph Dagnall, yeoman, Thomas Camden, gent, Margaret Cowardyn and Robert Morrys, all of Yoxall, were amongst those who failed to appear to answer charges of 'not resorting to their parish churches or other places of worship'. The men were outlawed and the women's charges were waived.[18] Catholic dissenters were regularly recorded in the parish and are included in the following chapter.

At the Restoration an immediate stop was put to all cutting and selling timber in the Needwood Forest, six months later timber from the Forest was granted to repair the church on the grounds that the parish was 'impoverished by the late wars'.[19]

When the windows were changed in the church is uncertain, but a catalogue of Green's museum (1748-93) lists 'A large quantity of stained and printed glass, chiefly from Yoxall church windows, among the rest, the arms of the Berrisford family'.[20]

In 1819 a vestry was added on the north side and two galleries were added, above the south and north aisles. There was already one in the west end which by 1820 held an organ.[21] These were removed during the 1860s renovation.

By 1829 Yoxall and Barton churches were lit with suspended lamps.[22] Following the invention of the argand lamp in 1780, oil lamps began to supersede candles in the nineteenth century. The Visitation of the Archdeaconry of Stafford of that year described the church as a 'Handsome Gothic building - two side aisles separated from body by pointed arches - Chancel'. The number the church could contain was 730 exclusive of 254 sittings for children. It had accommodation for 150 poor people. The dimensions of the church were 60 ft.

by 50 ft. The seats were oak with boarded floors and the pulpit and desk also oak, with velvet cushions and coverings. What was described as the churchyard fence was partly wall, partly hedge, rails and houses. 'In one part where a house has been pulled down the Churchyard is open - other parts need repair very much [- but about to be improved]'. There were several public footpaths and 'Cattle: None - except a poney'. The curate, John Riland received a salary of £100. He lived in the rectory, described as 'An old rambling brick building - rooms low and cold - many parts in an infirm condition - the east end very insecure and dangerous and greatly needing to be rebuilt'. The outbuildings were a stable, coach house, etc. and barn converted to a school. Orders were given for repairs including the removal of damp by an open drain round the walls, repairs to the chancel and vestry floors, also the floor over the Arden vault was sinking. Also in need of attention was some retiling on the roof and pointing and repairing of the walls and buttresses, and the porch either to be repaired or removed. Also repairs or renewal of the fences, plus new gates. By the visitation of 1837 work had been done externally but internally it was described as 'very far from being in a neat or becoming state'. By 1841 it was reported as very much improved.[23]

Sepia drawing, 'South East View of Yoxall Church, Staffordshire', J. Buckler, 1839. (Staffordshire Views, XII.153a. Reproduced by permission of the Trustees of the William Salt Library).

Rectors of Yoxall

The following list is taken from the board in St Peter's:

c. 1241	Roger de Yoxall	1727	Arthur Steevens
1321	William Davy	1740	John Botham
1329	John de Leycester	1746	John Foot
1340	John de Dredon	1768	John Dodson
1341	Guldimus de Shelton	1784	William Clare
1378	Walter Clifford	1809	Edward Cooper
1384	John Haselore	1833	Edward Willes
1394	John Williams	1848	John Bowdler Gisborne
	Roger Radelyne	1852	Henry William Sulivan
1413	Edward Rede	1880	Josiah Beatson Lowe
1448	Henry Ince	1893	Richard Johnstone
1474	Richard Brodoke	1894	Alexander Arthur Cory
	Hugh Coton	1922	Hugh Tunnadine
1515	John Johnson	1936	Gordon C. R. Cooke
1538	William Alynge	1941	John Cecil Hurst
1539	Roger Stockley	1950	Albert Edley Willings
1558	Oliver Whyddon	1958	John Osborne Nicholls
1575	Richard Barber	1969	James Reginald Hawkins
1589	John Waterhouse	1977	Brian Paish Brownless
1620	William Edge	1983	John Douglas Cutter
1636	Francis Coke	1992	John Marshall Evans
1682	Michael Edge	1996	Jennifer Grace Lister
1683	John Spateman	2008	Pauline Shepherd

A new board has been placed below this with the name of the present incumbent, Maldwyn Hawksworth.

Roger de Yoxall - John Bowdler Gisborne

Rectors were nominated by patrons of the living and were instituted by the bishops. Many of the early Yoxall rectors were absentees, having more than one benefice, from which they received the tithes. These were wealthy men who delegated the work of the parishes to their curates. The board in the church which lists the rectors is incomplete, and for some of the names there is no known information. The first listed rector, Roger de Yoxall c.1241 would, according to the probable age of the church, have had several predecessors. He appears to have been rector from at least 1216 when William Ferrers granted him land in Yoxall.[24] His successor has so far not been identified. The second listed is William Davy, who in 1311/12 had a grant of the manor of Hoar Cross.[25] The Papal Letters of 1455-1464 note that Henry Jule, rector of Yoxall, (who appears as Henry Ince on the Rectors Board) was a kinsman of William Booth, Archbishop of York.[26] In 1597 rector John Waterhouse was amongst those who assaulted two men who were taking Thomas Coxson of Yoxall to prison regarding a debt, and rescued him. In 1604 he was a preacher, pluralist and non resident. The rectory was then worth £60.[27] Francis Coke, a 'vicar of Bray' whose incumbency saw over half the reign of Charles I, the Commonwealth and the Restoration, was sequestered in the "Great Rebellion", but occurs as minister at Yoxall in a 1651-2 return and throughout the Interregnum the registers appear to be in his handwriting. Francis Coke was archdeacon of Stafford in 1660-82 and was one of the two representatives from the county in the Westminster Assembly. He was buried at Yoxall.[28] Michael Edge resigned the vicarage of Uttoxeter in 1682 for Yoxall, where he died in 1683.

John Spateman, rector from 1683 was born at Derby. His marble plaque, high on the wall to the west of the organ records that he married Mary Noble and the couple had twelve children. In 1714/15 his daughter Sarah married Michael Wood, rector of Blithfield. He retired in 1718, leaving a gap of nine years unaccounted for as Arthur Steevens, who appears as his successor on the rectors' board dates from 1727, the year before John Spateman died. John Botham, rector for six years, was succeeded by John Foot whose marble plaque is beside that of John Spateman, and bears a Latin inscription. He was educated at the College of St John the Baptist, Oxford and died in 1768 aged 48. John Dodson resigned in 1784 for a living in Sussex. His successor, William Clare came from Rugby.

Edward Cooper followed William Clare and was rector of both Hamstall Ridware and Yoxall and is included in other chapters. He was followed by Edward Willes who was succeeded in 1848 by John Bowdler Gisborne, born at Quorndon, Leicestershire, a grandson of abolitionist Thomas Gisborne of Yoxall Lodge. John signed the Census of Religious Attendance in 1851 in which it was stated that the total endowments were £582. There were a total of 740 sittings; 250 free and 490 'Other'. The estimated attendance for 30 March was 122 'General Congregation' and 102 Sunday scholars in the morning and 116 'General Congregation' and 77 Sunday Scholars in the afternoon. The average preceding that date was considerably higher, being 180 general and 120 scholars in the morning and 130 general and 80 scholars in the afternoon, there were no evening services. Enumerated with his wife Susan Elizabeth at Yoxall Rectory that year John died at Torquay in December aged 34. He was followed in 1852 by Henry William Sulivan.

Watercolour of Yoxall Church with north east view showing a small chancel with one window at the east end, four bays of the north aisle, and a small tower with a clock. The vicarage is shown on the left. Date approximately 1762-1802. Anonymous, [S. Shaw]. (Staffordshire Views, XII.151a. Reproduced by permission of the Trustees of the William Salt Library).

Watercolour of the interior of Yoxall Parish Church, dated 1860. Five years after this was painted the restoration of St Peter's began. (Copyright Lichfield Cathedral).

The Contentious Restoration of St Peter's

Henry Sulivan was incumbent at the time of the restoration of St Peter's, 1865-68, which comprised a new chancel, vestry, organ lobby, extension to the south aisle (which is now a chapel), north porch and a clerestory added to the naïve. In 1864 Queen Victoria donated 50 guineas to the Yoxall Church Restoration fund. Lord Palmerston, then Prime Minister, was also a benefactor and uncle to the incumbent, Reverend Henry Sulivan, but he did not live to see the project completed, as he died the following year. The *Burton Chronicle* reported that despite the fact that some contributions were lost, in the 'failure at Lichfield' by June 1865 the restoration fund had raised £3,200 of which £1,000 had been donated by the rector.[29] With the church often unusable and the churchyard in disruption burials could not always take place and in January 1866, Kate, the first wife of Charles Greasley Armson, surgeon of Yoxall, was buried at Christchurch, Newchurch, 'owing to the ruinous state of Yoxall church, and the commotion in the churchyard there, due to extensive reconstruction work, it was impossible to dig a grave'.[30] The church was closed then and at various times during the restoration and services were held in the boys' school.[31]

The disruption was greater than anyone could have foreseen. In November 1866 the masons and carpenters went on strike, claiming that Mr Beckensall, the clerk of works under Mr Woodyer, the eminent church architect, had allowed them to complete stages of the work and then condemned them. Feelings were so strong that on 5 November the men lit a bonfire on which they burned an effigy of Beckensall in front of his home, they also removed all the building materials and scaffolding. Meetings were held but the men were not prepared to resume work unless a replacement was sent for the clerk of works. The church was left exposed to the weather causing serious damage. At the end of November the contractor, Mr Ife, wrote to the *Burton Chronicle* correcting their report that he had also gone on strike, and claimed that the men had 'ceased to work on their own account', and quoted from a paper read by their representatives to the members of the Building Committee at the Crown Inn on 7 November; "The pulling down of the works by your servant, the Clerk of the Works, after having been erected under his superintendence, carpenters' work put together under his superintendence - the nave roof, for instance fitted together on the ground, which then taken into the interior of the church ready for erection, was compelled to be taken back and refitted, causing considerable annoyance to the men and unnecessary loss of labour and material". He claimed that he was powerless to intervene as the men had threatened to stop all work he had in progress elsewhere.[32] In early December the problem had not been resolved as letters to the *Burton Chronicle* followed, condemning the lack of authority which had allowed the men to take strike action. Eventually the contractor was replaced and Mr Beckensall remained as clerk of works.

More misfortune followed in September 1867, when the plasterers had erected a scaffold to plaster the upper part of the interior, a bearer broke and three men fell, landing on uncovered sleepers which had been laid to take the flooring boards. The injured included Mr Beckensall, clerk of the works, who had landed with force between the sleepers. John Tunnicliff, a labourer, received 'much injury', but by the time the event was published he was recovering, but Emery, an elderly plasterer suffered a broken hip and suspected internal injuries.[33]

Despite the problems St Peter's was re-opened on 13 April 1868, when the Bishop of Lichfield and about twenty local clergy formed a procession into the church. Rev. Sulivan was absent due to a 'serious indisposition', but later recovered and remained as incumbent in the newly restored St Peter's. The *Burton Chronicle* of 16 April devoted a lengthy article to the reopening of the church and descriptive information regarding the alterations. It states that with the removal of Mr Ife as contractor, the work was completed by David Sanders of Barton, aided by Green & Son of Uttoxeter, Mr Nichols of Burton, Mr Barnes (John Barnes, bricklayer of Yoxall) and Mr Perkins. (John Perkins, also of Yoxall, who was an ironmonger as well as agricultural implement maker). The old stone was, as much as possible, used for the walls with Bath facings to the windows and doorways. A stained glass window in the south aisle was the gift of Major Arden of Longcroft Hall, erected in memory of his brother the Rev. R. C. Arden, an original trustee of the restoration fund. The Meynell-Ingram family had generously supported the restoration, and the Misses Louisa and Georgina Meynell-Ingram had an elaborate monument erected at the end of the south aisle in remembrance of Admiral Henry Meynell, who died in Paris in 1865. It is the work of the famous Italian sculptor Baron Carlo Marochetti.

Monument to Admiral Henry Meynell, who died in Paris in 1865. The tomb is by Italian sculptor Baron Carlo Marochetti. He sculptured marble figures of Prince Albert and Queen Victoria, and the kneeling angels for the granite sarcophagus of the couple at Frogmore. The figure of Victoria was hidden at Windsor until her death in 1901. (Photo taken and reproduced by permission of Jim Hodgkiss).

When Hugo Francis Meynell-Ingram, the great grandson of Hugo Meynell, the 'Father of Foxhunting' died in 1871 he was initially buried at Yoxall, but later moved to The Church of the Holy Angels in Hoar Cross, which his widow built as a memorial to him. He is commemorated in St Peter's with a plaque 'In remembrance of him by whom the Restoration of this Church was completed'. The organ, 'an excellent and powerful instrument, and remarkable for its rich and superior tones' was a gift of the Rector at a cost of £400. His brother Stephen Henry Sulivan, Consul General to Peru, was murdered in Lima in 1857, and has a memorial tablet in the church, dedicated by the rector, his only surviving brother. Henry Sulivan died in 1880 aged 64 and was buried at Yoxall.

In 1886 an addition to the churchyard was consecrated. A house and garden had been purchased some time previously and eventually the house demolished and the land added to the churchyard.[34] The churchyard was further extended in 1896, when Henry Wright's tender of £6 9s was accepted for the building of a new wall around the new portion, together with a coal-house.[35]

The Green Man, also known as a foliate head or mask. Originally pagan it eventually acquired ecclesiastical connotations. This exterior carving in tracery above the west window of the south aisle of St Peter's was added during the restoration of the church, 1865-68. (Photo by author).

Rectors Josiah Beatson Lowe - Alexander Arthur Cory

Josiah Beatson Lowe

Born in 1814 and educated at Trinity College, Dublin, Josiah was admitted deacon's orders in 1839 by the Bishop of Kildare, and priest the following year by the Archbishop of Dublin. He was perpetual curate of St Jude's, Walton on the Hill, Staffordshire, (from 1850-1875), and from 1875 held the vicarage of St Michael-in-the-Hamlet, Toxteth Park, Liverpool. In April 1880 he took the crown living of Yoxall, stated to be worth £508 per annum, with the rectory, which was conferred by the Lord Chancellor.[36] He was the author of lectures on

"The Festival of the Jews", "The History of the Cross", "the Worship of the Virgin", "Mormonism Exposed", "The Church of Christ not a Catholic Body" and other controversial works. In 1881 he was enumerated at Yoxall Rectory with his wife, one son and five daughters, all born in Liverpool, including Elizabeth Isabella who in 1884 married William Ding, formerly curate at Yoxall. In 1889 his daughter Emily Beatrice married Percival William Henry Arden, son of George Pinkard Arden. After 13 years as rector of St Peter's, Josiah died in June 1893 and was buried in the churchyard with his widow Emily Mary and a daughter Louisa Wallace Lowe.

Richard Johnstone

Richard was the grandson of Dr Edward Johnstone, one of the founders of the first schools of medicine in Birmingham. Dr Edward lived at Edgbaston Hall for nearly 50 years and his youngest son James Johnstone was born there, and became associated with the General Hospital, the Queen's College, King Edward's School and many other Birmingham associations for 40 years. Richard Johnstone was his fourth son, and brother of Captain Charles Johnstone of the "Camperdown", (an Admiral class battle ship of the Royal Navy, noted for its collision in 1893 with HMS Victoria which sank taking 357 crew with it), also Major-General Sir James Johnstone, K.C.S.I., Fulford Hall, Warwickshire.

Richard was educated at King Edward's School and Trinity College, Cambridge. After he graduated he was for a short time a member of the Lloyds Banking Company in Birmingham, but took Holy Orders and was ordained at Lichfield. He held curacies at Little Drayton and Moreton Say and was rector of Stone, Staffordshire. Following the death of Rev. J.B. Lowe he was accepted to the living of Yoxall, which at that time had the net value of about £450 and was the gift of the Lord Bishop of the Diocese. It was formerly the gift of the Lord Chancellor, but an exchange was affected during the Episcopate of Dr. Maclagan, Archbishop of York.[37]

In May 1894 the Young Men's Friendly Society Anniversary was held, and in his after dinner speech Rev. Johnstone spoke of the pleasure it gave him to be present and expressed the hope that as long as he was in Yoxall he would be able to join them.[38] He died two months later, aged 49, leaving a widow and seven children. The youngest, Richard Michael was baptised at St Peter's in August, less than a month after his father's death. Rev. Johnstone was buried at his former parish of Stone and at the same hour a service was held at St Peter's. Rev. Johnstone was the author of several theological essays and a little book called "Parochial Addresses". A brass plaque in the chancel of St Peter's commemorates him and his incumbency of ten months.

Alexander Arthur Cory

Rev. Alexander Arthur Cory, incumbent from 1894 to 1922. (Photo by H.G. Pike, Lichfield, reproduced in Williams & Mallett, Staffordshire Towns and Villages, 1890).

Alexander Cory was ordained in 1875 and his first curacy was at Darleston. In 1887 he moved to Tipton where he stayed until 1894, when he moved to Yoxall. In the November of that year, at the commencement of an entertainment in the girls' school-room he spoke of the kind manner in which he and Mrs Cory had been received into the village, and said he looked forward to spending a long and happy time amongst them. He also commented on the able management of the schools, and the good teaching and behaviour of the children. By 1896 he was a member of the Parish Council and that year gave a piece of ground to be enclosed in the churchyard which was consecrated by the Bishop of Lichfield the following year.

Charities that had been distributed by the church were being handed over to parish councils and in 1901 Reverend Cory wrote to them asking them to take over St. Thomas's Dole which was left originally to the Overseers of the Poor. The money was to be distributed on St Thomas's Day to 55 poor parishioners. He was also a trustee of Mort's Charity, and that year he and two elected trustees attended the school to distribute the charity, which every January was given to the children who made the most attendances during the year.

Alexander Cory was subject to bouts of ill health and towards the end of his 27 years as rector of Yoxall the decline is evidenced in the deterioration of his signing in the parish registers. In 1922 he resigned the rectory, intending to move to Lichfield. However this was not to be as he became too ill for the move and died in Yoxall parish. An obituary states that 'During his stay there immense improvements were carried out in the church, and until his breakdown in health he worked the extensive and straggling parish single-handed'.[39] Apart from his work in the parish he had also been a justice of the peace for Staffordshire, and in his earlier days sat on Burton Bench. His son, also Alexander became a cleric and in 1889 married Dorothy Barnard, the only child of the Rev. Cannon C. W. Barnard, Rector and Rural Dean of Sutton Coldfield.

Curates

With many of the rectors being absentees, the curates undertook the parochial clerical duties. For many of the curates of Yoxall there is little known and there are gaps where the names are unknown. John Well was curate in 1533, John Marburye 1551, Ralph Parker 1552-68, Peter Pickering 1556, John Hatton 1573-8 and John Robinson in 1586. Most of these either were witnesses in wills or, as curates, paid the subsidies of 6s 8d. In 1585 the curate George Bargh was presented at the Quarter Sessions for administering a baptism using phrases contrary to the form in the Book of Common Prayer, including using 'you' instead of 'thou' and 'do you' instead of 'doest thou' etc., also omitting to make the sign of the cross.[40]

Thomas Shipton was a curate from at least 1707 to 1713, when his children were baptised in Yoxall. The burial of Humphrey Onely, clerk, in 1708 and the burial in 1710 of the daughter of Jacob Cressall, clerk, suggest two more curates. A handwritten list of rectors includes W. Greaves who was curate in 1727. James Lamb was the curate of William Clare (1784-1809) and lived at the rectory described as the 'excellent old parsonage, which exhibits a spacious and good front, with a suitable neat garden'.[41]

At least by 1830 the curates of Yoxall received all or nearly all the benefice income, the rector held another, richer benefice.[42] Almost all the curates in Staffordshire were licensed. Without a licence their income and security of tenure was at the mercy of the incumbent.[43]

During the dual incumbencies of Edward Cooper, who lived at Hamstall Ridware, most of the work in Yoxall parish was undertaken by his curate, J. Riland who lived at the rectory. From the baptism records the following names may have been curates; in 1846 William Mull Holland ' Yoxall Clerk'; 1853 William Capel; 1873 Walter Hamilton and 1894 John Gower Webb of Old Hall, Yoxall, the last three being 'Clerk in Holy Orders'. Also the burial in 1808 of Rev. John Araan, who may have been resident in Yoxall or a visitor.

Rev. Joseph Bainbridge was listed as curate in 1860, during the incumbency of Henry Sulivan, who was not listed.[44] In 1863 he married the daughter and co-heiress of the late Colonel Bund of Wick, near Worcester and left the curacy of Yoxall, which he had held for upwards of nine years.[45]

John Julius Baker

John was curate in charge at Yoxall for nearly 13 years and according to the baptism entries for most of his children born in Yoxall, he was living at the rectory. Like Rev. Bainbridge before him, it was he who was named in directories, and not the rector.[46] In 1880, he was curate in charge, possibly in between rectors, as William Sulivan had died in the March of that year. He left the neighbourhood due to the death of the rector and the appointment of Rev. D. Lowe to the living.[47]

William Ding

In 1880 William Ding was ordained at Lichfield Cathedral and licensed to the curacy of Yoxall.[48] By 1884 he was a clerk in Holy Orders at Stoke on Trent. He returned to Yoxall in August of that year to give an organ recital in the church, as part of a fund raising event for the parochial schools.[49] He returned again in October, when he married the rector's daughter, Elizabeth Isabella Lowe.[50] He subsequently held curacies near Market Drayton, and Barthomley near Crewe. In 1888 he was appointed to the private chaplaincy at Arley Hall, near Northwich. In 1892, he accepted the Consular Chaplaincy at Pernambuco, Brazil and in 1893 died there from yellow fever.

Over the years many parishioners served the church as churchwardens or in other capacities, these include William Merry whose burial entry in 1808 states he was '49 years Clerk to the Church of Yoxall aged 91', and John Snape, who in 1859 'died peacefully just before Christmas aged ninety-eight, but deprived of his ambition to help ring the bells of Yoxall church for his seventy-ninth successive Christmas day'.[51]

In 1891 it was decided to robe the choir in surplices and cassocks and money was raised for this by public subscription. A sewing committee was formed and work commenced in November at the home of Dr Armson. The intention being to have the surplices ready for the second Sunday in the New Year.[52]

A list of churchwardens dating from 1542 was compiled by Frank Greasley Armson, who for many years was a churchwarden and whose father, Charles Greasley Armson, was a churchwarden from 1892 to 1904. Earlier, long serving churchwardens include the Meynell Ingrams, Poysers and Shiptons.

In 1964 St Peter's became a Grade II* listed building.

Chapter 5

Dissidents and Nonconformists: Catholic and Methodists of Yoxall

Catholic Recusants

During the reign of Elizabeth I Catholic resistance resulted in heavy fines, confiscation of property and eventually the death sentence. Catholic resistance was noted in Yoxall and an enquiry was made in 1586 concerning the goods, chattels and landholding of Catholic priests, fugitives and recusants.[1] An oak panelled room in the roof of the rectory may have been a priest hole to hide a Marian priest during the early years of the reign of Elizabeth I. This would have been during the incumbency of Oliver Whyddon, (1558-75), who was possibly a crypto-Catholic.[2] In 1604 it was recorded that there were many popish recusants in Yoxall.[3]

Charles I was desperately short of money and from 1628 secured a steady income from recusants through the reintroduction of Composition. Recusants agreed to pay an annual rent based on the assessed value of their sequestered lands and goods. In Staffordshire in 1640 Peter Giffard was prosecuted for resistance, despite paying the king 'the greatest rents of any recusants saving two or three'. The next highest payments in the county were £66 13s 4d paid from 1636 by John Welles and his son Thomas, both of Hoar Cross.[4]

The Welles family and their servants at Hoar Cross continued to appear in the lists of recusants until 1657 and the Howard family who succeeded to the Hoar Cross estate were also Catholic into the 18th century.[5] In March 1696 instructions were given to search gentry houses for those loyal to the dethroned Catholic James II. Sir Robert Howard of Hoar Cross, a known Catholic, was ordered to the Fleet Prison.[6]

The number of Staffordshire Catholics increased during the eighteenth century and in 1706 the Privy Council ordered a return by the parish clergy of papists and reputed papists 'with their respective qualities, estates and places of abode'.[7] Yoxall was one of the main areas of concentration of papists listed in the returns, with 30 which included the Howards of Hoar Cross. In 1758 there was a Franciscan, Francis Copley, at Hoar Cross.[8] The Return of Staffordshire Papists in 1767 listed 47 in Yoxall.[9]

In 1791 the Roman Catholic Relief Act was passed, allowing Catholics to practise their religion, provided their chapels were listed, but it was not without restrictions. Catholic emancipation did not come until the later Act of 1829 and Hardwicke's Marriage Act which came into force in 1754 made it a legal requirement that all marriages should take place in the Church of England, except those of Quakers and Jews. It was not until 1837 that Catholic marriages were legal.

The Chapel of St Francis of Sales, Woodlane

Hoar Cross Hall had passed from the Welles family to the Howards and the Talbots, all Catholic families. When Charles Talbot, Earl of Shrewsbury, demolished the hall in 1794 before selling the estate he endowed the chapel at Woodlane, on the Lichfield to Ashbourne turnpike road, to replace the chapel at Hoar Cross Hall. Material from the hall was used in the building.[10] This Grade II listed building, The Chapel of St Francis of Sales, has an adjoining house which was home to the priest. Thomas Flynn, the last chaplain at Hoar Cross became the first priest at Woodlane. He died in 1797 and is buried at St Peter's. His tomb records that he was 'First Parish Priest at Woodlane'. In the burial register he is 'The Revd Thomas Flynn many years a Papist Priest at Horecross Hall aged 77'. Thomas Flynn was succeeded by Gaspar Bricknell. He died in 1833 and in his will bequeathed money from the sale of the farming stock that had supplemented his income to a cousin in London. Another beneficiary was his housekeeper, Sarah Shinglers, to whom he left £30 and his linen and apparel in a codicil. There was no indication in his will that he was the priest of Woodlane. A marble wall tablet in the chapel states 'the sincerity of his manners, and the integrity of his life endeared him not less to those, who differed from his creed, than those, who were consigned to his pastoral charge'.

James Jeffries followed Gaspar. He travelled to Burton to celebrate mass there and is said to have first used an old malthouse at the back of the Crown Inn, High Street, and then a cottage at the back of the Old White Lion Inn at the corner of Lichfield Street and Fleet Street. In 1832 he said mass in Burton once a month in premises that he described as 'so objectionable' that some felt 'a repugnance to attend'. He twice applied to the marquess of Anglesey for land but it was not forthcoming.[11] The chapel at Woodlane had originally looked from the road like a barn but was extended sometime between 1834 and 1840 and made cruciform in shape. Pugin's diary of 1841/2 records visits to Woodlane and "materials for the chancel at Woodlane". The angels at either side of the balcony may be his work.[12]

In 1851 the Census of Religious Attendance Return for 'St Francis's Chapel' stated that it was built about 1834 and was used exclusively as a place of worship except for a Sunday School. There were 100 sittings which were all free. There were no services on the 30th March and the average number of attendants during the previous years was about 80 with no Sunday Scholars. The return was signed by the priest, James Jefferies. Later that year he moved to Leamington Spa.

Patrick O'Sullivan who succeeded James was born in Ireland in 1793 and went to the United States in 1822 where he was ordained in 1824. He came to England in 1830 and worked in Wolverhampton during the cholera epidemic of 1832. Following twenty one years in charge of the Wolverhampton mission he came to Woodlane.[13] He bought a piece of land for a chapel in Guild Street, Burton. This was rebuilt in 1879 and dedicated to St Mary and St Modwen.[14]

After twenty-five years at Woodlane, in October 1876 Father O'Sullivan was presented with a purse of £170, subscribed by friends in honour of his "silver jubilee" at Woodlane and his "golden one" in the diocese.[15] He retired to Harvington Hall in 1879 where he died in 1881.

St Francis of Sales, Woodlane. (Ref: BB66_02003 – Yoxall RC Church, exterior EP: 5382_128. Reproduced by permission of Historic England).

Interior of St. Francis of Sales. (Photo by author).

Following the building of the Catholic church in Burton the number of baptisms eventually declined at Woodlane. During the time of Father O'Sullivan's successor, Hugh McCarten, Bishop Ilsley's visitation in 1881 revealed that the annual income stood at £158 9s 4d. The premises consisted of church and sacristy, the house, stable-cowshed, a building which had once been a dwelling, a coach house and pig sty, plus land totalling 11 acres, comprising four fields, the garden and graveyard, yielding the annual sum of £31 10s.[16] Father

McCarten hoped that a missions school would be built on the site of a cottage bequeathed by John Boulton, but despite his efforts and new plans, maps and a conveyance, this was not to be and in 1882 he left Woodlane for Holy Cross, Lichfield. His successor, Frederick John Morris, farmed most of the 11 acres to supplement his income. He did not like Woodlane and was not popular. In 1886 the Bishop received an indirect complaint from two old ladies who had not received a call from him for five weeks and feared death would visit them before he did. Fellow clergy also raised concerns and in 1889 he was ordered to leave.[17]

Father Joseph Parker followed, he had previously been secretary to the Bishop of Birmingham. At Woodlane he discovered that extensive repairs were needed to both church and house. There were ongoing arrears and the income was never enough to cover his stipend of £50. However he settled into the life of a priest at Woodlane and maintained the accounts. He was also a member of Yoxall Parish Council. He remained at Woodlane until his death in 1935.

Protestant Nonconformists

Originally Nonconformist meant anyone who refused to conform to the Act of Uniformity which came into force in 1662 and required all English and Welsh clergy to consent to the entire contents of the *Book of Common Prayer*. Later the term applied to a variety of sects who were Protestant but held different views to the established church. The Act of Toleration passed in 1689, (which did not apply to Catholics) permitted freedom of worship to Protestant dissenters from the Church of England, but required the registration of dissenters' meeting houses.

The Registration of Dissenting Chapels and Meeting Houses in Staffordshire, 1689-1852, lists eight registered dissenting places of worship in Yoxall Parish, the earliest recorded dating from 1794 when 'a certain house at Yoxall' in the occupation of William Elsinore was registered by him for Protestant Dissenters.[18] Other registrations were: a house at Yoxall, registered by the occupier, Mary Moore in 1806. She was listed as a witness to the petition, along with Thomas Simpson, Henry and George Kent, William Streetly and John Thompson;[19] a house at Hoar Cross in the occupation of Benjamin Corveser, registered for Primitive Methodists in 1820 by Sampson Turner of Cannock;[20] a house at Woodmill registered by Thomas Webb and John Wait of Bentley in 1821. The Bishop's Register stated that John Wait was an occupier of the house;[21] a house at Weaver Lake registered by James Hinckley in 1828, the entry also noted that in the Bishop's Register it is described as 'a building, not a house';[22] and a cottage at Merry (Morrey), for Independents, registered by Richard Morris, an Independent minister of Abbots Bromley in 1841.[23] The remaining two registrations were for Catholics at Hoar Cross and Woodlane (q.v.). In 1851 a Return for the Census of Religious Attendance was returned for a Wesleyan Chapel in Yoxall. It had been erected in 1845 and was used exclusively for public worship. It had 98 free sittings and 54 'other'. The estimated attendance for Divine Service on Sunday 30th March was 17 'General Congregational' in the afternoon and 22 in the evening and 15 Sunday Scholars in the afternoon. There was no morning service. The average number of attendants was left blank, suggesting that the chapel may not have been used on a regular basis.

Woodhouses Primitive Methodist Chapel

It is possible that one of the registered houses for Protestant Dissenters was at Woodhouses but only identified as Yoxall. In May 1869 tenders were being submitted for a proposed Primitive Methodist Chapel at Woodhouses and that of Mr. Maddox of Burton was accepted, the architect was Mr W. Kerridege of Wisbeach, Lincolnshire, the cost of building £245. In the June of that year the foundation stone was laid and despite bad weather the ceremony was well attended. In the stone, laid by Mr Hoult, was a bottle containing connexional documents and other papers relating to the new chapel and two copies of the *Burton Chronicle*. The event was followed by teas being served in Mr Hoult's barn. Among those who donated to the chapel were Mr. Hoult and Mr. Arthur Bass, M.P.[24] The chapel was opened in August and in June of the following year celebrated the first marriage to take place there, the couple being William Jeraz Booth of Wolverhampton and Miss Helena Louisa Ward, daughter of the Rev. R. Ward, a Primitive Methodist Minister of Lichfield.[25] The chapel, which was sited close to the road is no more, the only remains being the iron railed fence which once fronted the building.

Site of Woodhouses Primitive Methodist Chapel. The fence and gates are all that remain. (Photo by author).

Woodmill Primitive Methodist Chapel and the Wait Family

Joseph Wait was baptised in St Peter's Church in 1793, he was the son of John and Sarah who in 1821 occupied the house for Protestant Dissenters at Woodmill. His older brothers, William and Martin were also baptised at St Peter's. Like other dissenters, the Woodmill Methodists used the Church of

England for baptisms, marriages and burials prior to state registration in 1837 of births, marriages and deaths. Joseph and his brothers all played in the church band at St Peter's Church in 1815.[26] Joseph became a timber merchant and local preacher on the Burton upon Trent circuit plan. He married Elizabeth Rogers at St Peter's in 1816 and their first son William was baptised and buried there in 1818, their second son Joseph was baptised in 1824. Joseph senior's wife, Elizabeth died in 1843, aged 61 and in 1846 he married, farmer's daughter, Ann Tivey, who died in 1854 aged 47, both wives were buried at St Peter's. Joseph married for a third time in 1860, to Mary Ann Poole a 63 year old widow.

The 1851 Census of Religious Attendance named Woodmill chapel as Mount Zion. The return states that the building used for worship had been erected in 1822, the year following the registration of the house of John Wait. It is likely that this building was the chapel which preceded the present building and was still standing in living memory. The estimated number of people attending were 70 in the afternoon and 100 in the evening of Sunday March 30th. The average number attending during the previous twelve months were 50 in the afternoon and 70 in the evening, there being no morning services and no Sunday school. The return was signed by Joseph's brother Martin, whose 'Official Character' was recorded as 'Steward'.

Despite the Marriage Act of 1836 empowering superintendent registrars to issue licences for marriage either in a registrar office or a non-conformist church, Woodmill Chapel was not registered for the solemnization of marriage until June 1869. The first marriage to take place there was in October, between George Cox and Harriet Mottram, both of Yoxall. The revised service was read by Joseph Wait junior in the presence of George Raworth, registrar, also of Yoxall. The same month Joseph Law was the first person to be baptised there. It is likely that when Woodmill became licensed by the registrar there were plans for a new chapel, as in August 1870 Joseph Wait senior laid the foundation stone of 'a beautiful new sanctuary on the eligible site near a mill in the presence of a large number of friends'. The old one having the problem of overcrowding at the evening Sunday services.[27] The new Primitive Methodist Chapel, dedicated to St Paul, was opened for divine worship on Easter Tuesday, 1871. It was built by workmen chiefly from the neighbourhood and remains a meeting place for Methodists.

In his will of 1869 Joseph made provision for his wife, Mary Ann, leaving his 'several' cottages, gardens and premises at Woodmill to his son Joseph, who was to have paid her five shillings per week for the duration of her life out of the rents of the properties. Joseph died in February 1871 and probate was granted in November to his son Joseph, the surviving executor, his wife, the other executor had died the same month as her husband. He also bequeathed to his son Joseph his personal estate and to his nephews and niece, each a sum of money 'less the expenses of obtaining the same as maybe received by the executors in liquidation of a debt due to him from the Alrewas Primitive Methodist Chapel or from the trustees or other persons owing the same in equal shares…'.

Woodmill Primitive Methodist Chapel. (Photo by author).

Interior of Woodmill Primitive Methodist Chapel. (Photo by author).

For the use of the Woodmill Primitive Methodist Chapel Joseph bequeathed 'a plot of ground lying west and adjoining the Garden belonging to Mr. Thomas Whyman at Woodmill aforesaid extending in width forty two feet and continuing in that width from the main road to the Brook or Watercourse each plot of land to be used as a Burial Ground for the said Primitive Methodist Chapel or as the trustees of such Chapel shall or may lawfully direct'. His headstone stone records that he was the founder of the church and 'died in the faith of that gospel which he had for 50 years so faithfully and earnestly preached to others'. He never saw the completion of the new chapel, dedicated to St Paul and described as 'an ornament to the locality',[28] he died just four months before it opened. He was the first person to be buried in the ground he had bequeathed for that purpose, closely followed by his wife, whose name is not inscribed on his headstone. In 1878 Joseph's brother Martin, a farmer and sawyer, was also buried at Woodmill with his wife Martha who had died in 1872. The other brother, William was enumerated in 1851 as a timber merchant with a yard in Lichfield.

In November 1845 Joseph junior, a miller, married Martha, daughter of Abraham Hardy a farmer of High Hall Hill. Martha died in May 1875, aged 58, and later that year Joseph married widow Harriet Smelt at Woodmill. Harriet was the second daughter of William Ellis, a draper and grocer who occupied premises next to the Shoulder of Mutton, which at the time was in the occupancy of James Berrisford, a butcher and beerhouse keeper. In 1855 Harriet left Yoxall to live in Tamworth Street, Lichfield on her marriage to Anthony Smelt, who like her father, was a draper. By 1871 she was back in Yoxall in the family home, a widow with two sons. She was enumerated as an organist and teacher of music. She had formerly taught music in Yoxall and sometimes played the organ at the chapel, to which Joseph had succeeded his father as a local preacher, as well as, like his father, being a miller.

When Harriet's father died in 1880 he bequeathed everything to Harriet, his wife having predeceased him, he was buried with his wife in Woodmill cemetery, confirming that the Ellis's were also Primitive Methodists.

In 1881 it was announced that there was a debt of £70 on the chapel 'which, in addition to the damage caused by frost last winter, is a heavy burden to this hard-working and deserving people. We think that if the claims of this place were known by the rich of the locality they would gladly send help, which would be gratefully received and acknowledged by Mr J. Wait (Woodmill), and Mr J. Green (Yoxall)'.[29] Despite the publicity, the debt remained and in June 1882 it was reported that they had increased their liabilities through the frost of two winters in succession bursting the heating apparatus.

Joseph made his will in 1883, and died in 1895 aged 70 and was buried with his first wife Martha at Woodmill. Probate was granted to Harriet, his widow and sole executrix. Joseph bequeathed all money and personal effects to Harriet along with five cottages and gardens at Woodmill, also the garden 'of my own occupation adjoining the New Primitive Methodist Chapel at Woodmill' for the term of her life, and at her decease to her heirs and assigns absolutely. In November 1897 the chapel was re-opened after renovation by Yoxall builder John Wright.

Chapter 6

For King, for Queen and Country: From Muster to Mutiny

The Call to Muster

Originally a muster of able bodied men, aged between 16 and 60, who could be assembled as troops to defend the realm when needed, there being no standing army. Every town and city held a muster of fighting men on one day of the year and sent the figures of men available to the Commission of Arraye, set up for the purpose. In Lichfield the Court of Arraye was held at Greenhill, where a Bower House was erected and decorated with laurel and lilac. It was always held on Whit Monday and the men were paraded around the streets, accompanied by the Lichfield Morris dancers and people from the church carrying figures of saints, garlanded with flowers. The origins of Lichfield Bower go back to the reign of Henry II (1154-1189).

The Staffordshire Muster Roll of 1539 lists 40 legibly named Yoxall men (plus one name which was noted as crossed out).[1] Some lines missing and others partial in the original source suggest a total of approximately 51 men. Of the 40 named, three had horses plus a 'jestern', seven a 'salet' and nine had splents. Most of those with armour had more than one piece, and those bracketed as incomplete all had horse and armour, including a gorget and 'makys'. Three men were listed with 'bow and aroys', plus eight bowmen. Ten had a bill, and one (with a horse and armour) a poleaxe. Twelve had no armour and no weapon. Included in the names was Robert 'Morys' who although not stated in the roll, was a gentleman of Longcrofts who, as would have been expected, provided a horse. Of the fourteen men listed for Hoar Cross, only four had any armour. There were three bowmen, six with a bill, and five had no weapon, but two of these had 'splenttes' and one 'splentes salet Gorget'. In 1640 the trained soldiers impressed for service on 1st June had to be in Uttoxeter on 1st July, ready for service.[2]

Jestern: a coat of mail;
salet: a light helmet with or without a vizor and without a crest, the lower part curving outwards behind;
splents: two pieces of armour to protect the elbows, formed from plates or strips of overlapping metal;
gorget: a piece of armour covering the throat;
'makys': probably a mace; a club like weapon, with or without spikes;
bill: a blade with a long handle.

In 1600 Thomas Carter, constable of Yoxall was instructed to prosecute Hugh Kynnersley and Henry Wrighte of Yoxall for absence from the muster at Lichfield.[3]

Taking the King's Shilling

The term refers to payment of one shilling given to recruits to the armed forces of the United Kingdom in the eighteenth and nineteenth centuries and officially stopped in 1879. Some men of Yoxall 'took the King's shilling', (or were pressed into service with strong drink supplied by recruiters), and marched away to fight for king and country on foreign shores. The following five men all served in Canada, and are listed in papers from Canada, British Regimental Registers of Service, (1756-1900).

Edward 'Waite' was baptised at St Peter's in 1776, the son of John and Sarah Wait. He worked as a labourer before enlisting in June 1796 and joining Unit 29th Dragoon Guards. He was appointed Corporal to G Troop in June 1797.[4] He may have survived and returned to Yoxall as in 1806 an Edward Wait married at St Peter's.

Thomas Cooke was born in Yoxall, his military date 1796-1812. He served in Unit 22nd (later 25th Dragoon Guards).[5]

Thomas Boulton, son of Benjamin and Elizabeth, was baptised at St Peter's in 1788 and enlisted at Lichfield on 30 June 1810. Period of service: Unlimited. His occupation was butcher. His Unit was 12th Foot Soldiers.[6]

Daniel Dakes [Dukes], the son of Thomas and Mary Dukes of Woodhouses, Daniel was baptised at St Peter's in 1818. He was attested in 1839 at Birmingham and was a boiler maker by trade. He embarked with Unit 2nd Foot Soldiers.[7] By 1861 he had returned to Yoxall a Chelsea Pensioner and was living with his widowed mother. By 1871 he had moved to Birmingham and was enumerated with brother James, a carpenter.

John Snape was baptised at St Peter's in 1798, the son of Daniel and Sarah, John was a carpenter by trade and was attested at Lichfield in May 1824, his unit was 52nd Foot Soldiers Depot. In December of that year he married at Yoxall. He was discharged in 1825 at Portsmouth, Commissioned in Chief's authority having paid the regulated Sum of £20.[8] John changed his occupation from carpenter to tape weaver. From his will of 1829 it is clear that he was not merely a tape weaver, but had interests in tape manufacturing on a larger scale. He bequeathed his 'freehold messuages, shop and hereditements' in Yoxall in the occupation of himself, Elizabeth Young and Messrs Hindle and Bond, the latter of whom were tape manufacturers, also his personal estate to his executors, Daniel Knott, blacksmith and John Painter the younger, yeoman, to administer his estate and pay the rents, interests and profits to his wife Dorothy as long as she lived or remained his widow and provide for his children until they reach the age of twenty one. The witnesses to his will were Thomas Heaford, Morton Bond (tape manufacturer) and Edward Bond. He died in May 1829.

Gustavus Bode: Napoleonic Wars

German born Gustavus Bode served in the Napoleonic Wars. Service Date: 1793-1815. His Regiment was 2nd Light Battalion Kings German Legion and Regiment of Hussars (or Light Dragoons, K.G, Legion.)[9] In 1841 he was a musician at New Windsor and by 1851 he was a Chelsea Pensioner living at Morrey with his English born wife and children. The following year his daughter, Olivia Gerding Bode married John Harrison Robotham, a surgeon, also of Morrey, at St Peter's. By 1861 Gustavus had moved to Lichfield where he died in 1869 at the age of 83.

Sergeant John Worthington: Battle of Waterloo.

Sergeant Worthington served in the Coldstream Regiment of Foot Guards, his service record states that he was born in Yoxall, and from the information supplied he would have been born in 1785, but no record of a baptism has been found. He enlisted at Silverhill, Sussex for unlimited service in November 1803, aged eighteen and served until April 1817 when he was discharged on medical grounds '…in consequence of having asthma - the effect of service abroad'.[10] In 1805 John married Sarah Shouell at St Martin in the Fields. A son, Henry, was born and baptised in 1810 at the Lying In Hospital, Holborn, then part of Middlesex.

During his army career he worked his way through the ranks, serving as a private, corporal and finally a sergeant. His conduct was good. As a sergeant he was involved in the fighting at Hougomont. He was awarded the Waterloo Medal, the first true campaign medal issued to all ranks who took part in the battles of Waterloo. Approximately 39,000 medals were awarded.

It seems likely that following his discharge in 1817 he came immediately to Yoxall. Whether he resumed his previous occupation of nail making is unknown, but he appears to have managed to support himself, his wife and child for most of the few remaining months of his life, as he does not appear in the overseers of the poor accounts until close to death.

The accounts revealed that on 6 December 1817 John received 3s 6d, this was followed by a further entry on 11 December 'John Worthington £11 5s 6d.' On 20 December 'Widow Worthington' received 5s, also on that date was an entry for John's funeral, costing £1 14s 4d.[11] He had died on the 14th and been buried two days later. For John's wife and son poverty lay ahead.

James Thompson VC: Yoxall's Hero of the Indian Mutiny

James Thompson is the only known Yoxall person to have been awarded the Victoria Cross. Due to interest expressed by the Yoxall and District Branch of the Royal British Legion the author researched his military and civilian careers. The following is extracted from the booklet produced in 2006 as a result:

James Thompson, Yoxall's Hero of the Indian Mutiny wearing his Victoria Cross and Indian Mutiny medal.

An article in *Family Tree Magazine*, November 2000, claimed that James was William James Thompson 'who preferred to be called James', and was born at 'Hadley, near Yoxall in Staffordshire in December 1829'. The article continues 'Edward and Lydia had the good fortune to have their son christened on 25 December…'. The entry in the baptismal register records only one Christian name - William. There is no shortage of recorded evidence to contradict the claim that James was William. Firstly, in no document is he recorded as either William or William James and presumably the certificates of his marriages and death, and his military record would bear his official name. The inscription on his Indian Mutiny Medal is 'J Thompson, 1st Bn 60th Rifles'. Secondly, while sources vary with regard to his age, the majority of these, including his military record, suggest he would have been born 1832-3. Finally, in the population census of 1861 William was enumerated in the home of his parents, Edward and Lydia at Hadley End, as their unmarried son, aged 31, an agricultural labourer. By this time James had been in and out of the army and married. A further error was that James was the first Staffordshire recipient of the Victoria Cross. The earliest awards were backdated to include the Crimean War. The first investiture took place in 1857 and among the recipients was Samuel Parkes of Tamworth, whose action was chronicled in the *London Gazette* of 24 February 1857 for saving the life of a Trumpet-Major in the Crimea, during the Charge of the Light Brigade.

In July 1832 a James Thompson was baptised in Yoxall, the son of Edward, a tape weaver of Tamworth and Margaret Thompson. This would fit the age suggested by his military record. However descendants of James Thompson link back to Edward and Lydia, who had a son James baptised at St Peter's in September 1835. Possibly for some reason James chose to put his age back a few years, but clearly he was a Yoxall man. From at least 1835 the family were at Woodmill where they were enumerated in 1841 in the household of seventy-five year old Richard Thompson. The tithe apportionment of 1839 names Richard as the occupier of a house and tape shop, suggesting further that Edward and Margaret were relatives. In 1851 Yoxall born James Thompson was enumerated as an 18 year old servant and 'cow boy' in the household of Edward Mercer, farmer of Darley Oaks, Yoxall. Despite the age discrepancy, common in the censuses, it seems likely that this was James before he joined the army. In January 1852 James enlisted at Derby as a Private in the 1st Battalion 60th Rifles (later King's Royal Corp, now Royal Green Jackets). He served in the East Indies from October 1852 to December 1857.

The Indian Mutiny (1857-59) was a major revolt by Indian troops (Sepoys) against British rule, sparked in part by failure to respect native custom. Hindu and Muslim troopers, who were under the command of British officers, were arrested for refusing to use the bullets issued to them, as the cartridges were believed to have been smeared with cow fat and in biting off the protective cover they would swallow the grease of the animals that were sacred to them. The Indian troops rebelled on 10 May 1857 at Meerut and the massacre of the British army officers and European civilians rapidly spread throughout northern and central India. The Indian rebels marched to Delhi and declared Bahadur Shah II, ruler of the Mogul Empire, the new ruler of India. James was in one of the regiments that were dispatched to Delhi to recapture the city.

It was for his bravery at this time that James was awarded the Victoria Cross. The following account is quoted from the *London Gazette*, 20 January 1860:

'For gallant conduct in saving the life of his captain (Captain Wilton), on 9th July, 1857, by dashing forward to his relief, when that officer was surrounded by a party of Ghazees, who made a sudden rush on him from a Serai, - killing two of them before further Assistance could reach. Also recommended for conspicuous conduct throughout the Siege. Wounded. Elected by the Privates of his Regiment'.

The enemy was not the only problem. 'The heat at the time was terrific, with temperatures of 120 degrees; the plague of flies awful. Cholera increased'. The same source states that the 60th Rifles shooting ability was so efficient that the King of Delhi offered a reward for every rifleman's jacket brought into Delhi.[12]

James received a gunshot wound on 14 September 1857. As a result of the injury he had an arm amputated and was discharged from the army at Chatham in August 1858. James's military record is not without blemish. He is recorded as 'absent without leave' between 8-12 September 1855 for which he was tried by a Regimental Court Martial, convicted and sentenced to 42 days imprisonment and stoppages. This seems to have been forgiven by the time of his discharge as his character and conduct are described as 'good' and he was wearing 'one good Conduct Ring'.[13]

Although not the first man in Staffordshire to receive the Victoria Cross, James would have been one of the very few Staffordshire men whose outstanding courage had earned them this prestigious award, the highest award for gallantry in the British armed forces. It was instituted by Queen Victoria in 1856 as a reward for conspicuous bravery in the presence of the enemy and inscribed 'For Valour'. Recipients were allowed to use the letters 'VC' after their name and received an annual tax-free pension of £10. (In July 2015 it was announced the annuity would be raised from £2,129 to £10,000). James received his medal from Queen Victoria at Home Park Windsor, on 9 November 1860.

Following his army career James returned to Staffordshire and at the time of his first marriage in January 1859 was a postman at Tatenhill. The District Pension Returns for Derby 1852-62 record James's transfer to Edinburgh.[14] An undated newspaper cutting states that he went to Falkirk acting as head gamekeeper on the estate of the doubtless deeply grateful, Captain Wilton. In 1861 he moved to Jersey, but in 1862 his pension administration place appears on the Chelsea Regimental Registers as Derby.[15] He may have returned to Yoxall at this time. The earliest evidence of his return to the area is in 1865 when he was working as a game keeper on the estate of Major Arden of Longcroft Hall, and was charged with trespassing in pursuit of game in Barton. The case was dismissed.[16] He was also charged, with James Rice, with being drunk and riotous at Yoxall and although his accuser, Captain Oldham, a magistrate living in Yoxall, backed down to some extent, stating that he 'would not positively say that Thompson was drunk' he claimed his language was 'like that for which Sodom and Gomarrah suffered'. The public house the men had come from was most likely the Crown, which the accuser said was close to his home, and the alleged offence took place at the weighing machine on the opposite side of the road. During the trial reference was made regarding James having the VC and being a 'gallant and distinguished soldier'.[17] The summons against both defendants was dismissed. A further two cases of drunkenness both led to fines of 5s and unspecified court costs.[18] In 1870 he was in court as the gamekeeper of Major Arden who had caught two men poaching rabbits on the land of Daniel Ashton.[19] In 1871 he was enumerated at Woodlane as a Chelsea Pensioner with his wife Dinah, their two sons and a 7 year old boarder, who may have been a necessary source of income as James appeared to be unemployed. He later found employment as a watchman in Rugeley, where son George was baptised in 1875, and Alfred John in 1879. James was a labourer and the family were living at Sheep Wash, Rugeley. Enumerated there in 1881, James was a 'Colliery Watchman'. A daughter was born to the couple in 1882 and in March 1890, his wife Dinah died in their home at Marlow Street. In December of that year he married Hannah, a widow who was twenty-four years his junior. By 1891 James seems to have been unemployed as he was enumerated only as an army pensioner. The marriage was brief, James died in 1891, a year and a day after his marriage to Hannah. He was interred at Queen Street Cemetery, Walsall, where he is commemorated by a blue plaque. He is also commemorated in Yoxall with a plaque in St Peter's Church.

Chapter 7

Tax, Total/Totalis and Tokens

Tax

Poll Tax was first levied in 1377, at a flat rate of one groat (4d) a head, to be collected spring and autumn from all lay persons, male and female, aged 14 and over, excepting those who begged for a living. The same year the Poll Tax Return for Yoxall was 36s 8d.[1]

The Hearth Tax of 1662-1689, was charged at 1s per hearth, to support the household of Charles II, following the restoration. The Hearth Tax return for Yoxall for 1666 listed 144 names, suggesting that was the amount of households in the constablewick of Yoxall at that time.[2] The largest amount of hearths counted in any house was 14 in the home of Edward Mainwaring, gentleman, which was possibly the former Old Hall, followed by 7 for Henry Arden, gentleman of Longcroft [Hall]. The other gentlemen were William Brookes with 6, Thomas Ullock, 4 and 'Jo: Brown' with 3. Francis Massey 'for the mill' had a single hearth. Thomas Taylor, not listed in the return as a gentleman, but whose name appeared following the list as a constable, had 4 hearths. A few other households had 3 or 4 hearths, the majority had 1 or 2. A total of 109 households were chargeable and 35 were certified as not being chargeable under the Act. The window tax, considered as a tax on light, was levied between 1696 and 1851. To avoid, or reduce the tax some people boarded up some of their windows. How many buildings had windows bricked up is unknown as once the tax was discontinued people began to restore the light they had lost. An old photograph of the building formerly Norman's Store shows a blocked up window, and at least one remains blocked in Victoria Street. The window tax was replaced by House Duty, levied on uninhabited houses.

Marriage Duty/Registration Tax was levied from 1694-1706 on entries in parish registers. The cost of registering a birth was 2s, a marriage 2s 6d, and a burial 4s. The clergy were responsible for collecting this tax. Childless widowers and bachelors over 25 were also taxed. The tax on parish register entries was revived under the Stamp Duties Act of 1783, to raise money to pay for the American War of Independence, and repealed in 1794. Some of those not exempt as paupers did not baptise their children, but did so in the years following the repeal of the act. This does not appear to be the case in Yoxall. During the 18th century taxes were levied on carriages, silver plate, servants, game animals and birds, horses, coats of arms and hair powder.

Norman's Stores, now Tudor House and The Old Coach House, the building was a victim of the Window Tax. The windows remained blocked until around the 1950s. (Photo reproduced by permission of Marny Francis).

Yoxall was not financially untouched by the Civil War (1642-45). An entry in the Order Book of 1643 of the Committee of Stafford 1643-1645 entitled Col. Rugeley, Earl of Denbigh and Captain Roper to collect the weekly pay and arrears for the past five weeks for the officers and soldiers, 'either by distress or otherwise'.[3] In December 1644 it was assigned to the captains and officers of horse belonging to the garrison of Stafford, to collect returns and arrears from Offlow Hundred, towards payment of themselves and their troops. Yoxall was to pay £3 18s.[4]

Numeral Usage in Yoxall Probate Inventories - The Arithmeticke Project

The Arithmeticke Project: a collaborative research study of the diffusion of Hindu-Arabic numerals, was carried out by members of the Family and Community Historical Research Society (FACHRS). A series of micro-studies followed the transition of numerals from Roman to Hindu-Arabic in (mainly) probate inventories. The following information is extracted from the Yoxall micro-study.[5] The earliest surviving wills granted probate at Lichfield date from 1533, many of these have accompanying inventories of the testators worldly goods, and although they were written in English, with some minimal use of Latin, mainly for personal names, monetary values appeared in Roman numerals in all the earlier inventories. The transfer to Hindu-Arabic began in 1610 with the inventory of John Arnold, although tentatively. The value of items listed appear in Roman numerals and the total in both Hindu-Arabic and Roman, perhaps to ensure that the new form of numerals could be understood by those not so venturesome. In the same year the inventory of Robert Jackson, yeoman also used Roman for the values but Hindu-Arabic for the total, but without a duplicate total in Roman.

The first incidence of a truly mixed classification is that of Laurence Milnehouse, sieve maker, in 1613. Here the values of items are a mixture of Roman and Hindu-Arabic with a Roman total, which is, rather surprisingly, correct. It must have been a test of the numeric skills of the person responsible for adding up the column of Roman figures, interspersed with Hindu-Arabic. From 1613 to 1626 inventories appear either as Roman or a mixture of the two formats, not until 1626, was there a completely Hindu-Arabic inventory, this being of Richard Milnehouse, yeoman. By 1636 Hindu-Arabic predominated, and from that year only two inventories classified as Roman appear, those of John Ilseley in 1645, valued at £195 and Alice Shelley in 1647 whose inventory totalled £22.

The accuracy in general regarding the totalling suggests that addition using the new method was not a problem. It may be that the appraisers, or at least those totalling the inventories, were already familiar with the method, probably using it for their own household, estate or farm accounts, and possibly the Roman numerals remained in use longer for more formal, legal documents. Simultaneous with the phasing out of Roman numeral usage is a decrease in Latin. Where Roman numerals appear late in the period, so too does the remnants of Latin text, although this is rarer in the inventories than the wills.

A reluctance to dispense entirely with Latin is demonstrated in the will of John Clark in 1681. The name of the king, the countries over which he was sovereign and his role of defender of the faith are all in Latin. This is echoed in the inventory, taken almost five months later. The will is the work of John Ilsley who signed himself Joh[ann]es Ilsely scr[i]p[t]or, the last use of a Yoxall person's Latin name. His name does not appear on the inventory but his distinctive writing identified him as the scribe. The final use of Latin for the name of the sovereign is in the will of Thomas Wainwright in 1692. While in general both Roman numerals and Latin usage died out simultaneously, a few, possibly older scribes were reluctant to let go of the old ways. Yoxall wills continued to regularly have accompanying inventories up until the mid eighteenth century. Between 1750 and the last one in 1768, only four were either produced, or have survived.

Money Lenders: The Role of Women

The Yoxall micro-study also looked at the role of women as money lenders. Prior to the passing of the 1882 Married Women's Property Act a woman's property passed to her husband on marriage. The Act allowed women to retain ownership of property received as a gift from parents. A further Act in 1893 gave women full legal control of all property they owned at marriage or acquired after marriage, either by inheritance or by their own earnings. Women who left wills prior to this were either spinsters or widows. The will of a married woman before this date is a rarity. However many spinsters and widows were wealthy, either by family inheritance, if spinsters, or having been well provided for by their husbands. Often women bequeathed money already held by their sons. These sums may have been willingly given to help a son establish himself in his occupation or set up a home on marriage, or obtained by coercion. Doubtless the circumstances depended on relationships within the family. In a study of Yoxall women's wills 1540-1700 twenty one women had money owing to them, with amounts varying from 1s 8d to £225. According to inventory totals the two most wealthy women in Yoxall were Frances Welles in 1661 whose inventory value was £284 and Katherine Watson in 1691, by far the wealthiest with an inventory total of £728. In neither cases were any debts apparent. Clearly they had no need of increasing their income with interest on money loaned and possibly were not interested in gambling on the ability of debtors to repay money lent. The total amount of money owed to the 21 women was £1,068. These were £233 in debts by specialty bond, therefore a deed under seal or a sealed contract; £8 Bond without Specialty, and £24 in 'Desperate debts', a term suggesting they were unlikely to be repaid and were owed to a total of three women, and 'other debts' totalling £803.

Anne Welles probably had equal or greater wealth than her kinswoman Frances. No inventory survives but her will of 1640 includes a bequest of £355 to her son-in-law, of which he had owed her £225 for four years and to grandchildren and nieces a bequest of £290, owed to her by another son-in-law who was, by then, deceased. She was also owed £10 by Henry Shipton which he had borrowed to buy an oxen and £80 by a debtor in the parish of Abbots Bromley.

It was predominantly the widows who provided the finance. This is perhaps a reflection of the fact that the majority of wills and inventories surviving for women are those of widows. Wealthy spinsters are likely to have been a minority group as their inheritance from parents and other family members was likely to be their share of an estate which had been split between siblings. Widows would often be the sole or main beneficiary of their husband's will, provided they remain widows. Only three women in the study were found to owe money, the largest amount being £6 2s 4d. The only sum which is itemised is that of Isabella Stone, in 1620, who owed £1 6s 11d, of which 16s was for the surrender of a deed of gift, the rest for her funeral expenses and for the doctor who attended her for five weeks. All three women were owed money. Evidence suggests that while men were happy to accept loans from women, they were less inclined to lend money to them, probably due to their apparent lack of occupation which may have cast doubts on their ability to repay the loan.

It was not only women who were owed money, one example of the men who were also awaiting a settlement of debts was Thomas Leese the elder, a blacksmith, whose inventory taken in 1692 included 'Money owing by Book and Bill some hopeful to be gott & some Desperate in all £10 10s 2d'.

The inventory of cordwainer Thomas Brightland taken in 1768 suggests he was a money lender as well as a cordwainer, he was owed a total of £642 in securities 'upon Bond and Note' as well as 'Debts owing to the Intestate as appears by his Books and Papers, many are Dubious & many supposed to be paid but till further Enquiry is made the Exhibitants cannot specify or set forth the same more particularly'. A list of 41 people follows, their debts ranging from 3s 3d to £2 14s 3d.

Trade Tokens of Yoxall

Nationally trade tokens were produced in quantity in the mid seventeenth century to meet the need for small change. The smallest coins of the realm were silver and of much higher value than ordinary people needed for everyday use.

Yoxall had three tradesmen's tokens, including a copper coin of Theophilus Folkingham, described as a '17th Century Staffordshire/Yoxall Token Farthing', the value was ¼ of a penny. The name derived from the Anglo-Saxon, feorthing, a fourthling or fourth part. The obverse has the Tallowchandlers' Arms and a margin inscribed THEOPHILVS FOLKINGHAM.

Folkingham and Lightwood halfpenny tokens, the latter has been known erroneously for many years as 'The Yoxall Penny'. (Image courtesy of Dix Noonan Webb).

The reverse has the initials FTA circled by IN YOXALL 1667. On the shield of the Tallowchandlers' Arms are 3 doves bearing olive branches in their beaks. Tallow Chandlers were originally a guild of candle makers, formed to promote educational and charitable purposes in London around the year 1300. Theophilus also struck a copper halfpenny token of which the obverse is the same as his farthing, but the date on the reverse rim is 1667 with the words OF YOXALL and in the centre, instead of the initials FTA are the words HIS HALFE PENNY.

Reverse of Folkingham's farthing. (Photo by author).

Theophilus Folkingham was baptised at St Modwen's Burton in 1624, the son of John and Katherine 'Falkingham' and married Aves Ronolde in Rugeley in 1647. He included the letter of his wife's first name on the farthing. His will and inventory of 1680 reveal that he was then in Brereton, Staffordshire at the time of his death and was an 'Inholder' (innkeeper).

It may seem strange that men belonged to Guilds that did not reflect their occupation, but by this time the guilds were keen to attract more members to bring further wealth, influence, and power to their companies. Men from all over the country went to London to broaden their acquaintances and join a society or association which gave them status, and therefore joined the societies which offered them the greatest advantage. At some stage it seems this is what Theophilus, and later Zachariah Lightwood did. The inventory of Theophilus was valued at £471. The Inn which he kept was, according to his inventory, frequented by people of importance. The appraisers listed among the rooms 'Beding and other goods in Squire Ferrers his Chamber'. The Ferrers family, Lords of the Manor of Yoxall until well into the 13th Century, were still major landholders. How long Theophilus lived in Yoxall is uncertain, but the fact that he produced a token suggests he either was, or intended to be resident for some time, but possibly had left by the time Lightwood produced his own token.

In 1671 a coin was struck by Zachariah Lightwood, this time in brass, and unusually, octagonal in shape. This token has long been known locally as the 'Yoxall Penny' but is described as a halfpenny by traders of 17th century trade tokens and the Hunterian Museum & Art Gallery, University of Glasgow. Stebbing Shaw stated that he was given several tokens by an apothecary, Mr Lightwood, a descendant of Zachariah who also owned the iron stamp used to make the tokens. According to this source Mr Lightwood lived in 'the white house facing the parsonage', which suggests he lived in the Old Hall.[6] In describing the shield on the obverse, Shaw wrote that this was a 'chevron charged with hanks of cotton between three billets'.[7] This description is incorrect, and was correctly identified by Dr Gerald Armson as the shield of the Ironmongers'.[8] The Worshipful Company of Ironmongers' stated that the shield depicted 3 swivels on the chevron which is surrounded by 3 ingots. The shield is surrounded by the name ZACHARIAH LIGHTWOOD. On the reverse the initials LZK are set between 3 roses, and a margin with the words YOXALL 1671. Both men incorporated the first letter of their wives first names on their tokens, which was a common practice, although on his halfpenny Theophilus did not, the time probably being between the death of Avis and his marriage to Elizabeth. Although little is known of Theophilus Folkingham during his time in Yoxall, both he and Zachariah Lightwood were churchwardens at St Peter's in 1667. Nationally tokens continued to be struck until the Act of Suppression made them illegal in 1817.

Savings and Friendly Societies

An official return of 1880 showed 235 accounts remaining open at Yoxall and Barton bank, with £6,750 1s 8d due to depositors. The expenses of management during the year had been £42 18s.[9] Evidence of where people saved their money appears in some wills. In 1835 Mary Lester, a widow of Woodlane bequeathed to Hannah Brierley all the money she had in the Yoxall Amicable Society funds. In 1881 William Winfield, a grocer of Hadley End bequeathed to his wife the sum of £30 more or less, from an account already in her name in the Yoxall Savings Bank.

In 1803 Yoxall had 3 benefit societies with a combined membership of 235. Also an Amicable Society of Yoxall, was formed in 1819.[10] According to an 1874 report of Friendly Societies in Staffordshire there were 2 women's societies in Yoxall, these were the New Friendly Female Society, which met at the Boys' school, with a membership of 97 and funds of £79. The other society, the 'New Friendly', met at the Cup Inn, with 105 members and funds of £97.[11] Friendly societies were often known as benevolent societies, being a body of people who joined together, often for a common financial purpose, but some societies were formed for social reasons.

Another friendly society was the Oddfellows Lodge, which had 113 members in 1876.[12] This was the Meynell Ingram Lodge of the Manchester Unity of Independent Order of Oddfellows, a branch of the Manchester Unity of Oddfellows, which began in 1810 when a number of social groups formed together. The Meynell Ingram Lodge was formed in 1843 and in 1870 celebrated their 27th anniversary in style, wearing full regalia, accompanied by their banner and the 1st Militia Staffordshire Band they marched to Longcroft Hall for refreshments, their arrival and departure heralded by the firing of cannon. This was followed by a return to the village where members and villagers attended divine service, after which a perambulation of the village ended at the Cup Inn where a tent was provided in the field and 'Host Hancock' served dinner. Major Arden presided the meeting which included Dr Armson, Rev. Baker and Mr Perkins.[13] The Meynell Ingram Lodge became part of the Trent lodge of Burton in the late 1980s.[14]

Chapter 8

Authors, Abolition and Adultery

The literary interest of Humphrey Welles and George Arden are included in the chapter 'Yoxall Gentry'. During the eighteenth and nineteenth centuries Yoxall was home to, and/or the birthplace of, several notable authors of their time. Those who lived in Yoxall had the benefit of a close, like minded social circle, and a shared interest in the abolition of slavery. The adultery case also had literary connections, firstly through one of those involved and secondly in being written about by a famous author.

Thomas Astle

THOMAS ASTLE ESQ? F.R.S. &c.

Thomas Astle, line engraving by William Skelton, after Henry Howard. Published in 1803.

Thomas Astle was born in Yoxall in 1735, the eldest son of Daniel Astle, a keeper of Needwood Forest, and his wife Dorothy. The couple were buried in Yoxall church. Thomas was articulated to an attorney at Yoxall, but discovering his interests lay in deciphering ancient records, he went to London to improve his knowledge of the task. Fortunate in his acquaintances and patrons, in 1763 George Grenville, then prime minister and chancellor of the exchequer, nominated Thomas as one of the three men who would report on the records in the state paper office, which led to the trio methodising all the exchequer records. Thomas appears to have retained his part of these responsibilities throughout his life. In 1765 he married Anna Maria, the daughter and heiress of the Rev.

Philip Morant, author of the History of Essex, whose large estate Thomas gained after his death. Thomas was joined in his work by his son, also Thomas, who joined him as commissioner. Dr Samuel Johnson and Horace Walpole were both correspondents of Thomas, Walpole wrote regarding Thomas's enthusiasm for his work 'In the Paper Office there is a wight, [person] called Thomas Astle, who lives like moths on old parchments'.[1] Thomas became His Majesty's Chief Clerk in the Record Office in the Tower of London and a Trustee of the British Museum. His publications include 'The Will of Henry the Seventh' and 'The Origin and Progress of Writing', the latter published in 1783 was considered his masterpiece. His achievements are all the more remarkable as he had the disadvantage of having only one eye, the other he lost in an accident at school.

Thomas died at his home, Battersea Rise, in Surrey in 1803. His extensive library was purchased by the Royal Institution for £1,000. In his will he directed that his manuscripts should first be offered to George Grenville, Marquis of Buckingham, the son of his patron, for the nominal sum of £500, and should he decline to purchase them, they were to be offered to the British Museum on the same terms. A special room was constructed for them at the Marquis's home, Stowe House in Buckinghamshire. The collection became known as the Stowe manuscripts (Stowe MSS), and were privately purchased by Bertram Ashburnham, fourth earl of Ashburnham, in 1849 and sold to the government thirty years later by his son, for £45,000. Most of the papers which once belonged to Thomas Astle were placed in the British Museum and remain in the British Library's department of manuscripts.

Rev. Edward Cooper

Edward Cooper, the original painting was by T. Barber, 1819.

Edward was born in 1770, the son of Rev. Dr Edward Cooper and Jane née Leigh. The Leigh family were descended from Sir Thomas Leigh, who during the sixteenth century was Lord Mayor of London. One of the largest land owners in Warwickshire, the family acquired Stoneleigh Abbey in 1561 and became Lords of the Manors of Hamstall Ridware in 1601, and Yoxall in 1765. Edward senior was rector of Buckland St Mary in Somerset 1764-1782 and from 1770 to his death in 1792, prebendary of Wells Cathedral. Edward junior was the cousin of Jane Austen through his mother Jane's sister Cassandra, who married Rev. George Austen, rector of Steventon. Jane was the couple's seventh child.

Edward junior was educated at Eton and Queen's College, Oxford, graduating in 1792. He was ordained and became a curate of Harpenden, near Henley in Oxfordshire and in 1794 married Caroline, the only daughter of Mr and Mrs Lybbe Powys of Oxfordshire, who was 'an acknowledged beauty'.[2] The Hon. Mary Leigh held the lordships of Hamstall Ridware and Yoxall from 1786-1806 and offered the living of Hamstall Ridware to Edward who became rector there in 1799. In 1809 he also became rector of Yoxall and held the joint incumbencies for the rest of his life. He continued to live at the rectory at Hamstall Ridware and his curate, John Riland, to whom he paid £100 a year occupied the Yoxall rectory and took on most of the clerical work of Yoxall.

Edward was a friend of the Rev. Thomas Gisborne of Yoxall Lodge, and in 1802 baptised his third son Henry (who became perpetual curate of Barton under Needwood 1838-1876), at Hamstall Ridware with the second name of Gisborne as a tribute to his friend. Two years later his fourth son, Philip Arden Cooper (who became vicar of Orton on the Hill, Leicestershire), was baptised, suggesting a friendship with the Arden family. Edward wrote hymns and sermons and dedicated a collection of sermons to Thomas Gisborne. They had much in common, both being Evangelicals. Amongst his works are the hymns 'Father of Heaven, whose love profound' and 'This is the Day the Lord Hath Blest'. His *Practical and Familiar Sermons Designed for Parochial and Domestic Instruction,* Vol. 1 was first published in 1808 and Vol. 11, 1818. A book of sermons was published posthumously in 1838.

In 1812 he agreed resolutions regarding the singing in church with the principal inhabitants, including that the tunes in the church should be plain and congregational. There was also a declaration signed by the members of the Yoxall church band in 1815, agreeing to conform to all rules and regulations, including regular attendance and 'in all respects to behave ourselves in a manner suitable to the solemnity of the place and the office we have undertaken'.[3] Edward was also concerned with the education of children and opened schools in Hamstall Ridware and Yoxall.

In 1813 Edward was one of 30 men who watched over Ann Moore 'the fasting woman of Tutbury' whose claims to have eaten nothing from 1807-1813 were exposed as a hoax.[4] He was, like his curate John Riland at Yoxall and Thomas Gisborne, a keen abolitionist.

Edward Cooper died in 1833 and was buried in St Michael and All Angels Church at Hamstall Ridware. His monumental inscription states that 'as a faithful Minister of Christ and endeared to all his Parishioners he discharged with unremitting zeal the duties of his sacred office'. His wife Caroline Isabella, was buried at Hamstall in 1838, having died at Walton, Derbyshire, aged 62. The tablet in the church was erected by the couple's eight surviving children 'as a tribute of grateful affection and respect to the memory of their deeply lamented and much beloved parents'.

Jane Austen, Edward Cooper and Thomas Gisborne

Jane Austen, in a letter to her sister Cassandra in January 1799 wrote regarding the Coopers' move to Hamstall Ridware 'We collect from his letter that he means to reside there, in which he shows his wisdom. Staffordshire is a good way off; so we shall see nothing more of them till some fifteen years hence, the Miss Coopers are presented, fine, jolly, handsome, ignorant girls'.[5]

Seven years later, in the summer of 1806 the Hon. Mary Leigh died and Jane with her mother and sister Cassandra travelled to Stoneleigh Abbey, and then to Hamstall Ridware to visit the Coopers, where they stayed for five weeks.[6] No

evidence has been found to support the claim that Jane stayed in a coaching house in Yoxall, now known as The Old Coach House and Tudor House, and the visit of Jane and her mother was prior to Edward becoming rector of Yoxall. During the Austens' visit all eight of the Cooper children went down with whooping cough, which Jane caught from them and her cough lasted through the autumn.[7]

It seems unlikely that Jane's visit to the Coopers was a happy event as she appears, at best, to have no great liking for him, and it has been suggested that in his pomposity and insensitivity he resembled Mr Collins in *Pride and Prejudice.* Following the death of her sister-in-law, Elizabeth Knight in 1808

Jane Austen, from A Memoir of Jane Austen by her nephew, J.E. Austen-Leigh, 1870.

Jane expressed the hope that he would not send 'one of his letters of cruel comfort'.[8] In a letter she wrote to her sister regarding the children of Edward and his wife, apologising for failing to keep up with their progeny, 'It was a mistake of mine, my dear Cassandra, to talk of a tenth child at Hamstell. I had forgot there were but eight already'.[9] Jane disliked Evangelicalism, and in a letter to Cassandra in 1816 she wrote regarding a copy of Edward's latest sermons, which she had received 'We do not much like Mr. Cooper's new sermons;- they are fuller of Regeneration & Conversion than ever - with the addition of his zeal in the cause of the Bible Society'.[10] However Cooper's published sermons sold extremely well, and during his lifetime his work consistently sold better than Jane's.[11]

It seems likely that during her visit to the Coopers Jane would have met Thomas Gisborne, accounts of the Austens walking in woodland at Stoneleigh suggests she may also have enjoyed walking at Yoxall Lodge. Jane had read Gisborne's book *An Enquiry into the Duties of the Female Sex,* and she considered that as a conduct book it was less censorious than many. However Jane enjoyed public theatre, and would not have agreed with his pronouncements against it, but may have shared his opinion regarding private theatres: 'It is a custom liable to this objection among others; that it is almost certain to prove, in its effects, injurious to the female performers'.[12] His concern being the 'unrestrained familiarity with persons of the other sex, which inevitably results from being joined with them in the drama; to create a general fondness for the perusal of plays, of which many are improper to be read, and for attending dramatic representations, of which so many are unfit to be witnessed'.[13] This may have inspired Jane's private theatricals in *Mansfield Park.*

There is no evidence that Jane Austen ever visited Edward Cooper again. Although the company of her cousin was not entirely to her liking, it appears he was more popular with others. Friends included John Gisborne, younger brother of Thomas Gisborne, who after his marriage to Millicent, (the step-daughter of Erasmus Darwin), lived at Holly Bush Hall, on the north-western edge of the Needwood Forest until 1815. John recorded the death of his 'invaluable friend, the Rev. Edward Cooper, of Hamstall.' He added 'I am aware that I have lost one of the kindest and best of friends'.[14]

Gisborne Family of Yoxall Lodge

Thomas Gisborne and the Abolition of Slavery

Thomas Gisborne was born at Derby in 1758, the eldest son of John and Anne, daughter of William Bateman of Derby. Between 1776 and 1777 St Helen's House, which originally stood in 80 acres of parkland, was built in the Palladian style by Joseph Pickford for John, an alderman, and Thomas would have spent some time in the family home. John later lived at Yoxall Lodge, which had been built as a hunting lodge in the late eighteenth century and owned by the Hart family, and died there in 1779.

Thomas was privately educated by the Rev. John Pickering, vicar of Mackworth, Derbyshire before entering Harrow in 1773. In 1776 he entered St John's College Cambridge, where his rooms were next to those of William Wilberforce, who later came to prominence as a politician and philanthropist. Thomas spent his time studying while Wilberforce sought other distractions, a factor which sometimes caused conflict. After Wilberforce's death Gisborne wrote to the former MP, William Smith, (grandfather of Florence Nightingale), recalling Wilberforce 'with all his merits, lived at the time too much for self-indulgence in habits of idleness and amusement. By his talents, his wit, his kindness, his social powers, his universal acceptability, & his love of society, he speedily became the center [sic] of attraction to all the clever & the idle of his own College & other Colleges... With this great orbit the smaller and duller circle in which I moved came but incidentally into contact'.[15] However the two became close friends and when Wilberforce returned from visiting in the evening he would, in the words of Thomas 'summon me to join him by the music of his poker and tongs - our chimney pieces being back to back - or by the melodious challenge of his voice. He was so winning and amusing that I often sat up half the night with him, much to the detriment of my attendance of lectures the following day'.[16] Despite the distractions, Thomas was chancellor's medallist in 1780 and graduated with a BA as sixth wrangler and an MA. He had the opportunity of a career as politician but chose to be ordained as a priest.

The Rev. Thomas and Mary Gisborne by Joseph Wright, 1786. Yale Centre for British Art. The painting is in the style popularised by Gainsborough's Mr and Mrs Andrews, 1750, with the sitters placed in the landscape they owned. (Yale Center for British Art).

From 1783 he lived at Yoxall Lodge which he had inherited the lease of upon his father's death in 1779, and purchased the lodge and grounds in 1803.[17] He was presented with the perpetual curacy of Barton-under-Needwood in 1783, which he retained until 1820, when he resigned the incumbency to his son James. As a perpetual curate Thomas would have received a cash stipend, which was likely to have been maintained by an endowment fund, and unlike rectors, would have no ancient entitlement to income from tithes or glebes. During his incumbency he provided a curate to serve in Barton. Thomas was appointed prebendary of Durham Cathedral in 1823 and moved from the fifth to the first stall in 1826.

In 1784 Thomas married Mary, sister of his friend Thomas Babington of Rothley Temple in Leicestershire, who had been at Cambridge with Gisborne and Wilberforce, and was to work closely with them both in their efforts regarding the abolition of slavery. When Babington married Jean Macaulay, the daughter of a Scottish minister in 1787, she was considered not to have the necessary skills of running a busy English country home. Babbington took his bride to Yoxall Lodge to be trained by his sister Mary Gisborne. Only when her 'probationary period' was over at the end of six months, and 'she was judged capable of taking the head of her own household' did the couple return to Rothley Temple.[18]

The family life of Thomas Gisborne was a happy one. Prior to his marriage, Wilberforce spent much of his time either at Rothley Temple or Yoxall Lodge. When Wilberforce returned with Thomas to Yoxall Lodge from a visit to Nottingham he observed his friend's loving reception from his family, and 'felt sadly the want of a wife and children to hail my return'.[19]

Yoxall Lodge, date unknown. (Reproduced by permission of The Magic Attic).

Thomas, like Wilberforce, became a member of the Clapham Sect, a group of evangelicals whose priorities included the abolition of slavery. The Clapham community began informally as a group of friends who were drawn together by their shared views and aims. In 1792 a 'chummery' was set up in Clapham in and around Battersea Ridge on Clapham Common, a few miles south of Westminster. Some members, known as 'The Saints' lived there while others, like Thomas Gisborne, visited.

During the summer of 1790 Wilberforce, Babington and Thomas worked at Yoxall Lodge on the Slave Trade, rarely venturing out in favour of concentrating on the task of working through 1400 folio pages regarding the abolition.

Other local abolitionists included Rev. Edward Cooper and his curate John Riland who published a paper entitled *Reflections on Recent Occurrences at Lichfield; Including Illustrations of the Opinions of Samuel Johnson, L.L.D. on Slavery ... Addressed to the Rev. Thomas Gisborne, M.A.*, published in 1826. (Samuel Johnson had taken in, educated, and made his heir, Francis Barber, a freed slave who had remained with him until his death). John Riland also published *Memoirs of a West-India Planter* in 1827, which he prefaced as 'a narrative supported by impeachable evidence, and aspiring to awaken or increase its readers' sympathy with our colonial slaves'.

In 1794 Thomas Gisborne focused attention on the dreadful conditions suffered by children working in factories, stating that the case 'cried out loudly for the interference of the legislature'.[20] This led to the founding of the Society for Bettering the Conditions of the Poor, known as the Bettering Society. This called for legislation to limit the working hours of children in cotton mills and to regulate the age and conditions of apprenticeships, also to provide regular inspection. In 1802, Robert Peel, a vice president of the society carried through a Bill ending forced apprenticeships and forbidding night work for children in the Lancashire cotton mills.

The campaign towards the abolition of slavery continued but in 1795 Wilberforce was an absentee member of Parliament, a fact his critics noted, and he had to be persuaded into making the journey of reparation by an urgent appeal from Gisborne.[21]

Thomas has been described as a deeply shy man, except among his family and closest friends. James Stephen the younger, the chronicler of the Clapham Sect remembered Thomas Gisborne as 'never so happy as when sitting by the poor man's hearth', chatting about 'his crops and village politics' or talking to the poor man's wife 'about her children, her chickens and her bees'. Thomas loved the country but hated the popular sport of fox hunting for its love of 'inflicting torture and shedding blood'.[22] In his volume *An Enquiry into the Duties of Men in the Higher and Middle Classes of Society in Great Britain* published in 1794, he advised the master of the house not to attend the savage spectacle of cockpits and boxing matches and encouraged more gentle pursuits.

Thomas's *Enquiry into the Duties of the Female Sex* is informative regarding his ideas on the education of girls, although these ideas would only apply to the daughters of wealthy families. While he considered himself to be progressive, his ideas did not go as far as radicals like Mary Wollstonecraft, author of *A Vindication of the Rights of Women*, or the historian Catherine Macaulay who argued that girls should be taught the same subjects as boys. Thomas believed that girls should have an education that would 'enrich the mind with useful and interesting knowledge suitable to their sex'.[23] He believed they should be educated at home as he considered that away from parental control they would be 'thrown into the promiscuous multitude of good and bad'.[24] He disapproved of girls attending schools as he argued that 'one worthless girl is sometimes found to contaminate the greater part of the school'.[25]

Thomas was a prolific writer, he wrote at least six hymns and his published works include texts of ecclesiastical interest, moral philosophy, papers on slavery, and poetry, the latter often in the style of William Cowper. His *Walks in a Forest and Other Poems* was published in 1794 and proved so popular that it ran into an 8th edition. The following lines from 'Autumn' show his love of the forest at all times and in all seasons:

….I could rove
At morn, at noon, at eve, by lunar ray,
In each returning season, through your shades,
Ye reverend woods! I could visit every dell,
Each hill, each breezy lawn, each wandering brook,
And bid the world admire;….[26]

In May 1803 Thomas wrote 'To My Son on the Destruction of Needwood Forest' regarding 'The fate of Needwood's wild domain':

Man urges Man; stroke cries to stroke:
Loud crashing falls th' astonish'd oak.
Wide and more wide the slaughter spreads:
Successive woodlands bow their heads.
The birds their ruin'd haunts forsake:
The squirrel flies the echoing brake:
And glancing trouts their terror hide
Beneath the brook's impending side
Stretch'd on the desolated steep,
And drench'd in more than wintry sleep,
The mighty victims lie: nor dream
Of lightening braved, of freshening stream,
Of vernal gale, or summer sun.
Their joys are past: their course is run.[27]

It has been claimed that the Needwood Forest was to Thomas what Selborne was to Gilbert White. A keen botanist, his collection of plants, representing about 600 species, are in the National History Museum in twenty volumes of preserved specimens, about 100 species were gathered at Yoxall Lodge or in the vicinity and dated 1791 and 1792. It is likely that at least some are extinct today. Thomas was also a talented amateur artist and some of his work is in the British Museum. He was a friend of the artist Joseph Wright, who painted a portrait of him and his wife.

With the inclosure of Needwood Forest it was believed that the population would grow and the Crown gave land for a church and minister's house. Thomas Gisborne and his younger brother John were the leading members of a group of trustees responsible for building Christ Church at Needwood. The area became known as Newchurch. In 1843 Thomas's wife Mary, was buried there, the memorial bears testimony to her enduring love for her husband. 'During a union of nearly fifty-nine years her fervent affection for her husband knew neither change or limit in tenderness or depth'. Her memorial also records: 'Of her ten children, a daughter and two sons died before her and two daughters and five sons survived her'.

Thomas died in 1846 and was buried with his wife in Christ Church, Newchurch. He is also commemorated on a blue plaque which states he was a 'Landowner, philanthropist and anti-slavery campaigner' his name shares the plaque with William Strutt. It is situated on a wall outside of St Helen's House in King Street, Derby. The house was bought by William Strutt (1788-1829), an inventor, industrialist and chairman of the Derby Improvement Commission in 1801. St Helen's House is now a Grade 1 listed building.

Some Children of Thomas and Mary

The following are children who lived as adults in Staffordshire or South Derbyshire.

Thomas Gisborne Junior (1789-1852)

Thomas was the first son of Thomas and Mary. Like his father, he was educated at Cambridge, but unlike him he chose a career in politics. Thomas lived at Horwick House in Derbyshire until he inherited Yoxall Lodge on the death of his father. He married Elizabeth Fysche née Palmer who died in 1823 and in 1826 he married widow Susan Dukinfield Astley. The couple were enumerated in 1851 at Yoxall Lodge, Thomas was a 'magistrate, farmer of about 800 acres, colliery, land owner employing about 200 labourers'. He was interested in the advancement of husbandry and wrote articles on farming, published in the 'Quarterly Review' which in 1854 were published in a single volume. During his career he was elected MP for Stafford in 1830 and held the seat until 1832, when he was MP for North Derby until 1837. He was MP for Carlow Borough from 1839 to 1841 and MP for Nottingham in 1843 and held the seat until his death in 1852. He died at Yoxall Lodge and was buried at Christ Church, Newchurch.

James (1792-1872), the fourth son, like his father, became a clergyman and took the perpetual curacy of Barton under Needwood in 1819, prior to his father's resignation of the post in 1820. He held the curacy until 1838 and in 1861 and 1871 James was enumerated as the vicar of Croxall, then Derbyshire but now in Staffordshire. He died in 1872 aged 79.

Matthew (1794-1852) was the fifth son of Thomas and Mary, born at Yoxall in 1794. By 1851 he was residing at Walton Hall, Walton upon Trent and was a magistrate for Staffordshire and Derbyshire and a landed proprietor occupying 700 acres. Like his elder brother Thomas, he died in 1852 and was buried at Newchurch. His wife, Calcutta born Anne Frushard Gisborne, remained at Walton until her death in 1892 when she too was buried at Newchurch. Their second son, George Babington Gisborne, born in Calcutta predeceased the couple and was buried in the same place in 1843.

Although Lydia left Yoxall on her marriage to Rev. Robinson her story is included, as due to the famous connections, it was well known in Victorian society. Mrs Robinson of Thorp Green had more than a name in common with Mrs Robinson of the 1960s film 'The Graduate'.

Lydia Gisborne and the Brontë Affair

Lydia Gisborne, painted at the time she was Lydia Lady Scott. (Image courtesy of The Art New Gallery Walsall Archives).

Lydia was baptised in 1799 at Barton and in 1824 married at St Peter's the Reverend Edmund Robinson of Little Ouseburn, a tiny hamlet near York. The couple lived at Thorp Green Hall. Robinson rarely officiated at Little Ouseburn Church, but lived the life of a squire, much of his time being occupied in hunting. The only baptisms he performed were those of his own children, with one exception in 1842, being William the illegitimate son of Jane Kettlewell, a spinster of Thorp Green. This has led to the suggestion by some biographers that the child was his.

In 1840 Anne Brontë obtained a post with the Robinsons as governess to their daughters and may have been aware of whisperings regarding the illegitimate child. In 1843 her brother Branwell became tutor to the Robinsons' 11 year old son and both remained there until 1845 when Anne, who must have been aware of what was about to happen, resigned in June, prior to Branwell's dismissal in July. She later wrote in a diary of 1845 regarding her time with the Robinsons 'during my stay I have had some very unpleasant and undreamt-of experience of human nature'.[28] Letters had passed between Lydia and Branwell through Anne and 'Too often had she heard her unthinking pupils threaten their mother into more than customary indulgence, saying: 'Unless you do as we wish, we shall tell papa about Mr Brontë'.[29]

Charlotte Brontë arrived home to unexpectedly find Branwell also at Haworth and wrote to her friend Ellen Nussey: 'I found Branwell ill - he is so often owing to his own fault - I was not therefore shocked at first - but when Anne informed me of the immediate cause of his present illness I was greatly shocked. He had last Thursday received a note from Mr Robinson sternly dismissing him <from> intimating that he had discovered his proceedings which he characterised as bad beyond expression and charging him upon pain of exposure to break off instantly and forever all communication with every member of his family'.[30]

Branwell had a background of failure, having been previously dismissed from other posts; as a tutor with the Postlethwaites, possibly for drunkenness or sexual misconduct, although it is believed he fathered at least one child when with the family. A letter partially transcribed by Lord Houghton, noted that Branwell 'left Mr. Postlethwaites with a natural child by one of the daughters or servants - which died'.[31] When Branwell was appointed as a railway clerk, although not charged with the offence, he lost his post due to a discrepancy in the accounts.

After his dismissal from Thorp Green Branwell made no attempt to find other employment and remained at Haworth, in the knowledge that Edward Robinson was an invalid and unlikely to live for long. He lived in the hope and belief that Lydia would eventually marry him, hopes no doubt spurred by her many letters and the money she sent to him.

Branwell wrote some poetry regarding the affair, including one titled, in Greek, 'Lydia Gisborne'.[32] He had two poems published in the *Halifax Guardian* in the winter of 1845, both inspired by the abrupt ending of his affair with Lydia. It is likely that she was aware of these poems and the money sent to him was a bribe for him not to publish any more, which while they did not name her would be seen by all who knew of the scandal to refer to her.

Following Charlotte's death in 1855 her father Patrick Brontë wrote to her friend Elizabeth Gaskell, requesting that she write Charlotte's biography, as he hoped that it would end the speculative and often fanciful stories about the family which were appearing in the press. He had previously met Lydia, who was eighteen years older than Branwell, and apparently been charmed by her, but responded to the scandal by placing the blame on her and referring to her as a 'diabolical seducer'.[33] He regarded Mrs Gaskell's picture of Mrs Robinson in *The Life of Charlotte Brontë* as 'a masterpiece'.[34] Mrs Gaskell, as she is more popularly known, was a Victorian novelist, and is remembered for such works as *Cranford* and *North and South*, and is the source closest to the events which took place between the Brontë and Robinson families. Her book told of a clandestine meeting at Harrogate in which Lydia proposed an elopement to which Branwell refused to consent. She clearly respected the rest of the Gisborne family as she wrote: 'The woman - to think of her father's pious name - the blood of honourable families mixed in her veins - her early home, underneath whose roof-tree sat those whose names are held saintlike for their good deeds - she goes flaunting about to this day in respectable society; a showy woman for her age; kept afloat by her reputed wealth'.[35] An editor's note regarding the names held 'saintlike' refers to Lydia's father, Thomas Gisborne's friendship with eminent Evangelicals such as William Wilberforce and Hannah Moore. How much Lydia's father knew about the affair is uncertain but they appear to have remained on good terms as she was a beneficiary in his will.

Shortly following the death of her father in March 1846, Lydia's husband died in May. When the news reached Haworth Branwell believed his hopes were assured and confided to his friend, the sculptor, Joseph Bentley Leyland: 'I had reason to hope that ere very long I should be the husband of a Lady whom I love best in the world'.[36] It was not to be, Lydia sent a servant to the Black Bull at Haworth, and a messenger was sent to the parsonage for Branwell to go there. According to Mrs Gaskell, after the messenger left Branwell was discovered in a fit due to his grief on hearing that he was 'forbidden by his paramour ever to see her again, as, if he did, she would forfeit her fortune'.[37] In fact no such stipulation was made in Edward Robinson's will. The Robinsons left Thorp Green and Lydia moved to Great Barr, Birmingham, the home of Sir Edward Dolman Scott, who had married her cousin and on her journey south she returned to her old home of Yoxall Lodge, from which she brought some furniture. Over the next two years she spent most of her time at Great Barr and Allestree, Derbyshire, home of her sister Mary Evans.

Branwell had a reputation for intoxication and when his hopes regarding Lydia were shattered alcohol and drug addiction took hold and his family struggled with the effects of his addictions. Mrs Gaskell describes how Branwell, now in debt, would steal out of the house while all the family were at church to cajole the village druggist out of a lump of opium. While Branwell sank into self destruction news came to Howarth that Sir Scott's wife was near to death and Charlotte wrote to Ellen Nussey '…Sir Edward Scott's wife is said to be dying- if she goes I suppose they will marry-that is if Mrs R can marry-she affirmed her husband's will bound her to remain single-I do not believe anything she says'.[38]

In 1847 Mrs Gaskell published *The Life of Charlotte Brontë* which initially was well received. Although she never mentioned any of the Robinsons in her account of the affair the episode was common knowledge in Victorian society. Lydia resented being portrayed as the 'bold and hardened' woman who had seduced Branwell and 'who not only survives, but passes about in the gay circles of London society, as a vivacious, well-dressed, flourishing widow'.[39] Further publication of the biography was halted following a threatened libel action from Lydia, who was now Lady Scott. Apologies were inserted in *The Times* and *The Art Athenaeum* on Mrs Gaskell's behalf and all unsold copies of the book were withdrawn. As Mrs Gaskell began the task of revision, protest came from all sides. A letter from Mary Taylor, a friend of Charlotte's to Ellen Nussey '… As to the mutilated edition that is to come, I am sorry for it. Libellous or not, the first edition was all true'.[40] An expurgated version of the biography eventually appeared as the third edition, 'Revised and corrected'.

In 1848 Francis Grundy, a friend of Branwell's who had not seen him for some time, was shocked at his appearance. Branwell told him he longed for death and that the cause of it would be solely due to his disastrous relationship with Mrs Robinson. A few days later he died, according to Mrs Gaskell, with his pockets filled with Lydia's letters. Six weeks after Branwell's death Lydia married Sir Edward Scott.

Anne Brontë's experience as a governess to the Robinsons is reflected in her first novel *Agnes Grey*, (1845), which tells of the trials of a governess's life and has been read as autobiography, coloured by Anne's experience as a governess to the Ingram family of Blake Hall, Mirfield, and then to the Robinson family. In her second and final book *The Tenant of Wildfell Hall*, (1848), the main character, Gilbert Markham, bears a strong resemblance to her brother Branwell. After Anne's death Charlotte banned a further republication of it.

Gisbornes Commemorated Overseas

Henry Fyshe Gisborne (1813-1841) was the second son of Thomas junior and Elizabeth, born in 1813, he attended Harrow, Eton and Trinity College, leaving the latter in 1831 without a degree. He travelled to Australia arriving in Sydney in 1834 and was appointed a police magistrate the following year. After two years he resigned due to ill health. He became a police magistrate in Wellington in 1837 and in 1839 he was appointed sole commissioner of crown lands in the Port Philip district. His duties involved long rides and camping out. He took a leading part in the activities in the growing town of Melbourne. He resigned in 1840, due to ill health but used his time to support a petition for the separation of Port Phillip and New South Wales. Intending to return to England he sailed from Sydney and when the ship reached India he disembarked and either died there or at sea. A Melbourne street and the town of Gisborne were named after him.

William Gisborne (1825-1898) was the third son of Thomas John and Sarah of Holme Hall, Bakewell, Derbyshire, and grandson of Rev. Thomas. At the age of 17 William emigrated to South Australia. In 1847 he moved to New Zealand, choosing a life in politics and was appointed to many posts, including Secretary to the Cabinet and Secretary to the Treasury and Colonial Secretary. He took an active interest in the management of Wellington College, and was on the Board of Governors as well as an examiner. Apart from returning to England in 1852 for 18 months, he remained in New Zealand until 1881 when he returned to England to manage property on the death of his brother. He devoted his later life to literature and country affairs and wrote several books about New Zealand. As heir to his cousin, in 1892 he inherited Allestree Hall where he died in 1898. The city of Gisborne in New Zealand is named after him.

Last of the Yoxall Lodge Gisbornes

Thomas Guy, born in 1812 was the first son of Thomas junior and his first wife Elizabeth. He was enumerated in 1851 with his wife Emily Wingfield at his father's home, Yoxall Lodge, which he inherited on the death of his father in 1852. He was enumerated there with Emily in 1861 as a magistrate and deputy lieutenant. He died childless at Ryde in 1869 and was buried at Christ Church, Newchurch. He bequeathed Yoxall Lodge to his niece Elizabeth, who sold it to his widow, Emily Wingfield Gisborne in 1870. In 1872 she married John Harwood Griffiths, a gentleman of Hereford and the couple lived at Yoxall

Lodge, where they were enumerated in 1881. John Griffiths was a magistrate and occupier of a 401 acre farm and woods employing 5 labourers, 1 boy and 2 women, apart from the 13 servants listed in the household, these were: coachman, 2 footmen, a groom, game keeper, cook/housekeeper, a ladies maid, 2 laundry maids, 2 housemaids, a kitchen maid and a scullery maid. It appears they did not farm the entire estate as in that year Arthur Beard was also enumerated at Yoxall Lodge farming 188 acres. The Griffiths supported the local community, hosting bazaars at Yoxall Lodge and in 1880 the sum of £68 was raised and divided between Barton Cottage Hospital and funding repairs to Christ Church, Newchurch. In 1885 John died and Emily continued the fundraising, and in 1901 she established a home in Bournemouth for little girls who had lost their fathers in the war in South Africa. She died in 1917.

A dispersal sale was held at Yoxall Lodge in the 1920s. Rev. Elliot of Dunstall Vicarage was unsuccessful in buying the 'big house bell' made by Edward Arnold of Leicester, dated 1785. This was presumably the 'fog bell' which had rung to guide wayfarers. The Lodge had no dated stones but in the grounds were two that looked like church property, one having the Bishop of Lichfield's arms carved on it.[41] The Georgian mansion which had fallen into disrepair was demolished and the land with the remaining coach house, stabling, walled garden and gardener's bothy, which still exist today, were bought by Henry Walter Featherstone, founder of The Association of Anaesthetists of Great Britain and Ireland, in 1933. In 1951 a new house was built on the site of the former Yoxall Lodge. Each year the bluebells flower again on the land which once belonged to Thomas Gisborne, a fitting tribute to the cleric and botanist who put Yoxall on the map of the campaign for the abolition of slavery.

Yoxall Lodge is no longer part of the bluebell woodland but the bluebells can still be seen at events hosted by Lodge Hill Bluebells which is a field and forest wedding venue. (Photo by author).

Chapter 9

Poverty, Charity and the Poorhouse

In Medieval times monasteries gave alms to beggars but following the Reformation there was a gap in provision for the poor and the responsibility for poor relief fell on the parishes. Christian charity was encouraged and as well as providing for the poor during life, some of those more able to do so remembered the poor in their wills.

Endowed charities for the relief of poverty and the provision of education were usually established by the will of their founder, who bequeathed either property, land or money to be invested. The appointed trustees would pay the rent or interest from the bequest in keeping with the testator's requests. For the poor this was mainly received in the form of cash doles, distributions of bread and the provision of garments or the fabric to make them.

Thomas and Sarah Taylor

Thomas Taylor endowed a school for five poor boys and gifts for the poor of the parish. A charity board at St Peter's records his bequest as 'thirty two shillings to be distributed to the poor in white Bread at twelve pence the Sunday to begin the first Sunday after Lady Day and twenty shillings to buy coats for two poor Men or every other Year Cloth for poor Women'. His will bequeathed £32 to the overseers of the poor, from which the interest was to cover the costs of his bequest for the relief of the poor and the education of five poor boys. The will stated that two coats were to be made for the 'poorest and most indigent men in the parish of Yoxall'. Regarding the cloth for poor women Thomas stated 'if there bee any poore widows or other woman in the sayd p(a)rish, that shall stand in great need of cloathing, Then my Will is, that the sayd Twenty shillings be bestowed on such widow or woman every other yeare at the discretion of the Feoffes & overseers of the poore of the sayd p(ar)ish'.

Although Sarah Taylor is recorded on a charity board, it is only in connection with the school. However in her will of 1714 she further endowed the school and bequeathed thirty two shillings annually for a dole of bread to be administered by the overseers in the same way her husband had chosen in his will.

It is possible that during Thomas's lifetime he had been providing cloth for the poor as his inventory includes 50 yards of new flaxen cloth at 1s 3d per yard, 18 lbs of hempen and flaxen yarn at 8d per lb and 16 yards of hempen cloth at 1s per yard. Hemp, (apart from making rope), was used for making strong fabrics.

Dr F. G. Armson referred to a manuscript, written about 1706, which had belonged to Stephen Martin Leake, Garter King of Arms, which described a mural monument on the north wall of the church which was inscribed: 'Underneath layeth the body of Thomas Taylor Gent who departed this life. An. Dom. 1694 in the 84th year of his age. He did bequeath out of his store Bread, coals and learning for the poor. For to be given every year As by his will it may appear. He left behind his 2nd wife Sarah who was daughter of Isaac Clarke of Sutton Coldfield Gent and she has caused this monument to be erected in memory of her deceased husband'. The arms on it of Taylor and Clarke included three imperial crowns and three swans. Underneath the Garter of Arms wrote 'I question whether he has any title to this coat'. The suggestion being that the arms were probably spurious and would be classed as 'ignoblis', considered the greatest form of snobbery, being the personal invention of a coat of arms to which the bearer had no title.[1]

The Charity Boards

The charity boards list gifts to be distributed yearly to the poor of the parish of Yoxall and includes the names of those who gave and the amounts given. The majority of those named lived in the seventeenth century. The following are some of the names and their gifts:

Ralph Wright and William Roobotham, both of whom gave 5 shillings to be distributed every St Thomas's Day; Mr Cross whose gift was the interest of £40 to be distributed on St Paul's Day; Mrs Frances Biddulph whose gift of four pounds was to be distributed on St James's Day; Messrs Nicholas and John Millington, both gave 20 shillings to be distributed every St Thomas's Day, and Francis Millington gave 5 shillings to be given on the same day. Mr Salt's gift of £5 and Mr Goodinch's gift, the interest of £20, were to be distributed every Good Friday. Some gifts were directed to be given by the rector and churchwardens or rector and trustees, others by the overseers.

Also included was John Richardson, a tailor who died in 1698. In his will he left the reversion of three roods of arable land in a field called 'Narr Croft' (probably North Croft), which lay between land of John Arden, gent, and the rector John Spateman, to Henry Robinson, a weaver of Hoar Cross for this life, and then the yearly profits to the poor of Yoxall, to be distributed every St Paul's Day. He also left five shillings to be paid every St Paul's Day to the poor. His annual bequest is stated on the charity board as thirty five shillings.

These monetary sums distributed on certain days of the year were known as 'doles' and perhaps St Thomas's Dole was the last of these to survive. Rev. John Spateman gave £80 to purchase land, and 52 shillings of the rent was to be given in bread 'at twelve pence the Sunday the remainder to buy Books for poor Children'. One son, Francis Spateman gave £40 to purchase land, the rent to buy coats for three poor men. Thomas, another son of Rev. Spateman, gave £20, the use of which was not stipulated.

In 1691 Katherine Watson of Longcroft, a widow, bequeathed £10 for ten poor widows of Yoxall, the money to be let out at interest by some of the Ardens of Longcroft and the rector. She also left money to the poor of Littleover and Stoke. The Ardens were also to distribute 10 shillings to the poor every Whit-Sunday, the gift of John Arden, by his will of 1704. Mrs Althea Catherine Arden, gave the interest of £500 to be given in clothing to poor women and children, to be distributed at Christmas. Arden gifts were to be distributed by the family as long as there were any Ardens resident, and then by the resident minister.

Other Charitable Bequests

Although not included on the boards, in 1612 James Woodroffe a husbandman of Hoar Cross left to the poor of 'Whore cross' £3 to be paid in ten years at a rate of six shillings every year, the lack of inclusion may be because his gift could not continue indefinitely.

The two charity boards record payments to the poor which were to be continued through the years, usually through the setting up of a fund or charity. However many testators remembered the poor in their wills and are not recorded there as their bequest was a single payment. Up to the eighteenth century amounts to be distributed to the poor were generally either 3s 4d or 20s. The highest amount bequeathed was £5 in 1663 by Walter Ferrers, gent. In 1642 John Barkin, yeoman bequeathed 'six dozen of bread unto the poore of Yoxall'.

During the eighteenth century few testators left bequests for the poor, presumably considering they were already catered for by trusts and charities. Among the few who did, was John Onely, gent who in his will of 1722 bequeathed £4 to the poor of Yoxall, and a bequest to two poor maids at the Woodside, who were not named, but were to receive 10s each.

Thomas Newton Esq. 'Late of King's Bromley but now of Yoxall', in his will of 1780 bequeathed to his nephew John Newton £50 'owing me on Mortgage of the Tolls on the Turnpike road from Ashbourn to Sudbury in the County of Derby and from thence to Yoxall Bridge … to defray my Expenses of my Funeral'. Also to the same nephew £200 to pay the interest of £100 amongst the poor of King's Bromley and the other £100 to be divided equally amongst the poorest families not receiving 'Parish pay'. He requested to be buried in the morning in the parish he died in and not to have more than four bearers, who were to be poor old men, who would each receive one guinea. To the clergyman who officiated at his funeral one guinea and half a guinea to the clerk. If he died in Yoxall he bequeathed to the rector £20 to be distributed among the poor of the parish within three months of his death.

Perhaps the last bread dole was established by Charles Hunt in his will of 1877. He bequeathed £200 to the minister and churchwardens to be invested, the interest to be distributed in the vestry in quarter loaves of bread and 5s each to poor people attending divine service on Christmas day. His sister Ann Hunt had earlier by her will of 1870 left £100 for the same purpose. Both added that the charity would also be distributed to the poor too sick to attend the service, so far as the interest amount would allow and that the officiating minister was 'earnestly requested to remind the recipients of that spiritual bread which came down from Heaven as taught by the 6th Chapter of Saint John's Gospel'.

Lambard Bagot and the Abbots Bromley Almshouse

Born in 1649 at Buckinghamshire, Lambard was the seventh of the 17 children of Sir Edward Bagot, Baronet and his wife Mary Lambard. The family seat was at Blithfield Hall in Abbots Bromley. At the time of his death in 1702/3 Lambard was living in Yoxall. In his will, he requested burial at Blithfield at the expense of £200. His first bequest was for the building of an Almshouse at Abbots Bromley for six old men at the total cost of £800. The building to cost £200 and the remaining £600 'to be laid forth in Lands to purchase a perpetual Endowment thereunto'. He further stipulated that three of the six men were to be chosen from Abbots Bromley and one from each of the neighbouring areas; the parish of Yoxall, the town of Newborough and the township of Dunstall.

Lambard appears to have left no heirs, apart from bequests to servants, the rest of his estate is bequeathed to other lines of the Bagot family.

The inventory of his goods and chattels was valued at £2,390. The whereabouts of his house in the parish of Yoxall is uncertain, but appears to have been of the size and status expected for a man of his birth and wealth, the following rooms and closets being listed in the order that the goods in them were appraised:

Hall, buttery, cellar, far larder, green parlour, passage, little parlour, little closet, kitchen, scullery, larder, dark closet, stair case, best chamber, garrets over the best chamber, matted chamber, garret over the buttery, other garret, in the further garret, maid's chamber, buttery chamber, purple chamber, kitchen chamber, 2 closets, men's chamber, gate house chamber, over the cellar, cellar, dairy, brew house, wash house.

The almshouse was built in Bagot Street, and apart from the six single-person dwellings, a larger one was to accommodate a warden and family. The Queen Anne style building remains today. Over the oak doors is the inscription:

"Deo et eginis D D D Lambertus Bagot arm anno 1705"

This translates to 'Lambert Bagot Esquire gives, devotes and dedicates these houses to God and the poor in the year 1705'.

Lambert's executor, his brother Charles, discovered that the £800 was insufficient and added £300 of his own money to complete the work. He stipulated the type of tenants to be chosen in his will of 1722. They must be widowers or single men and if they should marry they would have to leave the almshouse. They were required to 'constantly and on Sunday assemble at the Church services' and must 'behave themselves soberly and honestly [and] injure no one by word or deed'. They were to receive free board and lodgings, a quarterly allowance of £2 10s, free coal and every two years an overcoat with the letters LB embroidered on it.[2] The men in the alms house were called inmates.

At the time of writing the almshouses (when the plural was first used is uncertain), support men and women in reduced circumstances, particularly those with a connection to the village of Abbots Bromley. The building is Grade 2 listed. An extensive renovation was completed by 2014 which included re-roofing the building, increasing the size to the houses and curing damp problems.

The burial register of St Peter's includes the burial of Henry Orgill in 1753 who was recorded as 'belonging to Abbots Bromley Alms House'.

In a meeting of Yoxall Parish Council in November 1899, consideration was given to the reply from the trustees of the Abbots Bromley hospital, which the almshouse was also known as, in response to a letter written by the Parish Council asking them to allow the Council to send Frederick Biddulph, an old man, to one of the vacant houses. The answer was not satisfactory and the subject adjourned until the next meeting.[3] In December 1900 a letter was read at a parish council meeting stating that there was a vacancy and Frederick Biddulph had been elected.[4] The following January it was announced during a meeting that Frederick Biddulph had been conveyed to Abbots Bromley and money had been received to buy furniture for him.[5]

Although Lambard Bagot's name is not included on the charity boards in St Peter's, it is inscribed on a board in St Nicholas church at Abbots Bromley, which states that he gave three almshouses and yearly maintenance for three poor men forever. This refers only to the three men from Abbots Bromley who would occupy the almshouse. The boards also includes the name of Richard Goodinch, (whose £25 for the poor of Yoxall is recorded on Yoxall charity board). He left £25 to the poor of Abbots Bromley.

Yoxall Town Lands: Coats, Gowns and the Poor House

There has been some residential accommodation for the poor in Yoxall since at least the sixteenth century. In 1562 Richard Agard bequeathed 4d to 'every poor body in Yoxall keeping house'.[6]

The Feoffe's accounts of Yoxall Town Lands from 1723 to the end of the century have many entries regarding relieving the poor:

1739	Spent att buying Poors Cloths			2d
1748-9	Spent att making the Bargain about Building the Poore Houses		1s	6d
	Paid George Bentley the Balance of his accounts for Building the Poors Houses	£3	12s	0d
	For writeing and Engrossing these Acc(oun)ts		5s	
1761-2	For Makeing the Poor Men's Coats and for thread for the Womens Gowns		4s	
1762-3	For Makeing Poor Men's Coats & etc.		4s	
	Straw for Poor House at Woodhouse		13s	
	For Thacking [thatching] he same		6s	2d
1763-4	For makeing the Poor Men's Coats		4s	6d
1765	Makeing Poor's Coats & Gowns		6s	1 ½ d
1769	Bricks and Mortar for the Poor House		1s	
	Payd Thos: Thompson for enlargeing the Gallery Window		5s	2d
	Payd Mr Whiteing for Glassing the Window		8s	
	Payd Robt: Bentley for raiseing & Winscoting the Gallery	£20	6s	
	Payd Thos: Baker for Iron Work		17s	6d

It is presumed that the above work was carried out on the poor house, as all these payments were in June of that year. Payments continued to be made for making clothes for the poor and in 1772-3 the payment of 5s 1d was towards the clothes for the poor, suggesting that money was coming from another source for the purpose of clothing the poor. Each year an amount of around £5 continued to be paid towards the clothes.

1775-6	For Twenty Thrave of Straw for the Town House	£1	10s	
1776	Payd Robt Bentley's Bill for Poors House		16s	2d
	Lime for the Poors House		16s	
	300 of Bricks for ditto	£1	19s	
	Carriage of the Bricks and spent at unloading them		12s	4d
	For three Loads of Sand		6s	
	Wood for Keying the House		2s	8d
	For Half a Strike of Hair			6d
	To Richd: Parkes for A Iron Casement		1s	

	Payd Thos: Baker for Iron work		2s	4d
	To Jos: Steaks for Carpenter Work		6s	4d
	To Willm: Willkinson for Mason Work	£1	0s	6d
	For Carriage of the Scaffolding and gave the Workmen to drink		2s	

In 1777-8 the amount of 9s 8d was paid for clothes for the poor.
1778-9 Pd Mr Dunn for Repairing poores Houses at Woodhouses £1 12s.

The accounts sometimes referred to the poor or 'poores' house and at other times houses. It may suggest that it was one house, built to provide separate accommodate for several poor people under one roof.

The account book of the trustees of the Town Lands, 1798-1894 itemises the material and making of clothes for the poor. In 1852 this included 12 yards of grey cloth, 4 ½ yards of black calico, 4 ½ yards of flannel, 3 dozen buttons, thread, tape and twist, padding, 28 yards of blue print, 7 ½ yards of calico and 5 reels of cotton. Making 3 coats cost 12s and 5 gowns 5s. The total cost, including 6d paid to Mosedale for carriage, was £3 14s 10d.[7]

Overseers Accounts

Under the Poor Law of 1563, two or more able bodied persons were to be appointed collectors of charitable alms from residents of the parish. Churchwardens were often appointed as collectors, but the Act gave them limited powers to compel generosity.

In 1572 the office of Overseer of the Poor was created. Overseers were elected by the vestry subject to the approval of the Justices of the Peace. Two people, often churchwardens or landowners were elected. They supervised endowments and other charitable funds, administering money, food and clothing as part of the Poor Law System.

Overseers of the Yoxall Poor Accounts include a payment to Edward Fletcher in 1804 for 8 quarts of ale for Ann Tomlinson and 7 ½ quarts of beer, presumably for the same person, at a total cost of 5s 3 ½ d.[8] An annual 'Salary' was allowed for medicines and attendance on the poor, which in July 1819 was £10.

There was also a payment of 10s 6d for attending delivering of Tunnicliffe's wife.[9] In December of that year the same amount was paid to Mrs Sutton for each baby she delivered, including that of Thomas Pott's wife who had a difficult labour and delivery, and a payment of £5 18s 6d for vaccinating 79 children.[10]

A bill for clothing for 'Nuttal's Boy'[11] was itemised as follows:

	£	s.	d.
To shoe bill		13	11
To Taylors		18	5
Cloth for shirts		5	2 ½
Paid for stockings		3	0
For curing the itch		5	0
[Total]	2	5	6 ½

The parish was also responsible for people who had left the area and fallen on hard times. In November 1827 a letter was sent to the Overseers of Yoxall from John Stretton in Derby applying for assistance having been out of work for a fortnight. He owed £3 10s for half a year's rent and stated 'I will do my endeavour to never trouble you again'.[12]

The same month a letter was received asking why the gentlemen had neglected to send money for Stoken's children. It stated 'the Children is both Naked For want of Clothes and shoes and if you do not send the Money on Thursday I must bring them For I can Do no longer without the money'. Where this parent or guardian of the children was living is unknown, though probably known to the overseers, the only address given being 'allison Street Number 3 Court and Number 3 house'.[13]

In December 1827 a letter was sent from Brierley Hill, Stourbridge, to the Overseers of the Poor of Yoxall stating 'Ann Lester widow has not received her parochial allowance since last July, she having written two letters and received no reply. I think that she is a proper object for Parochial Relief and hope that you will send it …'.[14] Also in December, a letter was sent from Elford regarding a Yoxall parishioner, John Bayley, whose daughter had 'been turned out hospital at Birmingham incurable, and is a very great expense to him as she requires somebody to attend to her every night…. she is a very poor Creature and cannot Continue long in the state she is in'.[15]

Widow Worthington

Following the death of Sergeant John Worthington his widow Sarah was referred to in the overseers accounts as 'Widow Worthington'. She received poor relief of 5s per week for herself and son Henry, who was not named in the accounts. Two payments were made in September 1818 for 'Worthington's boy 3s 6d'.[16] This may have been in connection with his mother's illness as later that month a payment was made 'By Widow Worthington being in the Infirmary'. It seems she recovered and received the usual 5s for herself and her son until March 1825, when the payments were reduced to 3s, being only for her. It is likely that her son was employed at that time. By September 1828 her payments had been reduced to 2s 6d. No reason for the reduction was stated in the overseers accounts and that amount was paid weekly until at least 26 September 1836, when payments ceased to be listed to the individual recipients.[17] On 12 May 1840 Sarah died at the New Union Workhouse at Lichfield and was buried two days later in the Parish of St Michael. Her death certificate describes her as 'Widow of Worthington Soldier'. Henry worked for John Poyser as a servant before marrying and later worked as an agricultural labourer.

The parish was responsible for the upkeep of illegitimate children. If the overseers could discover the fathers they would pursue payment from them. In 1820 'An Account of Money due to the Parish of Yoxall on Account of Bastard Children'[18] listed eleven fathers and the amounts the parish had paid out for their children, which ranged from £3 to £23. Obtaining money for the expenses and maintenance of these children proved difficult as in only two cases were amounts received recorded and in both of those there was money outstanding. The last named, Thomas Archer, owed £5 4s for his wife, which suggests he had either abandoned her or had left the parish in search of work but failed to be able to maintain her.

Often poor children would be sent out as apprentices by the overseers of the poor. In 1774 Mary Lester 'a poor child of the Parish' whose age was not included on the indenture, was apprenticed to William Madeley of Morrey, a farmer, to live with and work for him until she either reached the age of 21 years or married. Mary would be expected to serve her master to the best of her ability and be honest, orderly and obedient and 'in all Things demean herself toward her Master'.[19] William was contracted to teach her the art of housewifery, and provide her 'meat, drink, apparel and lodging, washing and all things necessary and fit for an Apprentice'. Similarly in 1798 another Mary Lester of Yoxall was apprenticed to John Poyser, grocer and mercer. Mary was aged 13 'or thereabouts, a poor Child of the said Parish'.[20] Other apprentices from the late eighteenth and into the nineteenth century include Ann Lester, aged 9, who was apprenticed to learn housewifery in 1795,[21] Sarah Lester, aged 14, also apprenticed to learn housewifery,[22] and Thomas Green aged 12 in 1838 who was apprenticed to the occupation of ironstone miller.[23]

Paupers

In 1722 St Peter's burial register includes an entry for 'Widow Bickley pauper'. In 1895 Mary Woolley was buried, although not stated as a pauper, she was of no fixed abode and had been found dead on the road at Hadley End. These would not have been the only paupers buried in Yoxall, although the registers do not record the impoverished state of others buried in the churchyard.

The population censuses reveal that the majority of paupers were elderly and therefore most likely to be unable to earn a living. Twelve paupers were enumerated in 1851, ten of whom were over the age of 70. Elizabeth Corbett, a widow of 74 was enumerated as a 'pauper (labourer's wife)'. She was one of seven women enumerated that year for whom age and the loss of husband had led to poverty. Also enumerated was Mary Killingly a 58 year old deaf pauper in the household of her sister, Ann Deakin, a lodging house keeper. Enumerated not as 'pauper' but 'alms receiver and shoemaker', Henry Twamley aged 69 was head of his household which included sons, John a small wear dealer and William a shoemaker and his wife and three children.

In 1861 Elizabeth Corbett was again enumerated and was one of thirteen paupers. In 1871 the number had dropped to four, and apart from Elizabeth Dukes, a 50 year old widow, all were aged over 70. In 1881 no paupers were enumerated and in 1891 again no one was enumerated as a pauper, but three people were enumerated as being recipients of parish relief, aged 75, 77 and 91. In 1901 Michael Kitteride was enumerated as a pauper, formerly wheelwright and George Robbins was 'living on charity'. Both were in their seventies.

Lichfield Union Workhouse

The Poor Law Amendment Act of 1834 created Poor Law Unions, which administered poor relief. The unions were groups of parishes who jointly provided for the poor in their area. Part of the provision was the Union Workhouse, or Poor Law Institution. Measures to make workhouses as unpleasant as possible in an attempt to deter people from seeking relief included separating married couples, and children from their parents.

Built in 1840, Lichfield Union Workhouse would have been the last resort for the poor who came under Lichfield Union. The censuses are generally not helpful for discovering how many Yoxall people were there on census nights except for those actually born in Yoxall. In 1871 Yoxall born Charlotte Fleming, an unmarried fieldworker and her 11 year old son, who was not born in Yoxall, were enumerated in the workhouse. He is identifiable only because his mother was Yoxall born. That year three Raworth children with ages ranging from 5 to 9 years old were enumerated in the workhouse. They were all baptised at St Peter's and were the children of engraver George Raworth and his wife Mary Ann. Another child, Charles was baptised in July 1868 and died in September of that year, followed by their mother in November. In 1870 their father also died and the children were left orphaned. Another inmate was Ann Lester, aged 12. She was the illegitimate daughter of Harriet Lester who was buried on 25 November 1858 the day Ann was baptised. Thomas Fearn a 37 year old unmarried cordwainer was enumerated there in 1871 and 1881, when he was listed as a 43 year old shoemaker who was deaf and dumb. Also in 1881 William Hill a 62 year old unmarried agricultural labourer, and two Pettifer girls aged 11 and 14 were also inmates of the workhouse.

Changing Times: The Parish Council

With the formation of Yoxall Parish Council the administration of charities changed. In 1896 the parish council were in communication with the solicitor to the trustees of the town lands, regarding separating the ecclesiastical and parochial charities. At a meeting regarding this it was also announced that a copy of Richard Cross's will had been received. He is listed as Mr Cross on a charity board and his gift, the annual interest of £40. It was discovered that the property left by him in the Yoxall Meadows, called Big Carr, was for 6 widows of deceased minsters, and not as had been thought, to widows of deceased parishioners. The interest had regularly been distributed to the poor every year.[24]

In 1899 the Town Lands produced a list for the Parish Council of the last distribution of coal and gowns to old men and women.[25] In 1900 a letter was received from Rev. Cory stating that St Thomas's dole was originally left to the Overseers of the Parish, and he 'begged' to hand it over to the Parish Council so that they could distribute the money on the following St Thomas's Day to 55 poor parishioners. The clerk was ordered to collect the money by 15 December, when Council next met.[26]

In 1900 St Thomas's Day dole was distributed by the Parish Council. That year thirty two people received Hunt's money dole and doles of between 1s and 2s were handed out on St Paul's Day (74 recipients), Good Friday (77), Whit Sunday (20) and St James's Day (54). In 1929 the surviving charities were brought together as the Yoxall United Charities for the benefit of the poor of Yoxall.[27]

Christmas Gifts

Lord and Lady Burton of Rangemore gave to the poor in the neighbouring villages and hamlets Christmas gifts of tea, beef, sugar and coal. In 1886 they were said to be a thousand miles from their friends at Rangemore during Christmas, but before going away they gave to the poor of Yoxall 648 lbs of beef, 7 lbs of tea and 144 lbs of sugar. They also gave half a ton coal to 150 families in their neighbourhood and on their return, a further half a ton to each family. Lady Burton also made her annual distribution of blankets and clothing.[28]

This annual event was appreciated and thanks were given to them through the press. In 1888 a letter from 'One who knows' wrote thanking the couple for the lavish distribution of coal etc. to the poor of Woodhouses and Yoxall village that winter.[29] In 1890 a letter signed on behalf of 'The Poor of Yoxall' stated 'Had it not been for the generosity of Lord and Lady Burton, many of us would have been without either dinner or fire on Christmas Day. As it was, all were enabled to sit down by a good fire and enjoy a roast beef dinner for which we heartily thank Lord and Lady Burton'.[30]

In 1894 the Misses Shipton of Bank House gave the annual gifts of Mr G. Shipton of Burton to the poor of Yoxall; about 300 lbs of beef, in 4 and 6 lb pieces to between 60 and 70 families in Yoxall. Lord Burton's annual gifts were distributed in the boys' school-room. Lord Burton had also arranged for the distribution of half a ton of coal to 60 or 70 families in the parish.[31]

Lord Burton was Michael Arthur Bass 1st Baron Burton, son of Thomas Bass and Eliza Jane, daughter of Samuel Arden and his wife Hannah, daughter of James Franklyn. Lord Burton died in 1909 and a memorial tablet was placed on an outside wall at St Peter's under the east window in gratitude of him 'whose faithful and wise stewardship of wealth contributed much to the comfort of the poor therein'.

In 1885 it was recorded that at Hoar Cross the 'usual abundance' of clothing, flannel, blankets and shawls etc., the gifts of Mrs Meynell Ingram were distributed.[32]

Mort's Charity

The life of Robert Sutcliffe Mort is included in the chapter 'At Home and Abroad'. He died in 1892 and in his will left £250 in a trust which became known as 'Mort's Charity'. Unlike most charities of the time this was intended for the amusement as well as education and advancement of children. Robert had stated in the will that it was for the benefit of children under the age of thirteen years and born in Yoxall or within a radius of two miles. In 1897 Dr Armson and Edward Pott were appointed by the Parish Council to act as trustees for the charity.[33] How the trust funds were to be administered was a subject for the Parish Council to resolve.

In 1896 at a Parish Council meeting the following scheme for administration of Mr Mort's Charities was read over and agreed to: (1) in making subscriptions or donations in aid of the funds of any club or clubs for promoting games upon such terms (as far as may be) as to enable the trustees to secure the benefits of the club for the objects of the charity, or in providing necessary materials or instruments for games; (2) in granting prizes or rewards, not exceeding in value 10s in any one case, to children residents who are, and have for not less than two years been, scholars in some public elementary school or schools, and have received from the managers of the school or schools such a certificate or certificates, in writing, of their good conduct, regularity in attendance, progress in learning as shall be satisfactory; (3) in providing or making contributions towards the cost of the supply of outfits for children, qualified as in the last preceding clause, upon their entering service or learning a trade.[34]

The following month the Parish Council again considered Mort's Charity. Dr Armson, the chairman, read a communication from the Charity Commissioners regarding Mr Mort's bequest. Mr Fearns asked if the rector was the sole trustee mentioned in the will, and the chairman said that he was. At this someone in the audience exclaimed, "If it belongs to the poor why don't you let the poor have it; but if the rich claim the same let them take it". Mr Simmonds said that as one of the representatives he was sure that the Council wished to carry out to the letter, if possible, Mr Mort's wishes. Rev. Cory subsequently proposed three resolutions that were carried unanimously. (1) "That the annual amount should be spent in apprenticing some poor boy in the village of Yoxall;" (2) "To procure an outfit for anyone going into service;" (3) "If there are any deformed, blind of orphan children in our midst, to send the same into some institution to enable them to obtain a livelihood in later years if possible".[35]

In 1901 Rev. Cory and Rev. Father Parker, the two elected trustees of Mort's Charity and Dr Armson attended the school to distribute the charity, which every January gave money to the children who had made the most attendances during the previous year. Charles Heathcote and Mary Fearns were given 7s 6d each and the 31 children who came next on the list were given 4s 6d.[36]

Both the Town Lands charity and Mort's Charity continue to be run in Yoxall for the benefit of individuals, groups, organisations, amateur sport and children/young people.

Chapter 10

From Five Poor Boys: The Growth of Education

Taylor's School

In his will of 1695/6 Thomas Taylor instructed that a payment of ten shillings be paid yearly 'for & towards the maintenance of a Schoolmaster within the sayd parish of Yoxall' also, 'All that my house or Cottage lying & being in Hadleyend within the sayd parish of Yoxall lately purchased of & from Thomas Lucas of the Parish of Yoxall aforesaid for ever for the teaching & instructing Five poore Children of the sayd parish at the discretion of my wife during her life, and after her decease, then at the discretion of the Minister & Feoffes of the said Parish'. A Charity Board at St Peter's states that Thomas Taylor left 'a house and ten shillings to the schoolmaster for teaching five poor Boys', but the will clearly states 'Children' not boys. Whether Thomas was financing the education of children prior to his death is unknown.

The school was further endowed by Thomas's widow Sarah, who died in 1714/5 with £3 12s to be paid annually to a schoolmaster in Yoxall for teaching nine boys to 'Read, write and Cast up accompts'. She referred to the 'five boyes schooling' in her husband's will, which suggests that although the will actually stated 'children' it was taken to mean boys exclusively. She also stated that five of the boys would be chosen from Reeve End and the other four to be the children of the poorest parents in the parish. The school would also be free for children of the Potts family, provided they lived in the house in which Sarah then resided. Following her death the house Thomas Taylor had left for the school was exchanged for the schoolhouse on School Green, probably either to cater for the extra boys, or due to its proximity to Reeve End. Sarah Taylor also made a bequest of £20 to Sarah Hall, 'Daughter of my neece Hall'. These Halls were connected to the later Hall family who kept the school from 1760. Whether the Taylors had actually taught children themselves is unknown, but William Bathoe, one of the schoolmasters who bridged the gap between the death of the Taylors and succession of the Halls, was a schoolmaster when he made his will in 1720, and may have taught in Yoxall during the life of the Taylors. From 1726 an unlicensed teacher, William Parkhouse, may have been William Parker who subscribed as master in 1732, and was succeeded by a younger William Parker in 1751.[1] He was in turn succeeded by Thomas Hall.

The Yoxall Town Lands Feoffees accounts include payments made regarding the school. They had borrowed £9 from Mr Arden to buy the house that Thomas Corbett lived in which was next to the school at School Green in Hadley Street. This became the schoolmaster's house. It had a large barn which was used as a school room. In 1724 they met at Mr Lightwood's to choose 14 boys for the school, for which a payment of 2s 6d for the meeting was made. That the barn was thatched is evidenced by the payment of 2s to the thatcher in 1725. In 1726 work, presumably repair work, was done at the school and John Mason's bill of 8s 4d was paid, also a bill of 6s 4d for glazing.

Further work on the school is as follows:

		s	d
1732 July 10	Rec(eiv)ed of Mr Parker in Bills of repair to the Schoolhouse	14	7
1732 December 28	Rich(ar)d Parkes for Glazing at Schoolhouse	1	0
1737 November 11	Richard Parkes for glaseing the Schoolehouse	2	3
1745 June 24th	Richard Parks for glassing the Schoole	3	5
	Mr Parker for Briks & etc. for the Schoole house	2	0

In 1764-5 a considerable amount of building work was done on the school. In 1765 the payments were itemised; 500 bricks at a cost £2 15s, for carrying the bricks 17s 6d, for four quarters of lime £1 4s, three loads of sand 6s, one strike and a half of hair 1s 3d, straw for ditto 6d, gave to the workmen 1s, and paid for the work done at the school last year £15 10s. Whether the following amounts were also for the previous year is not stated; for glazing, 6s 6d, Bentley's bill for the school £3 10s 4 ½ d, Thompson's bill for ditto £ 2 7s 4d. In 1771 the amount paid for repairs to the school barn was £3 11s 6d and in 1785 a new door for the school 6s 9d.

More work was done in 1794, £2 10s was paid for lime and carrying it to the schoolhouse. Also listed below the entry were amounts paid for tiles, bricks and nails and for work being carried out, although it was not specifically stated that this was for the school.

School Green in Hadley Street. The area was formerly known as Weaverslake. (Reproduced by permission of The Magic Attic).

Land tax for the school was a regular bill paid by the feoffees and in 1731 it was 1s 4d for the year. The amount paid was variable but between 1777 and 1788 the amount was 2s 5 ½ d. From 1789 this rose to 3s 0¾ d and was itemised as 'Land and Goal Tax for the School'.

In 1763 Thomas Hall married Elizabeth Green at St Peter's Church, where their children were also baptised, amongst them was daughter Jenny, born in 1774. Thomas became the schoolmaster and in his will of 1811 he bequeathed his estate to Jenny, who was to provide for her mother for the rest of her life. (Although not named in his will his estate included Churchyard Cottage, Yoxall, which Jenny sold in 1814). No mention was made in the will of the couple's other children. Elizabeth's death predeceased Thomas by two months, both died in 1812. They were buried in St Peter's churchyard and their headstone is inscribed: 'They kept the FREE - SCHOOL AT YOXALL; given by his ANCESTORS fifty two years; and had Issue Eleven Children … INSCRIBED TO COMMEMORATE, BY THEIR AFFECTIONATE DAUGHTER, JENNY HALL'. The use of capitals suggests a deliberate intention to draw attention to their role in educating Yoxall children. It also highlights the fact that although they had eleven children it was Jenny who provided their monument. Following the death of her parents Jenny continued to run the school and in 1818 was listed as schoolmistress and Michael Smith was schoolmaster.[2]

National School

In 1815 a meeting was held to decide how best to establish a National school in Yoxall. A Committee was appointed which included Rev. Edward Cooper, Rev. Riland (curate), and Messrs Harvey, Shipton, Brown, Simpson, Poyser, Riddell and Roobotham. Included in the report was that the institution would be conducted on the National Plan; that every boy in the parish would be admissible to a day and Sunday school, besides the 14 free scholars. That occupiers of large farms should be allowed to nominate one scholar for every guinea annually subscribed and tradesmen and occupiers of small farms should be allowed to nominate one scholar for every half guinea annually subscribed. That everyone in the parish would be allowed to send their boys to the school at a rate of not more than one shilling per quarter each. That the institution would contain a Sunday School for all girls resident in the parish, but that in both this and the boys' Sunday school the instruction would not include writing or arithmetic. Also there would be an evening writing school for girls during the summer months. The funds for supporting the institution would be supplied from the rents of the old free school lands, the surplus of the rents of the Town Lands, annual subscription and the quarterly payments (mentioned above). The school would be managed by a standing committee of the rector, curate, churchwardens and overseers of the poor and eight other subscribers, of whom at least five annually paid one guinea or more.[3]

Rev. Edward Cooper had opened a school in Hamstall Ridware and subscribed to a small Sunday school for girls in Yoxall, run by the Misses Arden of Longcroft Hall. Edward was keen to see a new school in Yoxall. He issued a printed appeal for subscriptions for the building of it:

An appeal for subscriptions to build a school at Yoxall in 1817.

In this large and populous parish there is no public provision made for the instruction of more than 14 boys: while all the rest of the Children of the Poor, amounting to perhaps one hundred and upwards, with the exception of such as may be assisted by private charity, necessarily brought up in a state of moral and religious ignorance.

There cannot then be a Measure in which Benevolence and Utility are more directly united, than the Providing of Means for suitably educating so large a number of poor children, who must otherwise remain destitute of instruction, and thus of training them up to be useful members of Society.

Such means the national mode of instruction peculiarly provides. The order and simplicity of the plan; the habits of Diligence, of Attention, of Regularity, of Cleanliness, and of Submission, which it inculcates; the improved and rapid manner in which it conveys instruction; and the comparative cheapness, on which the whole system is conducted, all these combined circumstances render the establishment of such a school in this place peculiarly desirable.[4] The National School was opened in a converted barn in the rectory grounds.

Jenny Hall

Although Jenny Hall was never officially appointed by the school's trustees she continued to occupy the house and retain possession of 4 acres of land and an allotment on the Inclosure of Needwood Forest. She continued to teach in the schoolhouse until 1820 despite not having abided by the terms set out in the wills of the Taylors; to give free education to children chosen by the feoffees or minister. It was stated in the feoffees records: '… she has usually taught such children as have been sent to her by the parishioners and in conformity to the said will she pretended to educate a number of them free of Expenses but none of such children have been sent by the Minister or feoffees and up to Lady Day 1814 she paid to Ann Smith as one of the Heiresses of Mr Lightwood the surviving feoffee of the Yoxall Charity Lands the sum of £1 15s per annum since which time she has not paid any rent but paid the £1 12s per annum issuing out of the land for Bread. Mrs Ann Smith will permit her name to be used if any action should be recommended on the part of the Trustees'.[5] The same document values the 4 acres of meadow land, which was New Rayles at £15 per annum, the schoolhouse at £7 per annum and the annual value of the allotment in Needwood Forest, comprising 1 acre 3 roods and 19 perches £5.

Jenny did not go without a struggle, she applied for possession of the property and at first proposed to give up part of the land and then agreed to give up all for a payment of £150. A letter was sent to her by Thomas Birch, one of the feoffees telling her she should give up possession of the school house 'and account for the use and occupation thereof from the time of your father's death when you wrongfully took possession of it'. This was dated 14 March 1820 and as no reply was received by 5 April Rev. Edward Cooper wrote to her of their resolve to take legal proceedings unless she gave up possession within 10 days. She was finally evicted by a law suit in the court of chancery in 1820 but started her own private school.[6] A front page of the *Lichfield Mercury* contained the following advertisement: 'Hadley Cottage, Yoxall, Miss Hall Respectfully informs her numerous Friends and the Public, that her Establishment for Young Gentlemen, will re-open on Monday 25th Instant July 2, 1831'.[7]

Apart from teaching, Jenny also wrote wills, which on two occasions landed her in court. The will of Mary Bacon of Tutbury, dated 1823, was the subject of a court case in 1831. Jenny had written and was a witness to this will, in which Dorothy Sharratt was the legatee and administrator. Jenny, who resided at Hadley Cottage and at that time kept a private school there, stated that she had made wills for people young and old and had always been paid what she charged and sometimes she had not charged at all. She stated that she knew of only one of the many wills she had made having the validity to become the subject of a court suit, this being the will of James Coxon. It was argued by Thomas Whetton, the executor of Mary Bacon's previous will in 1819, that he did not believe that Mary had asked Jenny to make a will giving all her property to Dorothy Sharratt. He agreed that Mary may have made her mark on the document but that at the time of the second will was in a state of imbecility and childishness, and completely incapable of giving instructions for her will.[8] In 1833 probate of the original will was granted to Thomas Wetton, the surviving executor.

Jenny died in 1832 aged 61 and was buried next to her parents in St Peter's churchyard. Her slate gravestone matches that of her parents but the inscribed text must contain more words than almost, if not any, other headstone in the churchyard. Having stated she was the daughter of Thomas and Elizabeth Hall, her age and date of death, it continues with the following eulogy:

'Combining strong intellect with extraordinary attainments in every branch of scholastic learning, and more especially in Penmanship, and Figures, she for many years conducted an Establishment for young Gentlemen, at Hadley Cottage, in this Neighbourhood, and was eminently successful in sending forth Youths of superior acquirements in the above branches of Education. What she was as a SISTER, a NEIGHBOUR, and a FRIEND, those only can know, who, most deeply feel and deplore her loss'.

After the eviction of Jenny Hall the National school seems to have moved to the Taylor's school building, where in 1821 there were 130 boys. Rev. Edward Cooper also converted the girls' Sunday school into a day school on National

Society lines and by the end of the year it had 70 pupils. This was housed in the barn previously occupied by the boys.[9] In 1824 there was an average of 86 boys at the day school and 142 at Sunday school and 69 girls at the day school and 129 at Sunday school.[10]

Michael Smith continued as schoolmaster and in 1822 was paid 10 guineas a year by the Town Lands feoffees in respect of the 14 boys on the Taylor's foundation.[11] He held the post until at least 1851 but by 1861, aged 76 he was enumerated as retired. In his will of 1866 he bequeathed £50 to the rector Henry Sulivan, for 'the benefit of the Boys school Yoxall and to be applied by him in such manner as he shall think best in the general good of the said school'. His house and garden at School Green were to be sold, and with the rest of the residue of his estate were bequeathed between the children of Sarah Green, wife of Thomas Green, schoolmaster of Kings Bromley.

Yoxall Girls' School

The following is extracted from the Diary or Log Book, Yoxall Church of England School Girls' School.[12]

Summary of H.M. Inspectors Report on inspection 4 December 1871:

'The girls are on the whole backward … arithmetic requires strict attention … ventilation of the room is defective … more desks are needed … a classroom should be added as soon as possible'. The schoolmistress was Louisa A Fletcher, a certificated teacher and Annie Batkin was a pupil teacher.
1871
5 July Very few children present, owing to the Wake.
17 July Many of the children who live at a distance are absent in consequence of the rain.
25 August - 25 September Harvest holidays school reopened with 66 children present.
23 November Not many children present owing to the custom observed here of keeping St Clement's Day.
30 November Many children absent through sickness.
11 December More sickness among the children only 2 present in the fifth class.
1872
15 January Received needlework from Rectory for children to do.
24 January Violent storm of wind rain and snow only 10 children in time for prayers.
27 February 27 Half day holiday for thanksgiving for the recovery of the Prince of Wales.
24 April Third class kept in for half an hour for punishment for inattention over their Arithmetic lesson.
15 May Children finished needlework they were doing for the poor.
24 June Most of the elder girls absent owing to the hay-making.

16 July Attendance of the upper class better though many of the elder girls are still employed in the hay fields.
23 August Closed the school for Harvest holidays.
23 September Re-opened school. During the holidays a class room was built and the school room boarded (recommended in inspection report).
4 October Children's annual tea party.

An extract from the report of the Scripture examination 14 October. 'On 10 October the Diocesan Inspector examined the children in Scripture, 39 children were presented. The Girls' School is more satisfactory, the children are neat and clean seemingly under a good influence with some exceptions, answered with fair accuracy and intelligence'.

1 May 1873 Attendance reduced the children in the village dressing a maypole.
29 May 1873 Children very unruly. They came to school in the morning, most of them with a piece of oak fastened to their pinafores which was obliged to be taken from them.

The oak mentioned in the above extract refers to the tradition of Oak Apple Day, which had previously been a public holiday, when people commemorated the escape of Charles II from the Roundheads, by hiding in an oak tree near Boscobel House. The custom often entailed wearing oak apples or sprigs of oak leaves. It has been remembered that if you went to school in Yoxall in the 1910s without an oak apple pinned to your coat your legs would be stung with bunches of nettles carried by the boys.[13]

The Log Book continues:

17 July 1875 The attendance still very low most likely in consequence of the hay making. The children being kept at home to convey the parents' meals to the field, or to take care of the younger children.

Court Cases

The problem of non attendance at school, often due either to illness or severe weather conditions was unavoidable and the use of child labour during busy farming periods was not considered truanting. Rural boards, run by parishes, accepted the release of children for agricultural labour. This appears to have changed with the Elementary Education Act of 1880, which made school attendance to the age of ten compulsory. At that age a child could obtain a certificate and leave, but if the pupil's record of attendances did not meet a certain standard the pupil was required to stay on at school longer. With the Act came school-attendance officers who could be appointed by the boards to check on truants. Parents could be punished under the Education Act under which officers brought cases of non or irregular attendance before the courts.

Between June 1880 and December 1881 several cases were heard at Rugeley Police Court regarding the non-attendance of children at schools including Yoxall. Parents were fined from 1s to 7s, others paying 5s and undisclosed costs. Some parents entered pleas of inability to pay the school fees, but the Bench said that poverty was no excuse, as fees would be paid by a proper application to the Union Office. In 1886 Joseph Law, nail maker of Hadley End was summoned for neglecting to send his son Charles regularly to school and was fined 5s.

Physical punishment in schools, including the use of the cane, was commonplace but it could be a contentious issue, sometimes leading to the matter being taken to court, and Yoxall was no exception in this.

In 1881 curate William Ding was fined for assaulting a boy at school who he had questioned regarding his absence the previous Sunday. The boy had told him he had attended Woodhouse Chapel anniversary because the curate had turned him out of the Sunday school previously. William said that it was not for his attendance at the nonconformist chapel, but for his disrespect that he had boxed his ears. The Bench considered the matter trivial but considered they must convict as he had broken the law by not taking the boy to the head-master for correction. He was fined 2s 6d.[14] The following week a letter to the editor from the rector J.B. Lowe was published in support of William, and on 22 September the following notice was published: 'We received several letters relative to the recent case of assault by a clergyman, but they are too personal for publication, and in the interest of all parties we think it advisable that correspondence on the matter should now cease'.

In 1887 another case came to court, Henry Bradwell, a schoolmaster at the National School was summoned for assaulting eleven year old Thomas Smalley, who had been using bad language. This was not uncommon and the police constable said he had made complaints about him but his father had told him he could do nothing with him. The child had been caned several times on both hands, and the boy claimed he had also caught hold of him by the neck and thrown him to the floor, put his foot on him and 'thrashed him while he lay there'. Witnesses said that the defendant had attempted to put the boy over his knee, having caned his hands, and the boy slipped to the floor, but no foot was placed on him. The Bench found the case difficult as they felt it necessary to maintain the authority of the schoolmaster in the school, but felt that the seven cuts on each hand had been a harsher punishment than he should have received. They concluded that the defendant was right to punish him for using bad language in the playground and dismissed the case.[15]

A school committee meeting in 1881, recorded in The School Managers Book of 1871-1898, considered the subject of the school pence which had not been paid by the children of both schools at the rate of thirteen shillings for a half quarter. It was resolved that no child would be marked present in the school register who had not paid the school pence. Also considered was whether to replace the schoolmaster as for several years the Inspectors Report had been bad. The grant to the boys' school had been reduced again by a tenth for 'faults of instruction' and the discipline, although slightly better was 'by no means Good'. That year Job Rowles had been enumerated as schoolmaster and assistant overseer. A letter was sent to him, hoping he would increase his efforts towards the necessary improvements, but he was replaced by his daughter Arabella Rowles.[16]

An Education Act of 1891 provided free education and further Acts during the nineteenth century raised the school leaving age in 1893 to 11 and in 1899 to 12.

In March 1896 the foundation stone was laid for a new school by Mrs Meynell Ingram and collections were made in aid of the school building fund. This was the beginning of the present school, St Peter's. The final entry in the Girls' School log book is:

30 September 1896 School closed. The girls to form part of the Mixed School in a new building.

The school opened on 1 October 1896, the children were given a tea, nuts and sweets.[17] Later that month the school board met and discussed the hire of conveyances to take pupil teachers to Uttoxeter for examinations. It was also agreed that the school would open at one o'clock and close at 3.30 in order to continue through the winter months.[18] Although one building, for some time the plural 'schools' was generally used, suggesting a divide remained between the boys and girls. Kelly's Directory of 1896 was too late to update its entry regarding Yoxall school but in 1900 the entry failed to be updated from stating the school was built in 1817. By 1908 this had been updated and was listed as the Public Elementary School, built for 175 children with an average attendance of 174.

The parish magazine reported in July 1897 that the new schools had been pronounced by H.M. Inspector as amongst the best in the district. The Organising Visitor had rated them second best in the county but added that in some points the best were not so good. In January 1900 the parish magazine included an extract from the report of H.M. Inspector for the last year: Mixed School: 'The children are very orderly and well-behaved, and if the Instruction were as good in the lower as in the upper half of the School a thoroughly good standard of efficiency would probably have been attained. The Instruction in Object Lessons should improve if the Higher Grants for Elementary Science and History are again to be recommended. Infant Class. The order and discipline are good, and the Instruction is very fair'. A note was added, that the lower half of the school had suffered from the disadvantage of changing teachers during the year.

In 1891 Henry William Jennings was enumerated as schoolmaster and later that year, at a managers' meeting, it was agreed that he should be requested to draw up a circular for the managers' approval to be sent to every parent urging the necessity of regular school attendance and stating that steps would be taken to enforce this.[19] At the back of the School Managers book is a letter of acceptance for the post of schoolmaster from Henry Jennings dated September 1896, which suggests that he had to re-apply for his post in the new school.[20] By 1901 Henry Jennings was living at King Street and by 1911 he was at Fernlea, the house he had built next to the school. He continued as master of the school until at least 1924,[21] and died in 1932 aged 67.

Yoxall School 1912.

Yoxall School, undated but probably around 1912.

116

Billy Meikle's Visits

William 'Billy' Meikle was a local historian, artist and photographer of Walsall. On one of his visits to Yoxall, which he stated as being in about 1875, he noted that he met the boys and girls coming from school, who mistook him for a gentleman, the girls bobbed to him and the boys took off their hats and bowed to him. This he claimed was because the school was run by the parson and squire who would have taught them to respect their betters. On returning twenty years later, this time on a bicycle, and wearing a cloth hat with ear caps tied on top, like the one worn by the politician Kier Hardy in the House of Commons, the children's greeting to him was very different, the girls shouted 'Does your mother know you have got it on'. and the boys shouted 'Gaffer!! Whose your B----y Hatter'. Billy supposed that the school board was in operation at this time, which suggests he believed this accounted for the difference in his reception to that of twenty years ago, rather than the difference in his apparel.[22]

Hoar Cross school

Although the school in Hoar Cross was not built until 1856,[23] in 1851 Ann Hulse, wife of Thomas, the Meynell family's groom was running a school, possibly in a house. She was still a schoolmistress in 1861, despite being aged 71, but had retired by 1871 and was replaced by Miss Alice Cooper.[24] The school was supported by Emily Charlotte Meynell Ingram from at least 1876, who made an annual gift of cloth for making dresses for the 12 girls who attended most regularly and achieved the best marks; the first six got a scarlet cloak, similar to those given at Windsor by Queen Victoria.[25] By 1880 Isaac Cresswell was the master,[26] and in 1882 Matthew G. Whitfield was appointed schoolmaster. An agreement was made between him and the Committee of Managers of Hoar Cross School. The duties he had to fulfil 'in obedience to the New Code of Regulations issued by the Committee of Privy Council for Education' included to provide teaching of plain needlework to the girls, to play the organ at church services, to instruct the choir in church music, to keep the school-room in a clean and orderly condition and regulate school services under the direction of the managers. In return he was to receive £90 per annum and eight weeks holiday.[27] The school was enlarged in 1883 for 100 children, with an average attendance of 88.

In 1893 it was reported that 45 of the 100 children on the Hoar Cross school register had made 400 attendances out of a possible 425 during the past school year.[28]

Titled The School Yard, Hoar Cross. The 'yard' appears to be almost on the road, unless it is behind the fence. Bottom left text 'Boys and Girls come out to play'.

In 1894 a new day school was opened in Hoar Cross for 120 children, paid for by Mrs Meynell Ingram. In opening a school in Leeds she stated that the battle for religious education was not yet won, as there were active and persistent enemies to it. She concluded that she would like to see facilities accorded to teachers to give religious instruction to children in Board schools, where their parents desired it to be taught.[29]

By 1896 it was a National School (mixed). By 1908 it was a Public Elementary School, with Matthew Whitfield still the master, a post he retained until his retirement in 1923. The school remained an all age school until about the late 1930s when pupils aged over 11 years were transferred to senior schools and in 1985, the year Hoar Cross became a separate civil parish, taking in parts of Abbots Bromley and Newborough, it closed and the children were transferred to Newborough.[30]

Sunday Schools

The Church of England would have been one of the early educators of children and continues to play an active part in the life of many schools, including St Peter's. Education by the various religious denominations took place in Yoxall, usually in the form of Sunday Schools.

In September 1870 the Primitive Methodist Sunday school at Woodhouses celebrated its first anniversary. Every year Woodhouses and Woodmill Methodists celebrated their Sunday school anniversaries. Newspaper reports of Primitive Methodist activities often fail to state whether they are referring to Woodhouses or Woodmill. In June 1890 a Sunday school anniversary treat was reported. Following a service, and recitations given by the children on Sunday, the following day the children, teachers and friends went to Hanbury Hills for tea.[31] In August 1891 a Sunday school anniversary took place; the scholars, who were trained in singing and recitation, being accompanied by a harmonium. The following day the annual treat, was held at Yoxall Lodge Park, where the Hon. Mrs Griffiths showed them Japanese curiosities and gave them sweets.[32]

The parish magazine of January 1900, under the heading 'Sunday School', reported that the number regularly attending had reached 92, besides the Bible Class. Thanks were given to the ladies of the working party for the gifts of clothing they had prepared, and which had been distributed on 27 December. Mr Meynell had added a penny and a bun for each child, to which was added an orange from Mrs Frank Armson.

Private Education

George Baker, music teacher in Yoxall during the 'Yoxall fever' of 1814 and listed in 1834, George Goodall, a dancing master of Hadley End,[33] would most likely have been teaching privately. An undated handbill states that Mrs Smelt (Harriet, née Ellis and later Wait), and Miss Ellis taught music and pianoforte. These were clearly private lessons for paying students. In 1871 the widowed Harriet was enumerated in her parents household as an organist and teacher of music. In 1891 Sarah Thomas, a 51 year old music teacher who was blind from childhood was enumerated, but whether she taught privately or at a school is unknown.

Governesses

In 1851 a governess of a school and three other governesses were enumerated. The 'governess of a school' was a very different post to the governess employed in a private household. Ann Winfield was enumerated in her family home as a governess, also in the household was her brother William Winfield, a schoolmaster, which suggests that she may also have been a school governess. There is no doubt that the other two were governesses and were listed amongst the servants of the households they were enumerated in. One of these, Apoline de Soycourt who was enumerated at Hoar Cross Hall. The role of the governess declined and in 1891 only one governess, a nineteen year old French subject, was enumerated in the parish at Cross Hayes, the home of the Hon. Algernon Littleton, J.P. and retired Royal Navy Captain.

Private Schools

The private school of Jenny Hall, which she ran exclusively for boys, was not the only private school to be opened in Yoxall. In 1835 Emma Garner ran a boarding school.[34] For a time girls from wealthy homes could attend Miss Loverock's boarding and day school for young ladies in Yoxall. She was clearly an enterprising lady as a further article of the same date advertised: 'To be let either furnished or unfurnished - a large sitting-room and bed-room. Apply to Miss Loverock, Bond End Villa, Yoxall'.[35] The school was still being advertised in 1879, when it was advertised as re-opening on 22 July.[36] In the 1881 census Louisa Loverock was enumerated as a 61 year old schoolmistress, born in Worcestershire. With her was Ann Dukes a 14 year old servant.

In 1896 a private day school was either run by Job Rowles or he was employed to teach in it, probably following the loss of his post of schoolmaster at the National school.[37]

Technical Instructions

At what age these courses were undertaken was not stated, but from April 1898 Staffordshire County Council Technical Instruction Committee ran courses in Yoxall. The following details were extracted from *Burton Chronicles* and dates given below are the date of the publications.

On 7 April 1898 it was reported that a 10 day course of dairy work had been concluded. The boys' school had been used for the purpose and of the 16 pupils entered only 8 completed the course, some of which had been entered for an exam at Stafford at the end of the month. Many of the parishioners had witnessed the various processes. By 13 October the second lesson in cookery and laundry work had taken place in the boys' school and had been well attended, the young ladies of the parish were 'taking a special interest in the work'. This course was repeated in April of the following year and again was well attended. In May 1899 a 10 week course commenced in dress cutting, which took place at Yoxall Library.

On 19 October 1899 a lecture was reported regarding winter work in the garden and was specifically a lecture regarding vegetable growing. By 30 November a lecture had taken place called 'Manure's Valuation', showing the results of experiments during 1899. There was rather a small attendance, and on 14 December of that year it was reported that a lecture had taken place in the rectory room on the subject of 'Management of hay and pasture land' but there was a very small attendance. On the following Monday there would be a lecture on 'Principals of breeding points in the breeding of farm stock'.

Apprentices

Education did not end with leaving school, as the children had to learn the jobs that they would go on to do for the rest of their working lives. How many apprenticeships were arranged by the overseers of the poor is uncertain, some examples are given in the chapter 'Poverty, Charity and the Poorhouse' but others would have apprenticeships arranged by or within their families.

Five households were enumerated with apprentices in the 1881 census: William Cooper, a wheelwright and blacksmith of Hadley End had three apprentice wheelwrights in his household, ages ranging from 13 to 18, who were all born in Staffordshire and Worcester born Robert Lyne was a visitor and blacksmith's apprentice in the household of Charles Hudson, a blacksmith journeyman. Family members could also be found apprenticed to their parents or grandparents. Henry Wright was a builder's apprentice to his father, John Wright and James Smith was a butcher's apprentice to his grandfather, James Berrisford, a butcher and beerhouse keeper at the Shoulder of Mutton. In some cases apprentices either lived with, or spent time staying with relatives to whom they were not apprenticed and in 1881 Edwin Leedham, a grocer's apprentice, was enumerated in the household of his grandmother Ann Leedham, a 71 year old widow, enumerated as a plumber, glazier and painter, as was her son William, also in the same household.

It can often be seen though censuses and parish registers that several generations of a family plied the same trade. How many of these were actually apprenticed is uncertain. Many would simply have learnt the trade from their families.

Adult Literacy

A study of the marriage registers at St Peter's gives some indication of literacy in Yoxall. This was chosen in preference to the signature or mark on wills, which were predominantly male, and are not an accurate source with regard to whether the testator was or was not literate. Wills were often made at a time the testator could have been unable to sign being too ill, or too near death.

The marriage registers, requiring either a signature or mark of both bride and groom give a more accurate picture of literacy, although a signature does not necessarily suggest that the person signing could do much more than that, but for the purpose of the study, it does suggest some degree of education and literacy.

Evidence for signatures and marks from 1760 to 1860 show that in every ten year period the number of grooms signing the certificate outnumbered the brides. The registers show a decline in marks for both sexes and by the mid 1860s most signed. The 1870s show a reversal of the pattern with 11 male and 5 female marks. Although the number is too small to be conclusive, it may suggest that female literacy was becoming a greater necessity as many girls would go into domestic service and would, by that time, be expected to be able to read and understand instructions, as domestic products increasingly came in tins and packages with labelled information. During the 1880s and 1890s few brides or grooms made their mark, the register for these decades ended in 1896 when all signed their marriage certificates. During the two decades 4 grooms made their mark and 8 females. Half of those who did not sign were aged over 30, the last, in 1895, was a female aged 60. Unlike the younger brides these women had not benefited from the better education available in the closing decades of the nineteenth century.

Boiling Peas

The *Staffordshire Advertiser* published the following report on 4th March 1865:

'YOXALL, - On Monday evening last, the Rev. J. Erskine Clarke, Vicar of St. Michael's, Derby, delivered his interesting and popular lecture, entitled 'How to boil peas', in the Girls Schoolroom at Yoxall. The proceeds of the lecture were devoted to the funds of the Yoxall Reading Room and Library'.

Rev. Clarke had been giving this lecture, described as genial and humorous, since at least 1859. He gave the promised instruction before telling a story of pilgrims who carried peas in their boots, one of whom boiled his peas and reached his destination sooner, (and doubtless in less discomfort). The Rev. then lectured on the 'peas' which his audience had in their lives, and offered common sense advice and earnestly requested them to 'boil their peas'.[38]

Chapter 11

A Living From the Land

This chapter includes those directly engaged in agricultural occupations, and those whose livelihoods were dependent, either largely or entirely, on the land or those who farmed it.

Agriculture in the parish, from the farmer down, occupied 33 per cent of the employed population in 1851 and 35 per cent in 1891, showing little change.

Farms and Farmers

During the 18th century 54 men aspired to the term 'yeoman', but of these, 4 testators who had used the term in their will were termed 'husbandman' in their inventory and a further two were considered only to be labourers by the appraisers of their goods and chattels. The yeomen include Edward Biddulph the younger of Morrey Hall, whose will and inventory of 1715 both state him to be a yeoman. The term yeoman, in connection with land, can be defined as a man owning and cultivating a small estate, a freeholder under the rank of gentleman, but the term was used loosely to define a countryman of respectable standing, also a farmer. Gradually the term farmer was used instead of yeoman, although a few were keen to be known as yeomen, possibly due to its links of status, differentiating themselves from the former husbandmen who also became farmers. One of these was Enoch Bailey of Cross Hayes Farm, Hoar Cross, a yeoman in his will of 1910.

Only 16 testators were stated to be husbandmen, with the exception of the 4 above, who had considered themselves of the higher status of yeoman, but whose appraisers had not. A husbandman was defined as being one who tills and cultivates the soil; a farmer. Henry Twamley of Morrey was the last testator to define himself as a husbandman, in his will of 1777, the term being gradually superseded by 'farmer'. John Bradbury of Hoar Cross, in his will of 1724, was the first testator to refer to himself as a farmer followed by three in the 1750s and three in the 1770s. From the late 1790s the term was frequently applied.

Farming was sometimes a dual occupation, other occupations included dealer, brick maker and nail maker. Also two butcher/farmers, whose main occupation appears to be in butchery, with perhaps a smallholding, which in fact many of the farms would today be classed as. However this is more fully explored through the acreage given in some censuses. Goods bequeathed in wills and enumerated in inventories often suggest dual occupations.

Some inventories appear to have a greater total value than might have been expected from the occupations of the testator. It seems unlikely that in 1642 Humphrey Oneley, a shearman, would leave goods to the value of £177 if he only sheared sheep, which was seasonal work. His shears, listed with other items of his trade were valued at £1. However the listing of a total of 52 yards of cloth and 6 lbs of wool suggest that his interest in fleeces did not end with the shearing. No items of spinning or weaving were appraised but these may have been passed on before his death, enabling someone to continue the craft, if he had been unable to. Alternatively other people may have provided him with spinning and weaving services from their own homes. The inventory also includes farm stock, crops and items of husbandry. Many other inventories where the occupation is not yeoman or husbandman include items related to husbandry, suggesting dual occupation was common. Yoxall wills continued to regularly have accompanying inventories up until the mid eighteenth century but between 1750 and the last one in 1768, only 3 inventories accompany the wills, the 4th being taken on an intestates estate.

While farmers were often listed in trade directories, these sources fall far short of giving a complete picture of how many farmers there actually were in an area at a particular time. Parson and Bradshaw's Directory of 1818 lists a variety of traders and professional people in Yoxall but no farmers.[1] White's Directory of 1834 provides a far more substantial listing of people living and trading in Yoxall and its hamlets and includes separate listings of several occupations, including farmers of which there were 43, but only 3 farms named, being Trent Bridge, Darley Oaks and 'Darley'.[2] It is likely that many farms at this time were not named but known by the name of the farmer. The same source in 1851 listed 44 farmers but 2 of these occupied the same farm. The total falls slightly short of the farmers enumerated the same year but it is likely that farmers of smallholdings were not included in the directory which also includes the distribution of the farmers as follows: Needwood 4, Hadley End 7, Hoar Cross 4, Linbrook 1, Longcroft 1, Morrey 5, Woodhouses 4, Woodlane 3 the remaining 14 being 'at Yoxall village' which include Darley Oaks and Trent Bridge farms. The totals for Hoar Cross and Longcroft have been adjusted as Phoebe Leedham was erroneously listed as being at Longcroft, not Hoar Cross.

In the 1851 census acreages were given of the 47 farms enumerated in the parish. These were 14 farms of 100 + acres, 12 of 51-100 acres, 12 of 10-50 acres and 9 farms of less than 10 acres. During the 19th century small holdings were defined as less than 30 acres.[3]

Thomas Gisborne of Yoxall Lodge, with his joint occupations including farmer had the greatest acreage with 'about' 800, followed by Edward Roobotham of Forestside who had 350 acres and employed 6 labourers. At Linbrook Farm William Twigg had 204 acres and employed 2 labourers, Thomas Mills of the Gullets Farm had 260 acres and employed 2 labourers and William Allsebrook of Darley Oaks Farm occupied 130 acres and employed 4 labourers. A separate household at Darley Oaks Farm was that of Edward Mercer who farmed 120 acres and employed 2 labourers. John Jackson of Trent Bridge Farm occupied 61 acres and employed 2 labourers, and at Longcroft Thomas Goring occupied 70 acres. Other farmers included William Riddell who farmed 234 acres and employed 5 labourers, William Pott of Hoar Cross, 110 acres and employed 3 labourers (his brother Edward, enumerated in the same household was a farm bailiff), and Richard and Joseph Shipton of Woodhouses who farmed 100 acres and employed a labourer and a boy. At the other end of the scale is Elizabeth Painter, a farmer of Morrey with 8 acres, and at Hadley End, James Winfield with 3 acres.

The amount of labour employed by farmers was likely to be variable and the censuses were not taken at the busiest time of the farming year, except perhaps for sheep farmers. The number of agricultural workers would be less than at busier times, such as haymaking and harvest, when additional labour was needed and often included women and children as well as men who otherwise did other labouring work during the rest of the year.

In 1871 farms enumerated varied in size from 250 acres down to smallholdings of less than 10 acres. In 1881 few farms were named but at Longcroft William Johnson farmed 102 acres and employed a boy and Charles Mills farmed 180 acres and employed 3 men and a boy. At Darley Oaks one farmer, William Hill, farmed 130 acres and employed 2 labourers and a boy. In 1891 forty farmers were enumerated but farms were not named and acreages not recorded.

Kelly's Directory of 1896 lists 29 farmers in Yoxall and hamlets, a similar number to the same source in 1880. From 1872 the directory listed commercial entries under the headings Yoxall, Hadley End, Woodmill and Morrey and in 1896 added Woodlane. Listed were Hadley End, with 6 farms, Woodlane 1, Woodmill 2 (one farmer having the joint occupation of carpenter), and Morrey 6. Under the heading of Yoxall 2 farmers were at Woodhouses the remaining 12 include 4 named farms: Bank House, also at Woodhouses but not stated as such, Whitewood, The Gullets, and Blakenhall.[4]

Most farmers occupied farm buildings and land owned by others, as many land owners were not themselves farmers, and although the Yoxall Tithe Apportionment of 1839 lists both owners and occupiers, it is not a true picture of just how much land some of the more wealthy residents owned, as some also had land in other parishes and in some cases, in other counties. This becomes apparent in the bequests of land and property in wills. An example of this is Mary Cooper who in her will of 1771 bequeathed to her brother-in-law, John Poyser an undivided part of land at Little Sutton in Warwickshire, which his father had given to her and her brother and sister. The inventory of Richard Marshall the elder in 1669 includes 'a bay of hay at Woodhouses £20; in the barn at Tatenhill payse & hay £10'. It seems likely that he farmed both at Woodhouses and Tatenhill.

Hadley Street showing Leafields Farm on the left.

Interior of Leafields Farm, probably taken when Ernest Roberts was resident, c.1912. (From Geoffrey Sowerby and Richard Farman, East Staffordshire to the Weaver Hills, 1995. Reproduced by permission of Richard Farman).

Crops

Barley, oats, peas and hemp were listed in inventories from the 16th century. The inventory of Robert Pack in 1744 includes wheat in straw £3, barley in straw £2 5s, oats in straw £1, peas in straw £2 5s and a parcel of hay £6 10s. Also listed was a parcel of muck £1.

The Summary of Crop Returns for Staffordshire in 1801 gives the acreage for the crops grown in each parish. The following is listed for Yoxall Parish: Wheat 268, Barley 69 ½, Oats 250, Potatoes 6 ½, Peas 5, Beans 33, Turnips 12 ¼, Total Acreage 644 ¼ .[5]

The Tithe Apportionment of 1839 lists the following bushels of crops in the parish and their price per bushel: wheat 279 bushels, price per bushel 7s 0 ¼ d, barley 495, price 3s 11 ½ d, oats 712, price 2s 9d.

An 1872 description of the land in the parish of Yoxall stated: 'The soil is a rich red marl and loam, producing good crops of wheat and beans, with a good portion of excellent pasture and meadow land. The area is 4,784 acres, about 1,200 of which have been enclosed from Needwood Forest'.[6]

In 1887 it was reported that at Hadley End a field of growing corn had been seen which the owner commenced cutting a few days before Christmas.[7]

In 1892 crops in Hoar Cross were reported as follows 'hay was 20 per cent under the average of the last three years, but gathered in excellent condition. Cereals of all kinds looked well but short in straw. Harvest likely to be late. Roots are healthy and promising, potatoes looking remarkably well, and up to the present free from disease'.[8]

Cattle Plague and Swine Fever

A hazard of farming livestock was the ever present risk of disease among the animals. In November 1865 a letter to the editor of the *Burton Chronicle* stated that the area had so far avoided the problem and listed recommendations for avoiding it as 'perfect cleanliness, perfect ventilation, and the best of nourishing diet'. These were far from the conditions the correspondent had seen: 'The most casual observer has only to look into the building arrangements and daily routine of most farms and places where cows are kept, to be very painfully convinced what dirty, neglected and sorry looking objects the poor dumb beasts are. The wonder is, that more do not die'.[9] By March 1866 cattle plague, otherwise known as rinderpest was in Hoar Cross on Gullets Farm. An inspector ordered several cows to be killed and burned, which was immediately done.[10] That month Mrs Mills of Gullets Farm was reported to have lost a total of fifteen cows. It was not understood how the outbreak had happened on the farm as it was stated that no fresh cows had been bought for years.[11] The disease seemed to have been contained as no other outbreak was reported in the parish.

In April 1881 Staffordshire was declared an area infected with foot and mouth disease,[12] and in July of that year a serious outbreak of pleuro-pneumonia was reported on the farm of John Anderson of Darley Oaks, who had two cows slaughtered. Cattle were not the only animals prone to disease at this time, swine fever broke out at Longcroft Farm and Charles Mills had two diseased and four healthy pigs slaughtered to avoid spreading the disease. It was reported that he was fortunate in having only six pigs at the time.[13]

In 1882 Charles Mills was prosecuted under the Contagious Diseases (Animals) Act for keeping fifteen cows infected with foot and mouth disease in a field, improperly fenced and next to the road leading from Yoxall to Dunstall. Charles claimed that the 'lane' was not a highway, and with no evidence of any cattle straying there the Bench gave the lenient fine of 2s 6d.[14] The same year John Ashmore was fined 2s 6d and 9s 6d costs for removing a pig from an infected area without having the requisite licence.[15]

Farm and Land Sales

In 1738 in neighbouring Kings Bromley agricultural land changed hands at prices between 7 and 14 shillings an acre and good meadow land at 18 shillings.[16]

The sale of farms, although sometimes reported in the *Burton Chronicle*, rarely included the names of the farms either sold or withdrawn from sale. The following are a few exceptions: at an auction sale held at the Swan Hotel in Lichfield in 1894 Morrey Farm; house and buildings, and 36 acres made £1,500, and timber £71 7s 10d. Weaverlake Farm; house and buildings, and 30 acres made £1,400 and timber £64 11s. A substantial amount of land was sold at the same auction, including 2 acres of pasture in Swain's Field which sold for £50. An acre of meadow in Pingle made £60 and 4 acres in New or Broad Meadow fetched £205.[17]

In 1896 an auction held at the Golden Cup was less successful. The first lot was Trent Bridge Farm, which was a dairy farm. The farmhouse and buildings were occupied by Messrs. S. and W. Dukes and the farm land contained 18 acres of pasture land, of which 6 acres was copyhold. With a bid of £1,000 the lot was withdrawn. Several meadows were also withdrawn from sale but a freehold meadow of 1 acre known as Coleholm was purchased by Dr Armson for £61.[18]

In 1901, reported as 'Extensive Property Sales' land and property were auctioned at the Crown Inn. Included was Rookery Farm, its buildings including cowshed, stabling and piggeries, also a large garden, an orchard and two fields of pasture land to the rear, the whole containing 6 acres in the occupation of Charles Upton. The lot, which was partly copyhold, sold to Mr Mellor for £417 10s. Morrey House Farm with recently erected farm buildings, yard, garden and croft, with freehold fields, known as Morrey Hall Croft, Bald Acre and Morrey Hall Piece, together containing 9 acres sold for £1,010 to Mr T. Shipton.[19]

Records of Staffordshire Estate Half Year's Rents record that in 1878 William Hall paid a half year's rent of £90 for Weaverlake Farm. The same source listed William Mayer who paid £83 12s 3d for the rental of Morrey Farm.[20]

Farm Servants and Agricultural Labourers

In 1851 there were 7 males who would be considered to be skilled agricultural labourers and in 1891, 6 males. This group included castrator, dairyman, gamekeeper, huntsman, shepherd and woodman. (Social and occupational groups based on groupings devised by P.M. Tillot for work on the history of Tickhill.)

Semi-skilled and unskilled agricultural labourer was one of the largest areas of employment in Yoxall in 1851 and 1891 being 25 per cent of those employed. This group included agricultural labourer, cowman, farm boy, farmer's son, gardener, gardener's labourer, plough boy, poultry keeper and helper to poultry keeper, also farm servants, who are generally considered distinct from labourers as they lived with their employers, and tended to be young and unmarried. However some agricultural labourers also lived in the household of their employer. In 1851 the number of agricultural labourers was 90, plus 20 farm servants. In 1881 the number of agricultural labourers was similar, being 86, but there were 44 farm servants.

Nationally, farm servants were declining in number, the majority of agricultural workers being day labourers, who despite being hired and paid by the day, often worked for the same employer for many years. By 1891 this trend was seen in Yoxall, as only 22 farm servants were enumerated. The number of agricultural labourers cannot be ascertained. It appears to be far fewer than in previous censuses, but the number of men enumerated as general labourers was also out of proportion to other censuses and the households some were enumerated in also suggests they probably worked on farms.

The youngest child employed in Yoxall in 1851 was James, a 10 year old farmer's boy who was enumerated in the household of his father, William Aimes, a cordwainer. In 1871 William Hollis, aged 11, was a servant boy in the household of his grandfather, Charles, who was one of the 48 farmers enumerated that year. In 1891 one of the two 12 year olds employed was a farm servant. Farmers continued to be enumerated into old age, but how much help they had is often uncertain and some may have employed others to do all or most of the work of the farm. A few farm workers in their 80s were enumerated in the censuses but the oldest was 91 year old agricultural labourer Thomas Biddulph who was enumerated in 1881 as a widower, alone in his household. Unless he had help in his home, he appears to have been looking after himself while continuing to be employed. Census information being limited, it is likely that he may have worked part time, even very short hours, or have an understanding employer who appreciated that he would be unlikely to work as hard as younger men. He may also have been retained for his knowledge and experience of agriculture, gained over many years.

Female servants who worked on farms could often expect both household and farm duties. Ellen Dukes was born at Woodhouses and in 1861, aged 15, she was enumerated as a general servant at Kings Bromley, in the household of a farmer of 50 acres. Her family remember that she worked on the farm and met her husband, John Mewis either at this or another farm, where Ellen said she had found her husband on the 'muck ruck'. The couple returned to Yoxall on their marriage and were living in Hadley End in 1871. By 1911 the couple had been married for 46 years and all of their 12 children had survived.

Ellen Dukes, who in her earlier years was a general servant whose duties included farm work.

Burton Statutes Hiring Fair

In Kings Bromley in 1738 the wage of an agricultural worker was 4d a day plus food.[21] The following extracts from the *Burton Chronicles* give some insight into the Burton Statutes hiring fair and the wages employees could expect:

1880 'Men seeking for situations were somewhat scarce, but experienced cowmen could command wages from £14 to £15 10s. Less experienced men and strong youths were engaged at wages up to £9 10s., while lads - and they were by far the most numerous - were picked up at from £6 to £8'.[22]

Burton on Trent Market Place. The scene suggests this was the Statutes Hiring Fair, held there annually for farm workers and domestic servants, who came from the surrounding area in search of employment. (Photo reproduced by permission of John Thompson).

1887 'Hiring secondary to the entertainment though many there to be hired. Wages lower than a few years ago. Men who had at the time commanded as much as £20 a year, now accepting places at £14 a year. Not many women in search of situations, and these were mostly dairymaids who asked for £12 to £14 a year'.[23]

1890 it was reported that men seeking situations were somewhat scarce. They included cowmen but lads were by far the most numerous. All groups were engaged for the same wages as in 1880.[24]

1897 'There was a fairly large number of boys, who secured places on farms at prices varying from £5 to £10, while some of the men were engaged for the year at £15 and £17. There were not so many farmers as usual at the fair'.[25]

Although it increasingly become a venue for shows and roundabouts towards the end of the 19th century, the Burton Statutes continued as a hiring fair until 1926.

Apart from hiring fairs it is most likely that many farmers employed local men and boys known or recommended to them. Some placed advertisements in newspapers: Wanted - a strong youth (about 16) to look after two horses and make himself generally useful. Apply in the first instance, to Joseph Clulow, Woodmill, nr. Yoxall.[26]

Various disputes between servants and those who employed them were sometimes settled in court. Once employed the employee had to complete the term of engagement or could be sued for being in breach of contract as in the following case:

In 1890 Mary Ann Potts, a farmer of Hoar Cross sued Thomas Lawrence, a waggoner of Hamstall Ridware for £1 damages. Thomas had been engaged four years ago at £15 per year. On the 15th March, when he entered the house he was asked the reason he was late in coming to breakfast. He commenced to use bad language and Mary told him he had better leave the house if he could not desist. He commenced to pack his things, although warned that he was breaking his contract and ought not to go, but refused to stay and left the place. In consequence the work he should have done that day was delayed, and the amount of damage mentioned in the claim incurred. Thomas considered that when Mary had told him to leave his contract was at an end. The Bench said they considered the breach of contract proved, but reduced the amount the plaintiff could claim to 10s, and added that if a labourer wished to void his contract he should first appear before the magistrates and state his case.[27]

John Perkins, Agricultural Implement Maker

Suppliers of agricultural equipment made a living from the farmers who bought their merchandise, as did the blacksmiths, waggoners and wheelwrights, who also supplied the farms, although not exclusively, so indirectly they also profited from the land. In 1851 John Perkins was enumerated in Yoxall as a blacksmith, with wife Harriet, infant son William and two blacksmith's apprentices.

Blacksmith's shop, Yoxall. Exterior of a blacksmith's shop in Main Street. This was one of a number of workshops which belonged to C.J. Perkins, agricultural implement maker. It was converted into a house during the 1970s. (Ref: P73001.0001. Reproduced by permission of Staffordshire Archives and Heritage Service).

Interior of above blacksmith's shop. (Ref: P73001.0019. Reproduced by permission of Staffordshire Archives and Heritage Service).

In 1860 John was listed in Kelly's Directory as a 'manufacturer of ploughs, harrows, cultivators, turnip and mangold drills, ridging ploughs, horse hoes, horse power machinery, machinist and agricultural implement maker & ironmonger'.[28] In 1861, with only one household between his and saddler and victualler Thomas Brandon, who although it was not stated by the census, was at the Golden Cup, John Perkins was again enumerated as a blacksmith. In 1871 his occupation was listed as blacksmith and grocer and in the column for road, street, etc. is 'Grocer's Shop and Hardware Dealers'. In 1869 he advertised that he had a general assortment of ploughs and harrows for which he had been awarded silver medals and numerous prizes at Staffordshire and other county agricultural shows. Also an assortment of chain harrows of various sizes from 5' 6" by 7'6" to 9'6" by 9'6", at prices varying from £2 to £3 10s.[29]

In 1876 he advertised his improved standard single and double furrow ploughs, which had gained champion prizes in competition with leading manufacturers and the silver medal at Staffordshire Agricultural Society's Show. He also had in stock single and double furrow ploughs, cultivators, harrow, chaff cutters, root pulpers, oil cake breakers, horse works, cow cribs, sheep racks etc., and was an agent for the principal implement manufacturers. He attended Burton market every Thursday.[30] In 1881 he was enumerated at Yoxall as an agricultural implement maker employing 4 men and 2 boys.

In 1893 John Perkins died at the age of 70. His obituary states that he had established himself as an implement maker, whose name was not limited to England. He was born in Warwickshire and when old enough was apprenticed to a blacksmith in Kenilworth, where he turned his attention to plough making. It was when he commenced business at Yoxall that he began to manufacture ploughs. He was credited with making the lever scuttle, the first treadle chaff-cutter, and the first disc wheel pulper and in 1865 made what is thought to be the first open finger for mowing machines, including a double furrow plough and a digging plough. He took his sons into the business and from 1876 also traded at Sandford Street, Lichfield.[31] The partnership had been dissolved in 1892 by the mutual consent of its founder, John Perkins the elder, and sons, William, George and John junior. William and John junior were to carry on the business alone.[32]

Agricultural machinery, like other machinery of its time, could be extremely dangerous if precaution was not taken, as the following case suggests. Edward Pott, a farmer of Hoar Cross was charged with having worked a threshing machine at Yoxall in October without having the drum and feeding mouth sufficiently fenced. PC Small stated that Edward had not been aware that he was doing wrong and the Bench dismissed the case, but the magistrate's clerk told him that if he contravened the Act of Parliament and anyone fell into the machine and was killed he would be liable for manslaughter.[33]

Mills and Millers

No Yoxall mills were mentioned in the Domesday Survey, but in the early 13th century a rent of 4 marks from the 'mills' of Yoxall was granted to Dale Abbey in Derbyshire, and in the 1320s the complex comprised two water mills and a fulling mill, presumably on the Swarbourn at the southern end of the village. The presence of a fulling mill suggests the production of cloth at this time. A weir on the river was mentioned in 1386 and during the 1440s a water course had to be cut for a new mill, described as being next to Hall bridge.[34] This was known as Yoxall Mill. The water course may have been a re-channelling of a brook from Needwood forest which powered the mill until 1813, when a new fleam was cut from the river Swarbourn north of Stair bridge.[35] The mill eventually fell into disuse as a mill and was used to house farm animals when it was bought with the surrounding land by Dr Gerald Armson's mother, Ethel Margaret nèe Arden, from the trustees of the Longcroft Estate. The Armsons demolished the mill in 1897 and used the material to build their house, The Moat, but they retained the mill wheel to generate an electrical supply to the house until the 1930s.

Yoxall Mill at Town Hill, prior to its demolition in 1897. (Reproduced by permission of Elisabeth Macfarlane, © Blurb).

Moat House, home of the Armson family was built from material of the demolished mill. Also shown in both images is the building now known as Corn Mill House.

Job Barry sites a mill as lying adjacent to the church and it being an old site as the following dispute took place about 1570.[36] John Greneway of Yoxall made a complaint to Sir Nicholas Bacon, Knight and Lord Keeper of the Great Seal, claiming that he had for 2 years rented a water mill and windmill off Sir William Hollyes from which he 'received sundry great profits towards the maintenance of himself, his wife and children'. John Hollys of Tatenhill persuaded Greneway to let him have the mill and verbally promised to pay him £3. Hollys denied this and claimed that Greneway had previously offered for £3 to get the goodwill of George Walton, bailiff to Sir William Hollyes, to admit him as tenant. The bailiff refused because the mills were in a bad condition, also Greneway's wife and friends had told him that Hollys had tried to get him to give up possession of the mills.[37] It transpired that Hollys had been admitted as tenant because Greneway was 'but a careless man' and had allowed the mills to fall into a state of dereliction and only the watermill could be repaired. Job states that a later windmill was built 'for the following millers are recorded' 1818 Josiah Atkin, 1835 John Atkin, 1850 George Roobotham, 1854 J. Wait, 1868-1872 William Simpson, 1892 Charles Minchin.[38] Joseph Wait occupied the mill believed to date back to 1341.

Mill at Woodmill. (Photo by author).

In a letter from William Salt Library to the owners of Woodmill in 1964, it was noted that in the Great Coucher Book of the Duchy of Lancaster, a medieval volume registering copies of the deeds relating to the property of the Duchy, was a grant from Henry, Earl of Lancaster to William Le Keu made in 1341 of property including a mill on the 'Swerborn' near Woodgate in Needwood. The letter suggested this was the site of their home. This is further substantiated by the later date of the mill next to Hall Bridge, which was also on the Swarbourne. The mill at Woodmill is currently known as The Olde Mill.

Miller's accommodation at Woodmill. (Photo by author).

Mill stones at Woodmill. (Photo by author).

Jessica Smith lived in Yoxall from her birth in 1915 to 1927 and recorded her memories of the mill as 'a very old building very low and built into the side of a hill, a pathway round the back of it, Mill Lane, was almost on a level with the roof of the mill, there was an old house built in to the end of the mill, tiny rooms so low that a man could hardly stand up straight, men must have been shorter at the time it was built, when we were there the Mill was still in use for grinding corn and Mr Roe the Miller, the farmers used to bring their sacks of corn in a pony and cart of course and leave them to be ground into flour. I didn't like to be in the Mill when it was working, the enormous wheels going round and round made such a noise and the building juddered and shook, I was always afraid it was going to collapse'.[39]

*The miller's house was built c.1858 by J. Wait. Photo dated 1902.
(Reproduced by permission of Liz Guy).*

Little is known about the windmill on Windmill Hill, but the Tithe
Apportionment of 1839 states plot number 198 as Windmill Hill occupied by
Thomas Pott and the adjoining plot 183 as Windmill Hill and Shed, owned and
occupied by blacksmith John Poyser.[40] Some residents remember three pine
trees which stood on the summit of the hill which led to it being known to many
locals as 'Jerusalem'. It is now a place of pilgrimage and worship for Christians
to commemorate Good Friday.

Maltings

A malthouse at Bond End was owned by the Brown family who were maltsters
and farmers. On the Tithe Apportionment of 1839 John Brown was listed as the
owner and occupier of 46 acres which included the Malthouse.[41] A description,
stating that it was built of brick and tile, also gives the measurement of the main
range which ran alongside the road as 83 ft long and 21 ft wide and the building
3 storeys high. The top 2 floors were laid with gypsum plaster, a surface that
was prized by maltsters from at least 1680 to 1870. (Gypsum is also used in
brewing both to lower the pH, the measure of how acidic the water is, also to
accentuate the bitterness of the beer). The kiln formed a cross wing at the west
end and was built in 1776.[42] The earliest malt houses, which included the one at
Bond End, resembled barns as they were disproportionately long with the kiln
at one end.[43] A further description stated that on the roof of the malthouse was a
flat cylindrical structure which was assumed to be something to do with the

malting process. Above this was the seated figure in silhouette of an old woman dressed in black with a huge nose which moved with the wind and kept the vent turned in the right direction.[44]

Bond End Malthouse, exterior view from south east. Photo 1967. (Ref: C/P/65/2/1/58/32. Reproduced courtesy of Staffordshire Record Office.)

The accounts of 1806 are the earliest legible accounts for the Bond End malthouse. They show that during that year 2,301 bushels of malt were sold, the usual rate being 11s a bushel. Of these the highest number, 298 ½ bushels, were sold in February and the lowest number, 86 were sold in June. The variation was due to the malting season being interrupted by the temperature being too high in the summer for the controlled germination of the barley and too hot for the fermentation of the ale. The customers were mostly the nobility and clergy who, being householders, escaped the beer tax.[45] In September 1853 the account for Mr Gisborne of Yoxall Lodge was for 16 strikes of malt, 16 of hops, 32 of old oats and a strike of barley. In comparison that month butcher and beerhouse keeper James Berrisford had 3 ½ strikes of malt, plus 2 ½ pecks of hops.[46]

Bond End Malthouse, top floor of main range from the east. Photo 1967. (Ref: C/P/65/2/1/58/38. Reproduced courtesy of Staffordshire Record Office).

Bond End Malthouse, tie beam of kiln from south east, dated 1776. Photo 1967. (Ref: C/P/65/2/1/58/36. Reproduced courtesy of Staffordshire Record Office).

Nathaniel Bladon Brown, a maltster, most likely operated the malt house at Bond End. He died in 1787.[47] In 1834 John Brown was listed as a maltster and hop merchant,[48] but by 1851 he was listed as a gent.[49] In his will of 1850 he named his nephew, also John Brown as his heir. The will was witnessed by Morton and William Bond. (There are several instances of marriages between the Brown and Bond families).

In 1861 nephew John Brown was enumerated as a maltster and farmer of 100 acres employing 5 men and one boy. In 1870 he was listed as a maltster and corn merchant.[50] He died in 1877, the census of 1881 enumerated his widow, Matilda as farming 180 acres and employing 4 boys and one man, his son William, also in the household was recorded as 'farmer's son'. From then the censuses recorded William [Shaw] Brown as a farmer, but he was listed in a directory of 1880 as a maltster and farmer.[51] By 1896 he was listed only as a farmer.[52] The building eventually ceased to be used as maltings and was demolished in 1977.[53]

The maltings at Bond End was not the only producer of malt in the area. In his will of 1858 Edward Roobottom a 'Gentleman' of 'the tithe Allotment in the parish of Yoxall', included in his bequests his malthouse at Yoxall. In 1851 John Roobottom was listed as a maltster at Woodlane,[54] and was listed in 1880 as a maltster at Wood Mill.[55] Apart from the malthouse at Bond End the Tithe Apportionment includes a malthouse, fold, barn etc. occupied by William Riddell and a malthouse and yard owned and occupied by William Yeld.

Apart from agriculture, the countryside also offered sport, often at the cost of the lives of the wildlife that inhabited it. Few people had sympathy for the fox and hunting it was a popular sport in the area. Foremost among those who made a living from the hunt was a branch of the Leedham family.

Leedhams of Hoar Cross and Yoxall

Hugo Meynell of Quorndon, Leicestershire, became known as the 'Father of the Hunt'. In 1793 his son, Hugo of Bradley came to Hoar Cross and demolished the 1740s hall and built a smaller hunting lodge. He died in a fall from a horse in 1800 and was succeeded by his son, Hugo Charles, who inherited his grandfather's fortune on his death in 1808. He also inherited Temple Newsam and assumed the surname Ingram in compliance with the terms of the will of the last Lord Irwin. By 1816 Hugo Charles had hounds kennelled at Hoar Cross and Tom Leedham was the first huntsman there, with his son Joe as whipper-in. A history of the Meynell hounds gives some indication as to the characters of some of the Leedhams who were connected to the hunt. 'They were always an outspoken race and between Old Tom the first and the squire there seemed to be some sort of feeling which so often exists between the faithful old family servant and the young master whom he had taught to ride and so on, and cannot help looking upon as a boy'.[56] The familiarity between the Meynell Ingrams and Old Tom is further illustrated by an incident when, during a gallop, Tom came up from behind and called to Miss Louisa, an excellent horsewoman and later co-originator of Yoxall Cottage Hospital, "Tho mun lick and lay on Missy".[57] This led to her becoming known throughout the neighbourhood by the pet name "Missy".[58] Tom had two other sons, Jack and Tom who also whipped in. When Jack fell from his horse the squire took him to Scotland to see if the change would do him any good, but it failed to work and Jack gave up hunting and became a bailiff.

Tom Leedham senior died in 1839 at the age of 73, his occupation in his will was yeoman, and Joe died in 1856 aged 51 and was buried in St Peter's churchyard at the side of his father. Joe was succeeded by his brother Tom, who was 'perhaps the best horseman of a family of good riders'.[59]

Elford, the favourite hunter of M.F. Meynell Ingram with Tom Leedham and Hounds, from a painting by Alfred Corbould. (Reproduced in J.L. Randall, History of the Meynell Hounds and County, 1780-1901, II, 1901).

Charles Leedham at New Lodge, Hanbury, from a photograph by W.W. Winter, 1898. (Reproduced in J.L. Randall, History of the Meynell Hounds and County, 1780-1901, II, 1901).

As the younger Tom grew older the idea of a successor did not please him and he 'had been regarding his nephew Charles with a jealous eye'.

On one occasion Charles had the misfortune to jump on his uncle, and it was with difficulty that the latter could be persuaded that it was not done on purpose. Everything that went wrong was laid to Charles's account. One day

Tom had a fall and dislocated his thumb. Going home he was laying the blame, as usual, on his nephew for something which had happened till at last the latter retorted with "I wonder you don't say it was my fault you put your thumb out". Tom … grunted out "Well, so 'twas if you hadna' joomped there I shouldna' ha' joomped, and then I shouldna' ha' fallen and put me thumb oot".[60] It had been noticed, and was the subject of good natured 'chaff' that towards the end of the day Tom was anxious to get home to his sister Phoebe and his tea. He was sixty four and lacked some of the enthusiasm he had in his youth. Ten years later, on a pouring wet day he remarked "And to think they call this pleasure". Tom's sister, Phoebe Leedham, farmed 37 acres at Hoar Cross from at least 1851 and by 1881 was farming 52 acres, when at the age of 73 she was employing a labourer, a boy, a widowed farm servant and two domestic servants. She was head of the household throughout the period, despite her brother living in the same household. Tom was remembered to have had a powerful and melodious voice 'and it was a treat to hear it ringing amongst the trees in Bagot's Wood or the Bracken Hurst'.[61] His career as huntsman terminated at the end of the 1871-2 season and in March 1872, at Sudbury village, Tom was presented with a silver cup containing £730.[62] He died in 1883, according to his will a yeoman, with an estate in excess of £18,000. Tom bequeathed to his nephew Charles, who had succeeded him as huntsman, the testimonial given to him by members of the Meynell hunt. The Armson doctors were keen huntsmen themselves, and Dr Charles Grealey Armson had set the bones of all the Leedham family.[63]

Other Leedhams supplied equestrian needs, these were William and sons William and Alfred who were saddle, whip and collar makers. William senior had been making collars for working horses from at least 1818.[64] The business, at Birmingham House, continued until the early 20th century.

Chapter 12

Manual and Mechanical: Trades, Crafts, Industry and Domestic Service

Joint Occupations

There was no shortage of dual occupations and those most commonly occurring were amongst farmers and publicans, although not necessarily in a combination of the two. Where one of the occupations was publican, it is likely that the wife or other family member worked at the inn or beerhouse, while the husband attended to the other occupation.

In 1851 the census enumerated 11 butchers, including James Berrisford, entered in a directory of that year as a butcher/beerhouse keeper,[1] and Edmund Pott of Hadley End who also farmed 74 acres. In 1891 only 5 butchers were enumerated, including James Berrisford Smith also an innkeeper (grandson of James Berrisford), and butcher/farmer John Ashmore.

In 1871 John Twamley was enumerated as a carpenter and beerhouse keeper at the Arden Arms and in 1901, at the age of 75, he was still a carpenter and publican there. In the next house his son Charles was enumerated as a joiner, although in fact he was a carpenter and coffin maker and ran a funeral parlour. Twamleys built the fireplace at Brankley Hall and worked at Rangemore Hall, Hoar Cross Hall, Yoxall Cottage Hospital, and in 1859 John Twamley received £10 for repairs on St Peter's steeple and £40 4s 6d 'for Church Roof'.[2]

Also working with wood were a decreasing number of coopers, including the Pott family who followed the craft since at least the seventeenth century, evidenced by the will of John Pott in 1645. Charles Pott was the last cooper to be enumerated in Yoxall. In 1861 he was jointly a farmer of 18 acres, and by 1881, aged 61, was enumerated only as a cooper. Buckets and other small household wooden vessels fell into disuse, which led to the demise of the village cooper, who either turned to another trade or may have been tempted away to the cooperages at Burton.

Pubs and Publicans

The Foresters

In 1871 the innkeeper of the Foresters at Woodlane was unmarried William Taylor, who was enumerated with his domestic servant, Mary Ash. Later that year the couple married and had a family of 5 children, but in 1880 William died and was buried with 2 of his infant sons. The following year his widow was enumerated as the victualler of the Foresters. Also in the household were her 3 surviving children, aged 3 to 9 and a 12 year old domestic servant. In 1882 she married Charles Upton, a sergeant in the 65th Regiment, whose father Charles was an innkeeper. Mary transferred the Foresters to Charles Upton in

1883,[3] but whether the transfer was to her husband or father in law is uncertain, but by 1891 William Fearn was the publican.

Fearn Family, Innkeepers of Yoxall

In 1881 William Fearn was enumerated as a bricklayer and innkeeper of the Horse & Jockey at Hadley End in the parish of Hamstall Ridware. By 1886 he was at The Royal Oak in Alrewas and by 1891 at the Foresters Arms in Woodlane, where he remained for the rest of his years as a licensed victualler. In 1891 his son, also William, was innkeeper at the Golden Cup, with the dual occupation of bricklayer. In 1892 at Burton County Police Court the licensing business transfers included The Shoulder of Mutton from James Berrisford Smith, who was enumerated there in 1881 as a butcher's apprentice to his grandfather, James Berrisford. The transfer to William Fearn (junior), was due to the fact that in 1891 an objection to the renewal of James's licence was served.[4] James Berrisford Smith was later to go to America, where after a time of being a 'cowboy' he took Holy Orders. He returned to England and took a living about 20 miles from Yoxall.[5] The Golden Cup transferred from William Fearn to Ellis Wakelin in 1892.[6]

The Golden Cup

The name of the Golden Cup was often shortened to 'Cup' in documents. It appears as Golden Cup in a directory of 1835,[7] but the previous year had been listed as the Cup.[8] While Kelly's directories consistently listed it as Golden Cup, censuses 1871-1891 listed it as the Cup. The name appears to stabilize in 1901 as Golden Cup, the name it bears today, although it is locally often shortened in conversation to the Cup.

Another victualler at the Golden Cup with a joint occupation was Thomas Brandon who by 1851 was a saddler and victualler, employing a barmaid, a house servant and an ostler to take care of the horses. Still with the joint occupation, Thomas was enumerated there in 1861. Also in the household was grandson Charles, son of his daughter Jane, wife of Charles Hancock. Separately enumerated in the village, Charles was a saddler and harness maker and Jane a shop keeper. By 1871 Charles Hancock was running the pub with the same joint occupation of saddler as his father in law before him but had left by 1877 when J.S. Richards paid a reserve rent of £1 11s 6d.[9] By 1880 Charles was living near the Crown Inn and continuing to work as a saddler with his son Charles. In 1882 James Eadie paid £15 for a half year's rent of 'the Cup' and £7 10s for Cup Croft, and was still paying the total of £22 10s in 1886.[10]

Main Street, with Birmingham House facing and the Golden Cup, far right.

The Crown

In 1871 George and Frances Roobottom were enumerated at the Crown but in the December of that year George died and in 1872 Frances was listed as the victualler. Between 1880 and 1896 Thomas and Jane Cooper were the innkeepers, and in 1891 their 15 year old daughter, Nellie was also in the household, most likely helping out with the running of the public house. The Coopers and the Crown and the Golden Cup are also featured in the chapter 'Legends and other Stories'.

The Crown, Main Street. Opposite is the weighing platform. This has been replaced by a small island.

Shoulder of Mutton, date uncertain. Thomas Taswell was the victualler.

Weavers

Thomas Taylor, founder of Yoxall's first school, whose will also bequeathed clothing for the poor, had in the kitchen chamber at the time of his inventory of 1699/1700, apart from the fabrice previously mentioned, one long wheel and two little wheels and a reel 2s 6d, suggesting that the cloth, possibly for the poor, was woven on his premises.

John Handley, a weaver in his will of 1715, bequeathed to his son John one linen loom that he had made himself and to his son William two looms with warp stock and bars. These did not appear in his inventory of that year, but two spinning wheels were enumerated with the furniture. John Jerom was also a weaver and in his inventory of 1747/8 the following items relating to his trade were enumerated: 'In the shop four looms with gears & stay etc. £5; Jersey spun and unspun £5; goods wove £4; one press, warp stock & etc. £5; three pair of scales 5s 6d; a quantity of wool £15; 'Sope' [soap] oil & charcoal £2 12s; one furnace and washing rings £1 15s.'

Morrey Tape Factory

The industrial weaving of tape was first associated in Staffordshire with J. & N. Phillips. A member of the Phillips family is believed to have introduced tape weaving into this country, after studying the industry in the Netherlands. In 1747 a Dutchman, van Sanfort, came to Tean to teach a local carpenter how to construct 'swivel looms'. By 1817 the Phillips had factories in neighbouring parishes, including Cheadle, and were the most extensive producers of tape in Europe, employing 'between 2,000 and 3,000'.[11] By 1824 the mills of Tean and Cheadle were extended to house the looms from other factories. Tape weaving sprang up in other areas of Staffordshire and in 1798 the first mention of a tape factory in Yoxall appeared. Stebbing Shaw noted there was a small tape manufactory at Morrey 'lately established by Mr Wright etc'.[12] In 1817 William Pitt stated that there was a small tape manufactory at 'High Wall Hill', established by Mr Wright.[13] Another source refers to this adding that after 1818 nothing more was known about it.[14]

At Morrey the factory was run in the early 19th century by John Emery & Co., who also had a tape warehouse in Morrey and a bleaching house beside the Swarbourn, north of Yoxall village, on land owned by William Bond.[15]

In 1800 Mrs Powys, mother in law of Rev. Edward Cooper visited Hamstall Ridware and wrote in her diary: 'July 22nd - We took a long hot walk to the village of Murry, [Morrey] to see a tape manufactury, of which seven gentlemen of the neighbourhood are proprietors. The noise of the machinery is hardly to be borne, tho' the workpeople told us they themselves hardly heard the noise! Such is use! The calendering part is worth observation, as the tapes all go through the floor of an upper room, and when you go down to the apartment under it, you see them all coming through the ceiling, perfectly smooth and glossy, where the women take them, and roll them in the pieces as we buy them at the haberdasher's, whereas in the upper room they all looked tumbled and dirty'.[16]

In 1818 Thomas Daws, and separately, Prince, Bond & Co were listed as tape and thread manufacturers.[17] Surviving accounts for the Morrey tape factory suggest that as the business expanded, so too did the space required and in 1820 £1 10s was paid for 1,000 bricks.[18] Also listed are monthly payments of loom and house rents, and in May 1822, 29 loom rents ranging from 3s to 12s were collected by Sarah Bond plus 5 house rents ranging from 6s 2d to 9s 3d. The same year Amos Brown paid £4 for 6 months rental of 2 cottages and 2 weaving shops at Hadley End occupied by himself, William Deakin and Joseph Harrison, also £2 10s for an undisclosed number of looms. Those renting shops over several years included, at Hadley End John Twamley, and at Yoxall ex soldier John Snape. In 1832 John Twamley paid £1 10s for a year's rent of his weaving shop and loom. Whether the majority who rented looms worked from home or hired them within the factory is uncertain. There were also 'sundry persons' who were paid for winding linen yarn. Regular payments were made for saddlers work to Thomas Brandon, William Leedham and Daniel Knott. Payments were made for candles, straw, lime and coal. In 1824 the sum of £1 16s 11d was entered for Hindle & Bonds' expenses in going to Earl Shilton, they were out for two days and nights 'with House etc'. The following year 10s 2d was entered for 'Mr Bonds expenses to Birmingham to procure Phillips' prices at 1 Day with Coach Hire'. He appears to have wanted to know what the competition were charging.

In 1827 £2 9s 9d was paid for dyeing 199 lbs of black tape at Hadley End. Payments were also made for 'sundry 2 & 3 Thread Twine & Single Twine &

Cotton', probably done outside of the factory by people working in their own homes. The following year the sum of £54 2s 6d was paid by William Bond for half a year's rent of 'sundry Buildings & Land in the Parish of Yoxall'. In 1831 Moreton Bond paid £46 for two years' rent of Morrey Hall and Church Field. While there is little evidence regarding the working of the factory, there is a record of a payment for turning calender bowls, and giving directions for the fire furnace. The calender bowls were part of the process known as calendering in which the cloth was passed between rollers, known as calenders, in which steel bowls rotated. This was usually done under carefully controlled heat or pressure, to produce a variety of surface textures. Amongst the many payments is one made to Mrs Colley of Yoxall which was 'the amount of her act for Oatmeal for Dog had from 9th September 1820 to 5th March inclusive 10s 10d'. In 1834 Francis and Moreton Bond were listed and separately Hindle and Bond as tape manufacturers at Morrey. The tape mill, described as large, was producing 15 cwt of tape weekly.[19]

The 1841 census for Yoxall reveals a total of 53 persons whose occupations were clearly involved with the manufacture of tape. Of these 21 lived in Morrey and 22 in Hadley End. Due to 'poor communications',[20] the firm, trading as Morton and William Bond, moved to Alrewas. The 1851 census reveals that Lichfield born Morton Bond had one daughter aged 9 born in Yoxall (baptised in 1841) and two sons, aged 6 and 4 born in Alrewas. This suggests the firm moved to Alrewas between the census of 1841 and 1845. The Alrewas premises, previously a cotton mill belonging to the Peel family, were conveniently sited near the river Trent, with a mill stream to supply the mill. A study of the migratory patterns of tape workers based on five Staffordshire tape factories discovered that the majority of tape workers travelled a short distance from their enumerated place of birth. In 1851 Alrewas had the highest number of migrants at 79 per cent, 28 of the 68 migrants were unsurprisingly born in Yoxall and five Yoxall households of 1841 had relocated there.[21] In 1851 it was noted that since the introduction of tape manufacturing into the country, English artisans had improved the production through modern machinery with which 100 people could produce as much tape as 1,000 formerly. This being the case at Tean.[22] That year only 2 tape weavers were enumerated in Yoxall; one at Morrey the other at Hadley End, also at Olive Green there was a silk weaver and twister.

In 1861 Morton Bond was enumerated at Alrewas as a tape manufacturer and miller master employing about 114 hands, but by 1871 the company had moved to Hanging Bridge, Ashbourne, where Morton, aged 70, was enumerated as a webbing and tape manufacturer with his son George. A report regarding the census of 1871 had the following footnote regarding the decrease in the population of Alrewas: 'owing to the removal of the tape works which had left 37 uninhabited houses in the village'.[23] By 1881, still in Ashbourne, Morton was retired and the company was run by George and employed 32 men and 12 boys. The company continues to trade at the same site as Bowmer Bond Narrow Fabrics Limited.

Dressmakers and Tailors

In the 1851 census 3 dressmakers were enumerated at Morrey, 2 being sisters in the same household, and a dressmaker/servant at Woodmill in the household of 84 year old retired Jane Johnson. Of the 4 tailors, John Woodings, a master tailor, was at Hadley End with an 18 year old daughter enumerated as a tailor's daughter, who was most likely working for him. William Sharratt aged 84 of Longcroft had a lodger who was also a seamstress, not counted amongst the dressmakers as she was probably helping him with the tailoring. Thomas Nutt, a tailor of Yoxall village came from a family of tailors dating back to at least 1815 with some members who were tape weavers. Samuel Lindsey was enumerated as a tailor of Hoar Cross whose eldest son was a tailor's apprentice. His eldest daughter whose occupation column was 'tailor's daughter' may also have been helping. In 1891 a total of 11 dressmakers were enumerated, 2 of whom were apprentices. The previous total of 4 tailors remained the same.

In 1891 John Roberts was working as a tailor at the age of 83, and was probably one of many people for whom it was a necessity to continue to work for as long as possible. Some were more fortunate and able to retire from their occupation at a time of their own choosing. One such was Jane Simpson.

A Note For Miss Simpson

When work was being carried out at a house now known as The Mooring in Main Street, an undated note was discovered which reads:

'Miss P Cooper is very sorry Miss Simpson has had the trouble about her body [bodice] she would be much obliged to her to send it as she would sooner alter the skirt than the body be touched again as it is not the best consequence at all. Miss P wishes to know by John if she did not have an apron like the coat whether there would be enough for a bonnet'.

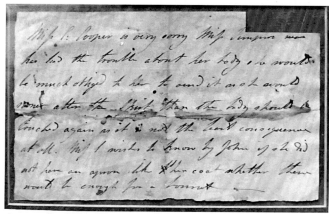

A note for Miss Simpson, discovered at The Mooring, Main Street. (Photo taken by author and reproduced by permission of Rev. Lisa Wright)

Clearly Miss Simpson was handy with a needle and has been identified as Jane Simpson, daughter of Thomas, a skinner and breeches maker who in 1810 bequeathed his estate, including houses to his wife Ann, and after her decease, the estate to be sold and divided between his eight children, namely Samuel, William, Thomas, Sarah, Ann, Hannah, Jane and Mary. Thomas died in 1823 aged 77 and his wife in 1842 aged 92.

In 1834 Jane Simpson was listed as a dressmaker living in Yoxall village.[24] The census of 1841 lists Jane, aged 50 in the household of Sarah Simpson, aged 55. No occupation was given for either of the women. Although no relationship is stated it is clear from other sources that they were sisters.

Sarah made her will in 1822 and at the time she lived in Burton. She seems to have expected to predecease her parents as she named them as beneficiaries for their lifetime. Her siblings she named as her ultimate beneficiaries. When Sarah returned to Yoxall is uncertain but clearly prior to 1841. Probate was granted in 1849 and it was probably on the death of Sarah that Jane lived with her unmarried sister, Mary, whose occupation is listed in the 1851 census as 'farming 7 acres'. Mary was head of the household, in which Jane is listed as a lodger. No occupation is given for Jane.

Both Jane and Mary remained unmarried and in the 1861 census Jane, listed as a 78 year old proprietor of land was still in the household of her sister Mary, who by then was a retired farmer, aged 68. Jane died in 1867, and her will of 1863 bequeathed her household furniture, linen and plate to Mary, also her money and fields named as Sutton's Intake and Swains Fields, as well as land in Woodlane and Scropton. The land was bequeathed for Mary's lifetime, after which the majority was to be sold and the proceeds divided between her nephew and nieces, though some fields were to pass to their brother William, for his lifetime, after which they were to be sold and the money divided between his children, namely John Simpson of Yoxall, Elizabeth wife of Herbert Deakin of Birmingham, Mary wife of Hugh Pott of Yoxall and Eliza, wife of John Watson also of Yoxall. In a codicil of 1865 Jane revoked the share of Elizabeth Deakin, leaving it to her trustees to pay Elizabeth personally, 'without the interference debts control or engagements of her husband'. This or similar clauses appear in several of the later wills.

In both the will and codicil Jane made her mark. It seems unlikely that a dressmaker would be unable to write and a more likely explanation may be that she was too ill, or her sight greatly deteriorated. This theory is supported by the will of her sister Mary who was able to sign her own will in August 1868 and bequeathed £15 to Lydia, wife of William Twamley of Hadley End, 'as an acknowledgement for the trouble she has already had with me and my sister as invalids and that she may still further have with myself'. Mary died the following month, a slate headstone in St Peter's churchyard records their deaths.

Apart from Jane Simpson being listed in the 1834 directory, her brother Thomas, a grocer, draper and ironmonger, was also listed, with an additional entry, still under Yoxall parish, as Tutbury court bailiff. Their brother Samuel was separately entered in the list of farmers.[25] By 1851 only William was listed, both as a 'bricklayer &c.' and as a farmer. In 1860 William, still a farmer was entered with his son William junior who was a miller,[26] and who later had the joint occupation of miller and farmer.[27]

Shoemakers and Cordwainers

In his will of 1553 Thomas Dane, shoemaker, bequeathed a jacket, a doublet and hose and 2 shirts 1s 8d. Also leather and tallow and all other things in the shop belonging to the shoemakers occupation 9s.

Thomas Brightland, a cordwainer, died intestate. His inventory of 1768 listed clothing including two pairs of leather breeches 6s; a claret coloured coat and waistcoat £1; four pairs of stockings 6s; two pairs of shoes 4s; a pair of buckles 6s and 'Two Old Whigs' 3s. His stock in trade was enumerated as: 17 pairs of shoes £2 7s; 2 pairs of boots £1; 2 hides 88 lb £4 4s 4d; offal leather 176 lb £5 17s 4d; offal leather dressed 46 lbs £3 3s 3d; four calf skins 8 lb £1 2s and working tools consisting of old pincers, hammers, old lasts and 'a few fa(r)ther inconsiderable things' 10s.

White's 1851 directory listed 9 shoemakers in Yoxall parish but 18 were enumerated, of whom 13, plus 2 apprentices were cordwainers, a name derived from goatskin leather first made at Cordova in Spain. Cordovan leather was of the best quality and very popular in the 16th century. This suggests that cordwainers supplied the 'well heeled' leaving the agricultural labourers and domestic servants to be shod by shoemakers. Also enumerated was a 19 year old whose entry in the occupation column was cordwainer's son, presumably learning the trade from his father. The 3 shoemakers included Henry Twamley who was also an alms receiver and small ware dealer. By the mid 19th century the terms had become interchangeable. In 1841 George Dean was enumerated as a shoemaker, in 1851 he was a cordwainer, also in 1861 when he was a registrar of births and deaths. However when he appeared in court in 1870 on a charge of fraud he was referred to as a shoemaker. In 1891 only 4 shoemakers were enumerated, the trade of shoemaking was fast dying as a cottage industry. Cordwainer generally fell out of use as an occupational name, but is retained by one of the oldest livery companies in London, the Worshipful Company of Cordwainers.

Nail Makers of Hadley End

Nail making in Yoxall appears to have been confined to Hadley End where 8 nail makers were enumerated in 1841. Of these 4 were in the household of nail maker, John Round. In another household three of the Law family were nailors. In 1851 the number had dropped to 6 and included Richard Winfield who was also a grocer who employed three men. His son William, also in the household, was a schoolmaster, who in 1861 had the unusual dual occupations of schoolmaster and nail maker. Richard died at the end of that year so possibly was too ill to work and for a time William continued the business for him.

James Law was another of the six nail makers enumerated in 1851, and by 1861 his son Joseph had joined him in the occupation. By 1891 Joseph Law was the only nail maker of Hadley End.

Wrights of Yoxall

In directories of 1896 and 1900 John Wright was listed as a china and glass dealer.[28] In 1908 the business was listed in the name of his son John Henry.[29] It was not until 1912 that John Henry Wright was listed as a builder,[30] and 1924 when H Wright & Sons were listed as builders, contractors, painters, decorators, wheelwrights, undertakers, and sawing mills.[31] John senior and Hannah were born and married in Uttoxeter. They were enumerated in Woodhouses in 1871, when John was a bricklayer and Hannah a dressmaker and schoolmistress, despite having 3 children aged from 11 months to 5 years. John died in 1900 and in 1901 Hannah was enumerated in King Street as a 'Fancy Shop Keeper' with daughter Annie, a dressmaker and son John a bricklayer. By 1901 John Henry was a builder, wheelwright and blacksmith living in Victoria Street with his wife Arabella and their children. Later that year Arabella died aged 34, and in 1911 John and his children were living with his mother Hannah, still a shopkeeper aged 74. He was enumerated as a painter and decorator, his eldest son, Richard Johnson Wright was a bricklayer's apprentice. Later the business moved to a building yard in Hadley Street. In 1975 the workshop was gutted by fire and eventually Don, the last of the Wrights of Wright's Yard retired and the business closed. Their workmanship remains in many houses in the area, including the old people's bungalows and the parish hall.

Alfred 'Pop' Lester

Amongst those who supplied farmers, as well as traders and other customers were the wheelwrights, waggoners, and blacksmiths. Many of the Lesters were employed in agriculture but the most written about Lester is the multi talented Alfred. Born in 1870 he grew up in the household of his grandparents, George and Elizabeth Dukes and in 1891 was a blacksmith in the household of his widowed grandmother, Elizabeth. How much work he did for farmers is unknown but his skills, like those of many other blacksmiths, far exceeded the shoeing of horses, as can be seen in the notice board he made for the church, which stands in the churchyard, opposite the Golden Cup. He used the skills of the wheelwright for farmers, being a jack of many trades. By 1901 he had become a self employed cycle maker and repairer, and by 1911 was a cycle and motor repairer. He lived and worked from his home at School Green, where he and his wife, Mary nèe Wright had brought up 10 children. His family continued in the motor trade and until recent years ran a garage at the bottom of Town Hill. Alfred 'Pop' Lester died in 1964 aged 94, his life having spanned a time when horses were the main form of transport, through to the growing motorised transport of the 20th century and had adapted his skills accordingly.

The Leedham saddlers and collar makers were not the only Leedhams who lived and traded in Yoxall. Others include Stephen who from 1841 was enumerated as a plumber and glazier. By 1871 his son Thomas, also a plumber and glazier had a separate household. Stephen died in 1877 aged 67 and in 1881 his widow, Ann was enumerated at the age of 71 as a plumber, glazier and painter, with a son William in the household with the same trade who was clearly doing the work of the business. Like the saddlers the Leedham plumbers continued to trade in Yoxall into the 20th century.

Grocers and other sellers

The census of 1851 enumerated 9 grocers, of these 1 was in Bloomsmithy Lane, 1 in Woodlane, the remaining 7 in Yoxall village. The village grocers included a grocer and draper and a wife whose husband was a brick maker employing 2 men and a boy. Also William Sutton, who is known to have occupied the premises which were later owned and run by the Norman family in Main Street which later traded as Tudor Stores. In White's 1851 directory William was also a draper and tallow chandler. The term in its stricter sense means candle maker but was also used for a seller of candles and groceries. Also enumerated in 1851 was a marine store dealer, which from 1837 was a dealer in scrap or old oddments. In Hadley End 2 small ware dealers were enumerated; Henry Twamley, and French born British subject, Anthony Mountsey, who also had the inclusion of '(sailor)' in the occupation column. Hadley End also had a hawker, a pedlar, and a cap hawker, the latter two shared the household with a cap maker, a mat maker and a tape weaver. In Bloomsmithy Lane a higgler hawker was enumerated. Higglers were usually pedlars with a horse and cart.

Norman's Store

Michael Poyser the elder who died in 1838 was one of the shopkeepers at what later became known as Norman's Store. Born in Ripley, Derbyshire, John Turton Norman was a chemist's assistant in London in 1881. He married Marion Copestake in Belper in 1885 and the couple lived in the centre of Yoxall in what had been the post office since its inception in 1855. John was the sub postmaster as well as running a general store. John also bought what is currently the post office, on the corner of Hadley Street and Sudbury Road, which was run as a haberdashery, and Birmingham House, which was an ironmongery, before the Leedhams ran their saddle and collar making business from the premises. At the part Tudor part Georgian building which was roughcast and painted and altered to a double shop front in the 19th century, John Norman sold a vast array of goods. In 1896 he was listed in Kelly's directory under the Yoxall commercial heading as 'chemist & grocer, & agent for W & A Gilbey Limited, wine & spirit merchants, Post office'. Separately, Yoxall Post Office was listed as a savings bank and an annuity and insurance office, with John T. Norman as sub postmaster. Letters arrived from Burton at 6.20 a.m. and were dispatched at 6.35 p.m. A wall letter box at Woodmill was cleared at 6.30 and one at Morrey cleared at 4 p.m. Letters for Morrey arrived via Rugeley at 9 a.m.[32]

Norman's Store, with Reginald, son of schoolmaster Henry Jennings entering. The original photograph was date stamped 1924, but a family member has stated that it was in fact an earlier image, which unfortunately fell victim to someone playing with the date stamp. The knickerbockers, popular before the slightly longer plus fours, suggest early 20th century.

A book running from 1888 to 1901 recording the accounts of Norman's many customers has survived, despite being damaged in one of Yoxall's floods. Apart from the immediate area, accounts were held in the neighbouring villages of Kings Bromley and Newborough, and farther away, at Moat Hall in Uttoxeter and Marchington Hall.

Although many accounts list only the amounts of money involved, in other instances the goods and their prices are included. The following does not represent the variety of the goods at Norman's but is informative as to what some of the account holders most regularly purchased. In 1889 at Hoar Cross farm one of the partially itemised accounts included foot rot liquid. One of the most regularly occurring purchases of the Cottage Hospital was seeds, mainly onion, parsley and turnip. In 1890 the hospital's account was predominantly for cake, jelly and birdseed, as well as seeds. In Hoar Cross at the Home of the Good Shepherd, the orphanage's most common requirement was generally paraffin and carbolic soap, the diet of the boys included rice, wheat, sago and barley meal. Large quantities of coffee were also purchased by the home but probably for the staff. Hoar Cross Garden's account included bass brooms, yard brushes, machine oil, rat poison, candles and soap. Yoxall's District Poor Account included tea and sugar, a bottle of brandy and a bottle of port. At the school ink was regularly bought by the gallon or ½ gallon and at Yoxall

Reading Room, the main purchase was, predictably, paraffin oil and wicks. The Church account was largely for gallons of oil, no doubt to fuel the oil lamps installed there.

The work of running a shop was far greater than in the present time of pre-packaging. Tea came in chests, butter in blocks and sugar in sacks. Rice, corn, flour and meal were also delivered in bulk. Paper was bought in sheets and often had to be made into bags of different colours, e.g. blue for sugar, purple for rice. The least paper that could be used, the better, as this had to be paid for and came off the profit as the customer was not charged for the wrapping. Everything had to be carefully weighed, to ensure the customer could not claim to have been given short measure. At Norman's great care was taken and customers were given a little more than they paid for, with the result that making a farthing on a lb of tea was considered good. Checks were made on the accuracy of scales and inaccuracy to the detriment of the customer was taken seriously as the following cases illustrate:

In 1875 William Potts, a flour dealer of Yoxall was charged with having an unjust ordinary beam flour scale. He was fined 5s and 12s costs. The same date Catherine Limer, publican and grocer of the Bell and Cuckoo Inn, was charged with having a number of unjust weights. The inspector said they were the worst he had found in the district. They had no sign of stamps on any of them. The Bench declared it the worst case of any that had been brought before them, and most serious that people should be robbed by the shopkeeper in so wholesale a manner. She was fined £3 and costs.[33]

John Norman had to go to Armitage or Barton station to collect stock that came from wholesalers in Birmingham and elsewhere, and this included bulky items such as cattle food. Apart from groceries and farmers and horse owners' requirements, the store also sold hearthstones, paint, carriage lights, paraffin lamps, and their glass, wicks, and chimneys, white lead and sand to name a few of the many products listed in the accounts. The account of Mr Boden of 'The Factory' includes 2 shirts and trousers made to measure, this suggests that whatever was asked for was supplied by Norman's.

The following are a few examples of some of the prices of household goods:

A tin of salmon 8d; 1 lb of tea 2s 6d; 2 lbs cheese 1s 4d; ½ lb cream crackers 3 ½ d; 12 lbs castor sugar 3s; 2 oz peppermints 4d; a gallon of vinegar 2s 8d; a bottle of spirits (Brandy, Whisky or Rum) 3s 4d; 3 wax candles 1s 4 ½ d; a gross of safety matches 8s; 2 lbs carbolic soap 1s.

Unfortunately another book did not survive the floods, this was a book of medicinal herbal recipes written by John Norman, which he never had patented. He used alum rock, oil of wintergreen, gentian of violets, cloves, oil of peppermint and poisons etc., and made imbrications used as a rub for flu or chest problems. His many preparations were popular with his customers, and he was known for 'Norman's Early Risers', a laxative of crystals of salt rolled in sugar.

John Norman's son Harold continued to run the store, including the post office, after his father's retirement, though not the pharmacy as he trained for the grocery trade and not as a chemist. The post office had to go to tender in 1947, and it was then that it moved to its present site.

Norman's Store, believed to have once been a coaching inn, later became known as Tudor Stores and for a time included a café. It became grade II listed in 1984 and in the 1990s trading ceased and it is now 2 houses, known as Tudor House and The Old Coach House.

Harold Norman. (Reproduced by permission of Marny Francis).

Page's Shop in Hadley Street

In 1870 the cottage that later became Page's shop was sold by John Simpson to William Barnes for the sum of £31. The Rectory Manor of Yoxall held a special court for the transaction and John Simpson came before the steward, John Humphries, and the receipt for the property was surrendered to the Lord of the Manor. The deeds state that the cottage was erected on the north end of a croft or piece of land belonging to Blythe Cottage, 'together with the way or passage at the south end of the said cottage sufficient for a wheelbarrow to pass and repass in and to the said garden … in a certain place called Reeve End within the Rectory Manor'. In 1872 William died intestate and unmarried leaving his father John Barnes his heir. Described in his will of 1887 as a gent of Yoxall, John appointed John Sabin, carrier of Woodmill and Joseph Green, farmer of Yoxall as executors, to sell his estate and to divide the proceeds amongst his children. In the September of that year John died and in May of the following year his executors came to the manor court for the transaction of a sale of the property which was bought by Frank Greasley Armson for £26.

In June 1900 the property was sold to Thomas and Sarah Page for £31, although it remained part of the Rectory Manor. Thomas was a shoemaker and shopkeeper, and he and his wife were admitted as joint tenants under a yearly rent of 5d 'and other services and customs therefore due and of right accustomed'. They paid £9 to the Lord of the Manor to respite their fealties and were admitted tenants. How long the shoemaking continued on the premises is uncertain, but Thomas had used an outbuilding in which was left evidence of his trade. The interior of the shop with its fittings from the time of Page's occupancy has been recreated in Shugborough Museum.

Page's shop with Sarah, wife of Thomas, a shopkeeper and shoemaker. The thatched building to the side was later demolished and became part of Wright's Yard when the business moved from Victoria Street. (Reproduced by permission of Sarah Lea).

Page's shop c.1912, with Thomas, son of Thomas and Sarah. The girl is believed to be Alice, daughter of Sarah's sister. (Reproduced by permission of Sarah Lea).

The cottage is remembered as The Old Store, considered by many as an 'Aladdin's Cave' which was reopened as a shop by Eric and Elizabeth Harvey during the early 1980s and traded into the early years of the 21st century.

Domestic Servants

From the evidence of the census female servants were almost entirely domestic. In 1851 and 1891 just over half were aged 15-24. In 1851 the two youngest girls employed were both domestic servants aged 11 and in 1871 Sarah Dukes aged 11 was the general, and probably only servant of Dorothy Brown. In 1891 the two youngest female workers were also domestic servants, aged 12, one of whom worked for John Perkins, agricultural implement maker, the other was employed at Old Hall, Yoxall, where a 12 year old boy was also a domestic servant. The oldest domestic servant enumerated was 74 year old governess Apoline de Soycourt, in 1851.

Domestic servants could be employed through registries, of which there were several in Burton, who advertised that all classes of respectable servants could be supplied with situations. Others attended Burton Statutes, where it was reported that in 1890 female servants could go free to the Shaftsbury Institute in Station Street, rather than the market place. 'Young girls according to their ages and experience commanded wages up to £6 10s, while women who were fit for trustworthy positions obtained situations at wages reaching up to £15'.[34]

In 1892 there was a great demand for girls, a fact not lost on some: 'One within a few months of 16 asked for £15 and refused £14'.[35]

In 1893 a room for girls was provided in the Market Hall by the Local Rescue & Protection Society and was 'largely utilised and much appreciated'.[36]

Female servants were just as likely to find themselves in court if in breach of their contract as males. Catherine Pegg of Rosliston was summoned by Edward Smith, farmer of Whitewood, Yoxall, for having unlawfully left his service without notice or reasonable excuse. Catherine, who had left after seven weeks servitude, did not appear in court and a warrant was granted for her apprehension. When arrested she was remanded on bail, and her uncle was bound over in the sum of £5 surety for her appearance.[37] The following week she was discharged from her service and ordered to pay 16s costs.[38]

Annie Chamberlain

Annie Chamberlain who came to Yoxall as a domestic servant and later became a shopkeeper.

One of the more fortunate servants was Annie Chamberlain. Born in Leicestershire, she was enumerated in 1901 as a domestic servant of Rev. Cory at the Rectory. By 1911 at the age of 42 she was a grocer and head of her household in Victoria Street, employing two people, one of whom was a 15 year old girl enumerated in the household. She remained unmarried and some Yoxall residents still remember the shop and Annie, who was a kind lady who liked children. Apart from her shop at Rook Cottage, which sold a variety of goods, Annie also ran a carrier's cart into Burton on market days, carrying goods and passengers. Described as 'a tiny person with golden hair in a tight bun and gold-rimmed spectacles'. The following unfortunate incident has been recorded: 'I remember once on one of her regular journeys to Burton she returned with a new set of teeth. As she passed the Cottage Hospital her horse slipped and she and all her goods were thrown to the road. Somehow her teeth met the ground before she did and before they were smashed to pieces they managed to take a dying mouthful out of her buttocks as she landed.'[39]

Victoria Street, showing Annie Chamberlain's shop, now Rook Cottage.

Chapter 13

In Sickness and in Health

During the second World War an evacuee from Birmingham recalled passing Brook House Surgery towards Woodhouses, and shortly afterwards coming to a five barred gate leading to the field where, he was told by another child, the victims of the Black Death were buried, the humps being the graves.[1] This was probably just the children's interpretation of features of the landscape. There is no known evidence that the plague reached Yoxall, although it was in Burton in 1349 and 1361 and outbreaks were recorded there in the 1640s and 1660s. It was also recorded in Lichfield in the sixteenth and seventeenth centuries, with a particularly severe outbreak in 1593. It seems probable that at some time plague may have visited Yoxall. A table of seventeenth century Yoxall baptisms, burials and marriages indicates a steep rise in burials in 1670, rising from 19 the previous year to 43 and gradually declining over the following two years. A similar pattern followed in 1680, when burials rose from 10 the previous year to 32 and peaked in 1681 at 42.[2] The cause of these is unknown.

Yoxall burial records rarely record the cause of death, even when the number was comparatively high. This was the case in 1814 when more children than usual were buried in January and February. However in this case the Paget Estate Papers, regarding Dr Baker, who was not a medical man, but a musician, solved the mystery and led to the following account of events.

Dr George Baker and the Yoxall Fever

Around 1794 Dr George Baker was appointed organist at St Mary's Church, Stafford. The Corporation Books contain several entries regarding habitual negligence of his duties and in 1800 an entry for his resignation. In 1810 he was appointed to All Saints', Derby, a post which was short lived as by 1811 he and his wife Elizabeth had arrived in Yoxall. Their names appear in the Parish Register for the baptism of a son that year. The beginning of George's musical career was rather unorthodox. At the age of sixteen he left the family home in Exeter to try to make a musical career in London, without the means to purchase musical instruments, and was said to have collected horseshoes of varying sizes and strung them across the street to attract attention. One day Lord Uxbridge, a lover of music, happened to be passing and heard him playing on the horseshoes. Impressed by George's ingenuity and skill he took him into his household and arranged for his musical training and procured the post at Stafford for him.

George was said to have been generous, 'even to the point of improvidence'[3] and perhaps for this reason he fell on hard times.

In January 1814 the Yoxall burial register recorded the burial of eight people; five aged from 14 months to 11 years, one aged 16, one 23 and one 62. This

160

number, not being substantially higher than expected would have escaped notice, but for the fact that three children of John and Esther Caldwell of Weaver Lake were among them. Of the five other fatalities, three were at Yoxall, one at Morrey and one at Hadley End.

The following month fifteen people were buried, the first having died on 31 January. Of those who died nine were aged between 3 weeks and 9 years, with a possible tenth child, George Pott, whose age is not stated. He was the son of George and Mary of Hoar Cross and the inclusion of his parents names on the register suggest he was likely to have been a minor. Two teenagers are also listed, aged 16 and 17 years, the remaining three were aged between 63 and 88. Again the spread of the area is fairly wide and includes Brookside and Forestside. Four in Meg Lane were the children of William and Mary Stretton, aged between 18 months and 16 years, whose burials took place over fifteen days. Whatever caused at least some of these deaths appears to have begun towards the middle of January and was at its height early to mid February, continuing until late February.

An anonymous letter dated 12 February was sent to the Earl of Uxbridge from 'A Friend to the Distressed' asking the Earl, the son of George's earlier patron, for financial help for Dr Baker, whose situation 'for a man of Genius is much to be lamented'.[4] The letter continues: 'His present residence is at Yoxall, where a dreadful fever now rages, and tho' I have not heard that his family are afflicted with it, yet they are in daily apprehension, and the fear of it is now so predominant in the neighbourhood as to preclude all possibility of his attending anywhere as a Music Master, so much are his friends in fear of infection'. The letter adds that his wife is recovering from a long illness and he has six small children. His own health has suffered as a result of caring for his wife. The correspondent also refers to George's horse, being 'no better an animal than a mule, who is in the habit of falling almost every time it goes out'. He or she thinks it 'a most degrading reflection that a Man of his merit should remain under a perpetual cloud in the obscurity of Yoxall'. The writer adds the following warning to the earl: 'a letter addressed to Dr Baker Yoxall near Lichfield would be received safe, and should it contain an enclosure, I would recommend a very careful folding as instances are not uncommon of notes being taken out of letters at Lichfield and its vicinity'.

Mysteriously the fever appears to have been confined to Yoxall as there is no trace of increased burials during that time in the neighbouring parishes of Kings Bromley, Barton, or Hamstall Ridware. Newchurch had no burials for 1814 before July. This suggests that the cause of the fever was probably due to some contamination either of food, or if in the water supply, had occurred locally and by the time it reached other areas was too diluted to cause any serious health problems.

In March there were four burials and only one of these was a child, the outbreak was over. There is no clue as to how many people, if any, suffered from the

'Yoxall Fever' and survived. The tone of letter to the Earl of Uxbridge suggests that it was, perhaps, far more virulent than the scant evidence suggests.

The Baker family all survived and a daughter was baptised at St Peter's in 1816. By 1824 George was living in Rugeley, where he was an organist. Afflicted by deafness in his later years, he died there in 1847, aged 96.

Surgeons and Apothecaries of Yoxall

The earliest known Yoxall surgeon is Edward Lightwood, grandson of Zachary Lightwood who struck one of the three Yoxall trade tokens. Stebbing Shaw recollected a Mr Lightwood, an apothecary and ancestor of Zachary giving him several tokens.[5] In a will of 1791 he was named in connection with an agreed property sale as Edward Lightwood the younger, surgeon, and in 1804 Mary Moore stated in her will that she had sold a cottage and land to him for £430 and added his occupation as 'surgeon and apothecary'. Edward died that year aged 47, the entry in the burial register states 'A very sudden death'. His name appears with those of his father Edward, mother Ann and grandfather Zachary on a bronze plaque in St Peter's which records that the family were buried beneath the north chancel aisle of the church.

The next known surgeon is William James Sutton, who died in 1818. He bequeathed his 'freehold, copyhold and leasehold messuages or dwelling houses, farm closes, lands, grounds and parts and shares of such' situated at Derby, Lichfield and Yoxall, along with his 'household goods, furniture, cattle, farming stock and other effects'. Clearly surgery was not his only source of income. His books and surgical instruments he left to whichever of his sons followed his profession. If either of them did they appear not to have practiced in Yoxall. In the year of his death two other surgeons, Edward Cleavin and John Garner, were recorded in the parish.

In the 1841 census four surgeons were enumerated in Yoxall. These were Cleavin and Garner, also Joseph Fearneyhough and Edmund Rice. In 1850 John Garner's wife, Emma, died aged 52. The following year he was enumerated as a widower living with his eight children. He died later that year, aged 58. No monument survives for him or his wife, but the graves of three of their children; Charles, Lucy and Mary Loat Garner, record that, unlike their parents they survived into their mid eighties. By 1851 Dublin born Joseph Allison, was also a surgeon and practitioner in Yoxall. Not only were the medical needs of the people well catered for, there was also a veterinary surgeon, James Ford, whose youngest son, Edwin, at the age of fourteen was his veterinary assistant.

By 1861 there had been more changes, while the same vet was in practice, the surgeons included John Barrow and Edward Hemmings Snoad. Also linked to the health of Yoxall was Samuel Shewin, grocer and druggist.

'Over the counter' preparations were generally available and often advertised in local newspapers. One such remedy was Hall's Lung Restorer, advertised under the ominous heading 'Voice of Death', which was sold in bottles ranging from 1s 1½d to 11s. These were sold at 'Chemists Everywhere'. The advertisement also included three 'letters' in praise of the product. Advertising, it seems, is little changed!

Prior to the founding of the Pharmacy Act of 1868 going to a chemist could be extremely hazardous, unqualified pharmacists were able to experiment and sell their own remedies. In 1862 Thomas Winter, a 26 year old farmer of Yoxall was advised to try a mixture compound principally of a mercurial preparation called AEsthops mineral. A Lichfield chemist's assistant gave him a preparation of a compound principally of Turpeth's mineral, which was the sulphate of peroxide mercury, and should not be taken internally. The dose proved fatal, the farmer died the same day of poisoning. The assistant came before the Crown Court accused of manslaughter. The jury had to decide whether he was guilty of gross neglect, therefore responsible for the death. They returned a verdict of 'Not Guilty'.[6]

Included in the duties of a surgeon was the occasional court appearance as a witness, such as in the case of 'cutting and wounding' at the Meynell Ingram Arms, Hoar Cross in 1861. Edward Snoad attended both Burton Police Court and the Crown Court as witness to the injuries sustained by one of the four men attacked. (The prisoner, David Woodings, was considered by the judge to have behaved 'like a wild savage' and was sentenced to three years penal servitude).[7]

In his spare time Edward enjoyed a game of cricket and was an active member of the Yoxall Cricket Club. He left the village in 1879, having resigned as medical officer of Yoxall District of the Lichfield Board of Guardians, and sold his practice to Mr. T. Wilson, who was appointed Medical Officer. On leaving the area he was presented with an inscribed silver inkstand and a purse containing twenty guineas, 'as a token of regard and grateful acknowledgement of his skill and prompt and kind attention to his patients during the space of twenty two years'.[8]

The Armsons: Doctors and Surgeons

Charles Greasley Armson

The first of the Armson line of Yoxall doctors, Charles married Kate Cottingham in 1861 and in 1863 he was amongst the local dignitaries who headed a procession through the garland festooned village to celebrate the marriage of the Prince of Wales (later Edward VII). It was also the year of the birth of Charles and Kate's son, Frank Greasley. Kate died in 1866, aged 24, her sister Mary Vere was present at her death. The following year Charles married Mary Vere, his widowed sister-in-law. The Armsons lived at Brook House where several doctors had previously lived and it is suggested that it had probably always been a doctor's house. There was also another firm of doctors in the village.[9] The same source records that one of the doctors who lived at Brook House was said to have been imprisoned for attempting to starve a child to death in the cottage at the back of the house and another imprisoned for debt.[10]

Meyell Ingram Cottage Hospital. (Reproduced by permission of Elisabeth Macfarlane, © Blurb).

In 1869 Miss Louisa Meynell Ingram of Hoar Cross told Dr Armson that if he could buy land near his house she would build a hospital "where your patients will be well nursed, well fed and get better sooner".[11] In 1871 Charles, enumerated as 'Licentiate of Faculty of Physicians and Surgeons and Licentiate of Midwifery in Glasgow', began the process of buying the land and in 1873, the year of the birth of son Charles James, the purchase was completed, and the hospital opened in December. Charles supervised the building and received advice from Florence Nightingale, who supplied six red blankets, which remained in use until World War 1.[12] Louisa Meynell Ingram had died in 1870 but her sister Miss Georgina had carried out her wishes and supported the hospital until her death in 1902. Armson doctors remained as trustees and hospital managers until 1948, and the inception of the National Health Service. The original hospital consisted of two large wards, with the matron's bedroom between them and one small ward. There was a sitting room for the matron, a bathroom with a bedroom over for a servant, a cellar, and across the yard, a wash-house. The hospital was lit by paraffin lamps, candles and nightlights and heated by open coal fires. Water was pumped from a well in the yard. There was no proper drainage so the drain discharged into the field below.[13]

Apart from his dedication to his patients, Charles was interested in sport, during the 1880s he was vice-chairman and later vice-president of the Yoxall Cricket

Club and in the 1890s was chairman of the Parish Council. He also invested in property including buying 2 cottages with outbuildings and gardens at Reeve End at a total cost of £31 in 1886.[14]

In 1891 Charles was enumerated at Brook House, and by 1901 he had moved to Trent Bridge and died at Brook House in 1905, aged 70. The burial register noted him not as a surgeon, but 'Church Warden of this Parish', in recognition of him having been a church warden from 1892.

Brook House. At least in its later days patients entered the surgery from the side of the house. Wealthy patients at the time of the photograph would most likely be attended by a doctor at their home. (Reproduced by permission of Elisabeth Macfarlane, © Blurb).

A window and brass plaque in St Peter's Church commemorates Charles Greasley Armson for his work as a surgeon in the village for 43 years, being 'dedicated by friends and patients as a token of their affection and esteem'. The window verse reads: 'Honour a Physician For the Most High cometh healing'.

Frank Greasley Armson and the Arden Connection

The eldest son of Charles, Frank Greasley, was a medical student living with his father and step-mother Mary, in 1881. By 1891, still in the family home at Brook House, he was a registered practitioner and surgeon. He was educated at Bloxham School and Middlesex Hospital where he obtained his M.R.C.S. and L.S.A. Almost immediately after qualifying as a medical practitioner Frank was appointed Medical Officer for the Yoxall district of Lichfield Board of Guardians, and public vaccinator. He followed in his father's footsteps when age forced Charles Greasley to curtail some of his public duties. He was appointed to the staff and made a trustee of the Meynell Ingram Cottage Hospital, and chairman of the Yoxall and District Agricultural and Horticultural Society. He was, like other Armsons, fond of the countryside pursuits of fishing, shooting, and hunting.

In 1897 Frank married Ethel Margaret Arden, daughter of the Rev. Edward Thomas Arden, vicar of Rangemore and his wife Emma, also an Arden before her marriage, her father being George Pinkard Arden. (Her brother George married Alice, daughter of Yoxall surgeon Edward Hemmings Snoad in 1878). Rev. Edward Thomas Arden was the son of Thomas, fifteenth child of the prolific Rev. John and Margaret. His wife Isabella was a daughter of Rev. Edward Cooper.

Edward and Emma had two daughters, Mabel and Ethel Margaret. Within weeks of the birth of Ethel in 1877, Edward died. In 1881 Edward's widow, Emma was living at Main Street, Yoxall with her sister Caroline and daughters Mabel and Ethel. Emma was well provided for as she was a land owner and railway shareholder having four domestic servants, including a groom/gardener and a cook. In 1891 her daughters, Mabel, aged 16 and Ethel, 14 were resident at a Ladies College in London. Their mother, Emma, married William Boden in Marylebone in 1883. During the census of 1901 Emma and her husband were visitors at the Crown Inn and soon settled in the area, living at Cross Hayes. Ethel's sister, Mabel, was enumerated in the household of her brother-in-law, Frank Greasley, who also played host to members of the Boden family. In 1905 Mabel married Albert Mayrall, of London, who would almost certainly have been related to Margaret Mayral, sister of Mary, the second wife of Charles Greasley Armson, who shares the burial plot of her sister and brother-in-law.

The marriage of Frank Greasley and Ethel was preceded by a presentation in the school of 'a handsome oak knee-hole writing table, subscribed for by the parishioners, and an elegant silver ink stand by the teachers and school children as a mark of their esteem and affection'.[15] The couple's return from honeymoon was greeted by the villagers who met them about ½ a mile from the village, led by Rev. Cory who welcomed them with a short speech. The horses were taken out of the shafts and they were drawn home by some of the villagers. Others lined the road cheering and showering the newly weds with rice. The bells of Yoxall and Kings Bromley rang during the evening.[16] Frank and Ethel lived at Moat House, opposite the Brook House Surgery. Like his father, Frank served on the Parish Council. They were the parents of the last Armson doctor. Frank served on the Medical Board and was regularly appointed as chairman of the Parish Council. He died in 1926 and Ethel in 1935, they share a grave beside the church, their memorial an intricately carved Celtic Cross.

Charles James Armson

Charles James, son of Charles Greasley Armson and his second wife, Mary, followed in his father and half-brother Frank's footsteps, and by 1891 was a medical student living at Brook House. In 1899 Charles married Margaret Eliza Anderson. Prior to his wedding a presentation was made by Rev. Cory, on behalf of the teachers and children of Yoxall schools. The returning couple were met, like his brother, by villagers. Garlands had been placed on the road and at Brook House, and at the old pinfold the horses were again taken from the shafts. These are the only two known incidences of a welcoming party replacing the horses with themselves. However it is a custom to be found elsewhere. Two of the couple's daughters; Margaret, (generally know as Miss Marjorie), and Beatrice (generally known as Miss Doreen) lived and worked at Brook House; Marjorie worked in the dispensary and Doreen ran a market garden business at the back of the property, as well as giving some assistance at the practice, often in the dispensary. In 1959 Charles died at the age of 86, having worked almost to the end of his life. He broke a leg during his rounds, having fallen at a patient's house. Despite this he continued visiting his patients, his nephew, Philip Arden Armson of Barton (son of Frank Greasley) drove him on his rounds. He did not complain and asked his nephew to make several calls with medicine on the way home. Charles was taken to St Modwen's Nursing Home in Burton where he died due to a combination of the fall and heart degeneration. The coroner said: "I think he was a wonderful man of his age, to have been doing his rounds continually, even after he broke a leg".[17] Under the middle window on the south wall in St Peter's Church a bronze plate is inscribed: 'The Festival Frontal on the altar of this church was given by grateful friends and patients of Charles James Armson of Yoxall, surgeon in the village for 43 years, who departed this life 1st Feb 1959, aged 86 years. Let everlasting light shine upon him'. Daughters Marjorie and Doreen had a double bereavement, as their uncle, William Anderson, brother of their mother Margaret, who had spent his final months at Brook House died the same month. Margaret Eliza died in 1967 aged 100.

Frank Gerald Arden Armson

Dr Gerald Armson, the last of the Armson doctors, with a keen interest in local history. (Reproduced by permission of Elisabeth Macfarlane).

Dr Frank Gerald Arden Armson, son of Frank Greasley, and known as Dr Gerald, lived at the family home, Moat House and continued to work at the Brook House Surgery, where Marjorie and Doreen continued to help with the dispensary. Gerald is remembered not only for his medical skills but also for the reminiscences and research which formed his lifelong study of the parish of Yoxall. His work became the basis of an adult education course which resulted in the University of Keele's publication; *Yoxall: a walk through history*, edited by Denis Stuart. His retirement in 1971 ended 120 years of Armson doctors who had served Yoxall and Kings Bromley. In the middle of the south wall in St Peter's Church a bronze plate is inscribed: 'The iron gates at the south east corner of the churchyard were given in memory of Frank Gerald Armson physician life long parishioner of Yoxall 1901-1982'.

Dr Khan and Brook House Surgery

When the 20th century dawned Brook House Surgery continued to be run on the same lines that it had in the previous century, that is until Dr Arif Khan, the last doctor to join the surgery, came to Yoxall in 1972.

Dr Khan had been GP trained in an organised practice with secretaries and notes and would naturally assume that the same applied in other surgeries. Arriving at Brook House was a complete shock, not least because the 'system' was to rely on memory. Being used to notes, Arif started to write things down and built up a rudimentary card box. In an article written by his wife Shamim, published in the parish magazine of November 2012, the surgery in 'Dr Finlay's Casebook' was described as modern by comparison with Brook House Surgery, where the dispensary was kept in a cupboard and the books on the shelves were in Latin. If a doctor drove past a gatepost and saw a newspaper on it he would know that a home visit was required.

Dr Khan, the last doctor to join the Brook House practice, and founder of Yoxall Health Centre at Savey Lane. (Reproduced by permission of Shamim and Roxi Khan).

Patients still remember the queues which stretched around the corner at the foot of Town Hill, in all weather. At 9 am the surgery was unlocked and patients filed through the now bricked up doorway in the wall at the side of the house, and then into a narrow, unevenly tiled hall which led to a small waiting/reception room and sat on the few chairs and the fender. A fire blazed in the hearth and Marjorie Armson sat at a large desk organising the proceedings. Although Brook House ran smoothly, Dr Khan saw the need for a new, modern surgery and set the wheels in motion but nothing would have happened had he not kept up the pressure over several years until Yoxall Health Centre was built in Savey Lane in 1980. It is entirely thanks to his efforts on behalf of the practice patients that Yoxall has a modern, well equipped surgery.

Marjorie Armson, died in 1981, aged 78, her sister, Doreen in 1986, also aged 78. A marble headstone inscribed with their birth names Margaret Armson and Beatrice Doreen Armson marks their shared grave, next to that of their parents, Charles and Margaret Eliza. Only one plot separates these Armson graves from that of their kinsman William Anderson.

Having founded Yoxall Health Centre Dr Khan remained there as a very popular GP until his retirement in 2005 and continued to live in Yoxall until his death in 2015.

The consulting room at Brook House Surgery
(Original framed photo by Dr Arif Khan was photographed
by Rob Grenfell and reproduced by his permission).

Chapter 14

Crime and Punishment

This chapter includes some of the early crimes in Yoxall, which were recorded in volumes of the Staffordshire Historical Collections. The conclusion of a case is often not recorded in the volumes due largely to the accused not appearing at the court sitting from which the information was extracted.

In 1374/5 Alice 'daughter to William Wylmott of Yoxall, sued William de Bernewell of Yoxall, carpenter, for insulting, wounding and ill-treating her at Yoxhall and taking chattels to the value of 100s. William did not appear, and the Sheriff returned he could not be found'. It was ordered that if he was found he would be produced to answer the charge, if not he would be outlawed.[1] To be outlawed for a criminal offence not only put the person outside of the protection of the law, they could be killed by anyone with impunity and no one was allowed to give food, shelter, or any other support to an outlaw.

In 1414/15 Thomas Dethick, late Sheriff of Staffordshire was accused by Thomas Coleman, chaplain, of assaulting him and imprisoning him at Yoxall, until he paid a fine of 40s for his release, and for which he claimed damages. The Sheriff claimed he had lawfully arrested him, having a writ from the King and admitted taking 33s 4d from Coleman's friends for 'easement of his imprisonment and in order that he might not be put into fetters or manacles', but denied taking a fine for his release.[2] The same year the Sheriff had been ordered to arrest upwards of 300 who were to be produced at court for 'divers felonies and murders'. If they did not appear to answer the charges they were to be outlawed. William Benbowe, miller of Yoxall, was named as one of the men considered to be of most note.[3]

In 1481 Robert Myner, a gentleman of Yoxall was sued by widow Joan Coton, for taking fish from her fishery at Hamstall Ridware and threatening her servants to the extent that they feared for their lives and for a time she was without their service. Like many other accused, Robert failed to appear at the court and the Sheriff was ordered to arrest him.[4]

Richard Arnold, husbandman, late of Yoxall, appears on the Staffordshire Quarter Sessions Roll for 1586, along with Ann, wife of Nicholas Barbour, yeoman and Margaret Madder, late of Yoxall, spinster along with three people from Rugeley, for gathering at Rugeley in 1585 with arms and attacking Nicholas Adye, clerk, wounding him to the extent his life was despaired of.[5]

In 1601 Hugh Kynnersley and Roger Wrighte were accused under the collective term of 'certain trespasses and other misdeeds and offences'.[6] As was the custom, when they failed four times to attend the court for their offences they were outlawed in 1600/1.[7]

The Staffordshire Jurors' Book of 1784 lists the jurors of Yoxall and includes names still remembered in Yoxall today. With the exception of Nathaniel Bladon Brown, a malster, they were all farmers: John Sharratt, Nathaniel Brown, William and John Shipton, (both 'gent' in 1785), Robert Tarlington, William Jerom and Joseph Woolley who was also an 'innholder'.[8]

The 1822 Calendar of Prisoners at Stafford Goal records a Yoxall felony case. William Yates aged 21, Daniel Smith, 18 and Edwin Moore, 17 were charged on suspicion of stealing eleven fowl, the property of William Woodward and two geese the property of John Shipton of Woodhouses. They were found guilty on both charges; William Yates and Daniel Smith were sentenced to seven years transportation and Edwin Moore was to be kept in the House of Correction. The written term of the sentence is indistinct, but was for a number of months.

The Hoar Cross Murder: The Facts and the Fiction

The Hoar Cross murder has been written about on several occasions. It was thoroughly covered at the time by local newspapers, but more fancifully by Billy Meikle in his book 'Middle of the Midlands'.[9] Written when in his eighties, Meikle was looking back over the years to his experiences as a young man living in the area. Doubtless failing memory may have played a part in the inaccuracies, but clearly his intention was to add his own fictionalised version of some details.

The facts of the case as provided by the *Burton Chronicle* are that on the afternoon of the 23rd of November 1874, Mary Kidd, the 55 year old wife of John Kidd, a labourer of Hoar Cross, was returning home from a shopping trip to Yoxall with 8 year old Sarah Hollis, a neighbour's daughter, when she was approached by Robert Taylor, described as a 'tramp'. He asked her for money, and on her refusal threatened to cut her throat if she did not give him half a crown. She offered him 2d, telling him it was all she had. He then threw her to the ground and cut her throat with what appeared to the child watching, no doubt in horror, as a pocket knife, nearly decapitating her in the ferocity of the attack. At that point a man driving a horse and trap approached and Taylor fled the scene, jumping over a gate and running across a field towards Yoxall Lodge. It is probable that the child's life was saved by the oncoming driver.[10] It seems unlikely that Taylor would have spared the life of the only witness to his heinous crime. Throughout the December the *Burton Chronicle* continued to report on the case.

The inquest took place at the Meynell Ingram Arms, Hoar Cross. The witnesses who came forward included the Rev. R.F. Mumford, Vicar of Newborough, who said he was returning from Yoxall when he saw something black lying in the road which his pony refused to pass. On discovering it was Mrs. Kidd, a lady known to him, apparently dead, he drove off for assistance, meeting a person with a cart whom he asked to go to Yoxall for a doctor and policeman.

Mr. Edward Hemmings Snoad, surgeon of Yoxall, arrived on the scene, which is described as being 'in the road near the reservoir at Lower Hoar Cross'. He discovered three distinct cuts and stated that she would have died in minutes. There was no shortage of witnesses; Henry Mottram, a farm labourer, said that earlier that afternoon he had seen the prisoner near Dunstall Church and had been asked where he was going. He lost sight of the prisoner at Woodlane.

Arthur Fearns also saw the prisoner on the afternoon of the murder, in Mr. Wait's Mill Yard. The prisoner had not spoken to him. Thomas Croxall, groom to Major Griffiths of Yoxall Lodge saw the prisoner at about half-past three on the road from Dunstall to Barton, and again at about six o'clock when he came to the stables at Yoxall Lodge, claiming he was lost. He asked the way to Burton and was seen leaving in that direction.

The sole witness to the deed, Sarah Hollis, first said that when she and Mrs Kidd got to the wood at Copy Plain they saw the man sitting on a stile against Wood Mill. Mrs Kidd had asked him if he was going to sleep and on receiving no answer told him to go home, to which he replied, "I haven't got no home". They walked on and the man followed until they reached the spot where he demanded the half-a-crown. Asked if she could recognise the man, Sarah immediately pointed to Taylor. She said that at the time he was wearing a red handkerchief, a dark jacket and old brown trousers, which were torn, with a tight fitting cap and clogs. He had black hair and no whiskers. Police constable Hales, the Newborough policeman, said he had examined the gate the child said Taylor had jumped and discovered a bloody hand print and clog prints.

On the morning following the murder Taylor was seen near Mr Watson's public house in Branstone Road. Taylor saw the officers and went into a nearby shop and asked for tobacco. It was there he was arrested, still wearing the blood stained clothes of the previous day.

It was around this time that Billy Meikle was travelling around Kings Bromley, Alrewas and Yoxall. He claimed to have arrived in Kings Bromley the day after the murder and 'had to listen to the story of the crime at every house [he] went to'. According to his story the tramp wanted 3d and Mrs. Kidd only had 2d, which she offered him. He remembered there had been a heavy fall of snow, which is nowhere mentioned in the official account of events, and that he was told the exact spot the murder was committed, 'by a large tree - where the folk had scraped away the snow to see the blood'. In his fanciful account Meikle wrote that the killer could not resist singing 'The Thorn', especially if accompanied on the piano, so pianists in all public houses that had pianos were asked to play the song at regular intervals, and this according to Meikle, is how the prisoner was caught, at Wilnecote in Tamworth. The truth was more prosaic, and nowhere in the *Burton Chronicle* reports on the case is there mention of Meikle's story that while awaiting execution Taylor scratched on his wooden spoon the figure of a man being hanged with the words "A bloody long drop for this kid for killing another Kidd". It seems doubtful that prison spoons would be large enough to accommodate the diagram and text. However Meikle drew an image of the alleged spoon.[11]

Burton Chronicle articles reported that Robert Taylor, aged 21 had previously committed thefts, and was a sinker, (a well or shaft digger), who had previously lived in Wigan, Lancashire. In court he claimed he was reared by his grandparents until he was six or seven years old, when he went to work in a coal pit and earned sufficient to maintain himself. Throughout the proceedings he 'manifested a degree of callousness which at times appeared to make him think the affair was only a joke'.

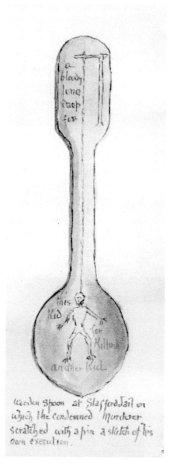

Wooden Spoon at Stafford Jail on which the condemned Murderer scratched with a pin a sketch of his own execution.

Initially he had entered a not guilty plea, but perhaps due to the overwhelming evidence against him, changed it to guilty. It took the jury only two minutes to return a guilty verdict, he was then sentenced to death and left the dock smiling. Following his conviction he was taken to Stafford Goal. Asked if he had relatives or friends he might like to see, he said he had no relations. However, a woman from Wigan wrote to the governor of the goal, stating that her husband had left her the previous June, and from what she had read in the newspapers, feared that the convict might be her husband, but on receiving a photograph of the prisoner, said he was not the man. Despite this she clearly had a lingering doubt as she travelled to the goal, where she asked to see one of the chief officers, and was allowed to see him in his cell, where to her relief she discovered he was not her husband.

Watercolour of wooden spoon by Billy Meikle who claimed this was carved by the killer of Mary Kidd while awaiting his execution. (Meikle Collection: Middle of the Midlands 63/1. Reproduced by permission of Walsall Local History Centre).

During his time in Stafford Goal as a condemned man his experience of prison life was far more comfortable than for people convicted of far lesser crimes: 'In compliance with custom, Taylor has been allowed a rather liberal dietary since his condemnation, and he availed himself of the concession to the fullest extent. His appetite seemed to be insatiable, and the meals he consumed were enormous. He was further allowed two pipes of tobacco per day, which he seemed to thoroughly enjoy. On each of the three Sundays following his condemnation, and also on Christmas-day, he twice attended service in the prison chapel, occupying the same pew in which William Palmer (the infamous 'Rugeley Poisoner') and other murders have sat before him, and which is screened by curtains from the view of the other prisoners. The chaplain advisedly refrained from making personal allusion in his sermons to the convict's awful position, but at the appropriate place in the order of service the prayers of the congregation were desired for Robert Taylor, now lying under sentence of death'.[12]

Taylor's cell was situated in what was known as the new prison, and was 'a bare looking apartment with whitewashed ceiling', where he slept on a straw mattress. On the morning of his execution, 29 December 1874, Taylor was baptized in the prison chapel, and on returning to his cell asked to be allowed a good breakfast, and consumed over a pound each of beef and bread, and a quart of cocoa.

Despite the bitterly cold morning around 200 people had congregated, to hear the thud when the bolt was drawn and to see the black flag raised, reminiscing about the "good old times" when men had been executed in public, a fate which Taylor had escaped thanks to the Capital Punishment Amendment Act of 1868. Taylor was handed over to William Marwood, who was in his first year as official public executioner, and who became the first English executioner to refine the 'long drop', a more humane method that usually resulted in instant death. Taylor showed no outward sign of fear as he was led to the scaffold, but turned to Marwood with the request "Snap me off quick". Following the drop of five feet, Marwood remarked that death was instantaneous, and following an examination of the body by the goal surgeon, and the coroner's inquest, Taylor was interred in a part of the goal premises set apart for murderers. Mary Kidd was buried at Newborough, a headstone marks her resting place.

Unfit for Human Consumption

In 1872 John Ashmore, a butcher of Morrey was charged with sending four quarters of beef that were unfit for consumption to Birmingham. The meat had been examined by the inspector and the cause of death was influenza so was ordered to be destroyed. The defendant claimed that a butcher named Potts of Hadley End had bought the meat to his house at midnight and called him to see it. He agreed to give Potts £9 for the carcass if he got a market for it. Potts said that the beast had been ill for several days and he had given it gruel and gin but as it did not get better he killed it. The defendant had given Potts £5 10s for the carcass. The Bench gave John Ashmore a two months sentence with hard labour.[13] In 1885 Alfred Bird of the Bell and Cuckoo, Hadley End, was summoned for sending the carcasses of two cows to market for sale as human food, which were diseased and unfit for human consumption. He was sentenced to three months imprisonment.[14]

Poaching

At Elford Petty Sessions on 26 May 1881 James B. Smith, butcher, William and Abraham Birch, labourers and George Fearns, bricklayer, were charged with attempting to catch fish in a tributary on the Trent. It was an offence to take fresh water fish between 15 March and 15 June in each year, it being the close season. William Boston, an under farmer at Yoxall Woodhouses, said that he saw the four defendants a little distance from the Trent and another man by the side of the water. One of them had a long rod which he kept lobbing in and out of the water, evidently trying to catch fish. He watched them for a considerable time, and when they saw him they ran away. They denied the charges and said they were gathering watercress. William Birch, who had a previous conviction was charged 5s and costs, the others 1s each and costs.[15]

In 1896 Thomas Wright, a labourer of Yoxall was summoned for trespassing in search of rabbits in Rough Park Wood at Yoxall. He was caught with a snare and rabbit on land over which Mr Robinson of the Smithfield Hotel, Burton, had shooting rights. There had been many complaints of poaching in the neighbourhood of Yoxall, and Thomas was fined 10s and 8s costs or 14 days imprisonment.[16]

Drunkenness, poaching and trespassing with the intention of poaching were amongst the most regular cases to come before the courts. Some would have poached as a way to feed a hungry family when their income was insufficient to supply their basic needs, others no doubt did it as a side line to their employment, selling on their catches.

Samuel Finney and Francis Birch

Samuel Finney had the dubious distinction of holding the maximum number of court appearances for any one person in Yoxall. The following are just a few of his cases:

In 1873 he was charged with doing wilful damage to a fence at Yoxall and ordered to pay a fine of 6d or go to goal for fourteen days. In 1875, described as a fish dealer of Yoxall, Samuel was fined 20s and costs, or one month imprisonment, for illegally taking a pike from a pond belonging to Major Arden of Yoxall.[17]

In 1879, under the heading 'Impudence and Felony' Samuel Finney, alias Wood, labourer of Yoxall was charged with stealing 14 lbs of parsnips and a steel potato fork, valued at 5s 9d, the property of Samuel Reeves, landlord of the Crown Inn. Mrs Reeves had seen the prisoner in the garden and informed her husband who went to search for him. Samuel had tried to conceal himself on a heap of manure, but the prosecutor saw his coat, and found the pockets filled with parsnips. Samuel threatened to stab the prosecutor, and took a knife from his pocket. The prosecutor got back into the house with the coat and

Samuel picked up a fork, saying he would keep it until his coat was returned. The fork was later found in the garden and Samuel found at Alrewas. The magistrates were of the opinion that the prisoner did not take the fork away with felonious intention, but had aggravated the offence by threatening to stab the prosecutor. He was sent to goal for two months for stealing the parsnips.[18]

The above case reveals some mystery regarding Samuel Finney. In 1861 a Samuel Wood, aged 9, was enumerated in the home of his parents, Thomas and Sarah, at Trent Bridge. His father was an agricultural labourer. In 1871 Samuel Wood was enumerated as a waggoner in the household of Thomas Green, a farmer of 150 acres at Yoxall but by 1881 Samuel had returned to Trent Bridge, the home of his parents and was enumerated with them, not as their son, but as a lodger, with the name Samuel Finney. Over three censuses Samuel Wood/Finney's year of birth varies from 1848 to 1855. In most of his court cases Samuel appears as Finney, which seems to be the name he used permanently from the 1890s, and the name the courts always used, though sometimes with the alias of Wood.

In January 1886 Samuel, again alias Wood, a labourer of Hadley End, who was then on remand, was charged with stealing a watch and chain, valued at 30s from Francis Birch, a labourer, of Yoxall. Both men had been in the Bell and Cuckoo at Hadley End, when Francis left to have his hair cut, leaving his waistcoat behind. In his absence Samuel stole his watch and chain and sold it to Charles Mills, a farmer of Hadley End. With his previous convictions mentioned in court, he was sentenced to three months imprisonment with hard labour.[19]

Undeterred from a life of crime, Samuel was in July of the same year back in court with Francis Birch. It seems an unlikely friendship had developed between the two as they had been summoned by the conservators of the Trent Fishing Boards for trying to take fish from the Trent by means of a snare. It was taken into consideration that there was a 'severe' list of convictions against both defendants, and Francis was fined 10s and Samuel, who clearly had the bulk of the convictions was fined 40s, and they were each charged 9s 6d costs.[20] The pair continued poaching together and later in 1886 were back in Burton Court and in 1887 were tried at Rugeley. In both cases the sentences were fines or in default imprisonment.

In June 1889 Samuel was charged with again stealing from Francis Birch. This time it was a single-barrel gun valued at 5s.[21] He was remanded and taken to temporary confinement at Derby goal, where he wrote to Francis asking him not to press charges. He subsequently admitted his guilt and was sentenced to two months hard labour.[22]

Again the hard labour did nothing to show Samuel the error of his ways, or deter him from risking a repetition of the sentence. In 1891 Samuel was enumerated as a lodger and general labourer in the household of Thomas

Wardle of Hadley End. By 1892 he was sharing lodgings with Francis Birch, when he was charged with stealing, at different dates a table knife and fork and a pair of scissors, the property of Alfred Raworth, proprietor of the Bell and Cuckoo. Mrs Raworth mentioned the loss of the items to Francis and he returned the property to her. When arrested Samuel admitted his guilt and was sentenced to a month's hard labour.[23]

Samuel's cases also included drunken and riotous behaviour and in June 1893 he married Agnes Upton, also of Hadley End, at St Francis Chapel. Agnes was the daughter of James Upton, a coal higgler. A thick black line is drawn across the sections where Samuel's father's name and occupation should have been entered. In July of that year he was charged with embezzling 6s from his employer, Alfred Rayworth of the Bell and Cuckoo. He had sent Samuel with the 6s to fetch grain which Samuel got from the brewers but did not pay for. He sent his wife with the grain and later admitted he got drunk with the money. He was remanded for a week.[24] Later that month he was convicted to 14 days hard labour. He had 42 previous convictions.[25] Later that year Francis Birch, died in the prison hospital at Stafford prison. He was 35 years old and had been admitted to the prison in November on a charge of poaching and had undergone half of his sentence of a month's hard labour when he was taken ill with influenza.[26]

In 1899, Samuel Finney's name appeared under the heading 'A Worthless Felon'. This time he was charged with being drunk and riotous in Yoxall. Police constable Moyle, who had taken him to the police station, stated in court that Samuel had only just come out of goal for neglecting to support his wife, who was in Lichfield Union workhouse. As he had already been convicted 47 times he was now fined 10s and 7s 6d costs with the alternative of 14 days in goal.[27]

In 1900, Samuel was again charged with being drunk and disorderly in School Lane, Yoxall, and the case was published as 'His Jubilee "Drunk"' in celebration of his 50th conviction. He was fined 10s and 8s 6d costs with the alternative of 14 days imprisonment.[28] In June of that year his wife, Agnes died of epilepsy at the age of 45 in the Union Workhouse. Samuel's criminal career continued and in July 1901 he made his 51st appearance in court and was charged with being drunk and disorderly in Main Street. He was fined 5s with 8s 6d costs or seven days.[29] He had entered the 20th century with a record of more offences than any other Victorian resident of Yoxall.

William Brannon: Father and Son

In 1886 William Brannon was summoned for being drunk at Hadley End and fined 5s and 9s 6d costs.[30] In 1895 he was again at Burton Police Court for damaging a fence at Yoxall, the property of Lord Burton. Police constable Moyle gave evidence that there had been much damage done to fences in the neighbourhood of Yoxall, about which farmers complained bitterly. He had seen William pulling sticks out of a fence at Yoxall, which he had said he was going to take home for firewood. He was fined 5s and costs or 14 days imprisonment.[31] The following year he was charged with stealing a shovel of the value of 1s 6d belonging to John Sabin, a farmer of Hadley End and was sent to goal for 7 days.[32]

William's son was soon to be in trouble himself. An entry in a school managers' book in September 1897 records that William Brannon was a subject for discussion at a meeting of the school managers. He had repeatedly been complained of for truancy and pilfering, and the previous month he and Arthur Pott had taken a younger boy with them. That day a garden was robbed, which the boys had previously been seen to rob. The managers resolved to write to the Department for consent to expel the boys.[33] The fact that he was sent to a truant school is evidenced by his court case in 1898 for breaking into the house of Edward Hodgkiss and stealing an egg. He asked to be not sent back to the truants school, but to go to the reformatory. The Bench ordered that he be detained in an industrial school until he was 16 years old, he was 11 at the time.[34]

Another Young Offender

At the age of ten John Prince was in custody for stealing bacon. He was found amongst straw in an outbuilding on Dr Armson's premises, and it was afterwards ascertained that he had stolen and eaten 1 ½ lbs of bacon from the bacon room. It was stated in court that John had no father and his mother was living in Cheshire and paying 3s a week to John's uncle for keeping him. The uncle was Dr Armson's coachman, and John was constantly hanging about the doctor's premises instead of going to school. There had been several cases of burglary in Yoxall, but he had not been prosecuted on account of his youth. In one case he had found the wine and was so tipsy he could not get away. At the time the case was heard he was suffering from scalding feet and being attended by Dr Belcher. He was remanded for a week.[35] The case continued the following week at Burton Police Court by which time his feet had improved and it was thought that he had not been scalded but that he had been affected by an irritant in the straw. His mother, a widow, appeared and informed the Magistrate of the efforts she had made to have him brought up honestly and properly, by entrusting him to the care of the parish authorities at Yoxall, but she claimed they had declined to do anything, even though she offered to pay 3s per week towards his maintenance. He was sent to the workhouse for 7 days, during which time efforts were to be made to get him to an Industrial School.[36]

A Case of Fraud

In 1871 George Dean, a shoemaker, was reported under the headline 'A Rate Collector Committed for Fraud'. He was charged with fraudulently obtaining 4s from John Foster, a farmer of Hadley End. He had been an assistant overseer for the parish of Yoxall, in the Lichfield Union since 1863 but had been suspended by the vestry in 1870 'in consequence of many complaints from ratepayers as to his conduct'. A rate book in dispute had been in George's possession but he would not produce it in court, but offered to return the overcharge, which was not considered a satisfactory way of settling the matter. He was committed to the Quarter Sessions for trial, and bail was accepted. At Staffordshire Sessions he was found not guilty, but the assistant chairman expressed astonishment at his mode of transacting business and at the fact there was no satisfactory check on the collector.[37]

Theft

In 1863 Ann Lester was committed to Stafford prison for one month for stealing one peck of potatoes from a field. The severity of the sentence was due to her having been previously convicted of felony.[38]

Richard Baker, a seventeen year old fruit hawker of Hadley End was charged with stealing a shawl. Hannah Smalley had missed her shawl and the prisoner, who lived at the adjoining house, was arrested at Woodmill. He at first denied the charge, but on the way to the lock up admitted he had stolen it and sold it in Newborough for 2s on the same day. Sarah Hodgkinson, wife of a labourer at Newborough, remembered the prisoner calling at her home at the end of August. He had a bag with him and was collecting rags, bones and old boots. He pulled the shawl from the bag saying he had come from Birmingham, and that his mother was dead and he wanted to sell several articles of her clothing. After asking her for a higher price he accepted the 2s for the shawl. Richard said he was sorry he had committed the theft, but he had no money to pay for his lodgings or get anything to eat. He was cautioned as to his future conduct and sentenced to one month's imprisonment with hard labour.[39]

Thomas Brandon, alias Shaw, a general dealer of Yoxall, was charged with stealing an iron cooking pot, of the value of 2s, the property of George Upton of Woodhouses. It was reported as missing from the coal house and constable Moyle, stationed at Yoxall, discovered it on the premises of Mrs Simpson of Hadley End, who stated that she had bought it off the prisoner. Thomas said he stole it because he was 'hard up' and could get no work and was nearly starving with hunger. He was sentenced to 14 days imprisonment.[40]

Misconduct and Theft from Employers

Stealing from employers was not uncommon. In 1867 Catherine Ratcliffe was charged with stealing from her master Amos Arlblaster, of High Hall Hill, two bottles of wine, a cheese and a half, numerous articles of clothing and a pencil case. An adjournment was requested and bail allowed as Catherine intended to be married, the banns having been published at St Peter's.[41] The following week she pleaded guilty. She had been employed at High Hall Hill as a housekeeper dairy maid for nearly four years and had previously conducted herself as an honest and industrious servant. It was stated during the hearing she had transferred £130 invested in her bank account to avoid it being forfeited by the Crown. She was sentenced to a month in prison.[42]

In 1869 John Birch a 'servant-in-husbandry' to John Moore of Yoxall was charged by his master with misconduct and neglect of his work. He did not deny the charge and was discharged from his service and ordered to pay 20s as compensation and 10s 6d costs out of his wages.[43]

In 1869 Emma Heathcote, a married woman of Yoxall was charged with stealing raisins, soap, soda and matches from her employer George Forman, a grocer of Yoxall, who was also the employer of her son, an errand boy. Emma had placed the articles in a basket and given them to her son. The court discharged the son who she had made party to her theft, as she had 'been teaching him to do that from which she should have protected him'. The magistrates would have sent her to prison for three months, but as she had many recommendations in her favour she was sent for one month.[44]

Also in 1869 Mary Windley, described as a young girl, was charged with stealing a gold diamond ring of the value of £5 from her master, Henry Green of Yoxall. She was a daily servant at his home and had taken it from a dresser and after at first denying the charge, fetched it from the garden. The stones were missing and she claimed she had bitten them out and swallowed them, and later, that she had thrown them away on her way home. The prosecutor wished to withdraw the charge but the magistrates remanded her for a week.[45] The following week the court heard evidence of her previous good character and that of her family. Her mother was a widow and had struggled to provide sufficient maintenance for herself and Mary. In her defence it was requested that the case should be taken under the Juvenile Offenders' Act. She was sentenced to 21 days imprisonment.

The Chimney Sweeps Act

Henry Johnson, a chimney sweep of Yoxall, was charged with permitting a boy under age to climb a chimney for the purpose of sweeping it, which was in breach of the Chimney Sweeps Act. The case was proved by Frederick Butcher, coachman to the Rev. W. Oliver of Needwood vicarage. Fined 20s and 15s 6d or one month in prison.[46] In August Henry was again convicted of knowingly allowing a person under 21 years to climb a chimney for the purpose of sweeping it. The offence took place in Alrewas. He was fined 20s and costs and it was noted in court that this was the second offence proved against him.[47]

Paternity Summons

In 1866 James Lindsay of Hoar Cross, aged 'about' eighteen was charged with being the father of Emma Haddock's illegitimate child, and ordered to pay 1s 6d per week towards her maintenance.[48] In 1890 George Boston, a farm labourer of Yoxall Woodhouses was summoned to show cause why he should not contribute to the support of his illegitimate child of Elizabeth Cawser, a single woman of Barton, of which he was alleged to be the father. The evidence necessary to establish the case was given and an order made for the payment of 2s 6d per week, and costs of £1 5s.[49]

Cases Dismissed

In the case of 'A Women's Quarrel at Yoxall' Hannah Smalley was charged with assaulting Ann Johnson at Hadley End. The women were related and their husbands were chimney sweepers. Ann was out acorn picking when a quarrel started between them. The quarrel led to a fight and in the struggle they tore one another's clothes and were said to have fiercely 'Ingged'. Hannah produced in court a handful of hair, sufficient to make a chignon with, which she said Ann had pulled out of her head. The case was dismissed and the women each ordered to pay 3s 3d costs.[50]

In the trial of the attempted suicide of 83 year old William Woodings, the Bench heard that he had attempted jumping into a pit of water at Hadley End. He appeared to have taken to heart the accusation of his master, Mr Brown, that he had stolen apricots and plums. He assured the Bench that the accusation was false. He was reprimanded and discharged and constable Steele was directed to take him home.[51]

William Radford of Yoxall was summoned to show cause why he should not be bound over to keep the peace towards Ann Millington, who it was alleged, he had threatened to kill and to 'kick into a warm but necessarily nameless region'. He showed that Ann had annoyed him that day and that no threats were used and the Bench dismissed the summons.[52]

Henry Mosedale was charged with assaulting William Taswell. The men were employed by Mr. Riddell, farmer of Woodlane, and on the day in question had quarrelled, which resulted in blows being struck with hoes. Case dismissed.[53]

James Upton, carrier of Yoxall was brought into custody charged with attempting to commit suicide there. The magistrate's clerk explained that he had been detained for a week in a Derbyshire prison on the order of the magistrates. He was discharged, the Chairman cautioning him as to his future conduct, hoping he would abstain from drinking in future.[54]

In 1888 Oswald Henry, a baker of Kings Bromley, was charged with assaulting Jane Hinsley, a single woman who kept the tolls at Yoxall, through which he was in the habit of passing. He had asked her to distribute some bills recommending herb syrups but she told him he could do it himself. She claimed that he had endeavoured to indecently assault her. Constable Moyle said he had seen finger marks on her arm, but he had known the accused for several years but never heard anything against his character, and the vicar also spoke of his good character. Under cross examination Jane admitted she had an illegitimate child and the Bench dismissed the case.[55] Typical of the times, Jane's moral character appears to have been as much on trial as the man accused of her assault, and at least a contributory factor in the outcome.

Yoxall Police

In the 18th and 19th centuries, before the creation of a national police force, rural communities formed mutual subscription societies to prosecute criminals. These associations were created out of resolutions passed at parish vestry meetings to prosecute felons out of the public purse. An early 19th century account book for the tape factory at Morrey includes payments to Yoxall Society for the Prosecution of Felons.[56]

In 1842 the foundations of Staffordshire Police were laid and by 1851 Matthew Hook was a police constable in Yoxall. In every census year there was one police constable but in 1871 there were two. This may have been due to the influx of workers living in the area while working on the building of the new Hoar Cross Hall, adding to the pressure of maintaining law and order.

Churchyard Cottage was first used as a police house during the 1880s. In 1911 the 'Police Station', not named as Churchyard Cottage, appeared in the census at 'King Street'. Sometime after that it was moved to Main Street. The house still bears the name of 'Police House' and a previous resident said that those arrested were kept there prior to being taken to Burton cells. A further lock up at the end of the alms houses, now one house known as 'Warwick Cottage', is in the living memory of a few Yoxall residents. This may have been used instead of the police house, to give the resident policeman and his family some peace from reluctant prisoners and riotous drunkards. The house in Main Street remained the police house until a new one was built in Sudbury Road after the second World War.

Chapter 15

Drunkenness, Temperance and the Band of Hope

The Beerhouse

During the 1820s and 1830s the government was keen to promote beer drinking instead of spirits. Gin was cheap as it was not taxed and had become the drink of the working class and had led to the rise of the Temperance Society, which campaigned for the closure of 'gin shops'. Beer, the former drink of the working man, was taxed and for many people was not affordable, despite the fact it was considered, even by the Temperance Movement, to be healthy and nutritious and safer than water, which was untreated and dangerous to drink. Children were often given 'small beer' which had a lower alcohol content. The Beer Act of 1830 abolished the tax on beer and extended the opening hours of licensed public houses, taverns and alehouses, from 15 to 18 hours a day. It also introduced the beerhouse, which could only sell beer and cider, which some houses bought from brewers, but anyone could brew and sell beer for a fee of 2 guineas payable to the local excise officer. Some beerhouses offered food and a few offered lodgings, though most were just one room in the home of the licensee.

Listed in a directory of 1834 are the names of nine people selling alcohol in Yoxall and the hamlets. 'Mary Brown, victualler, Cup' and 'Thomas Stubbs, victualler, Crown' are the only two people whose premises were named. Of the other seven listed as 'beerhouse', two were in Hadley End and one at Longcroft.[1] Both the Crown and Cup, were inns and therefore offered temporary accommodation to travellers as well as alcohol. The Wine and Beerhouse Act of 1869 reintroduced stricter controls on the sale of alcohol and required a licence for the premises from the local magistrates, who now had some control over licensing hours. Licensees were expected to be on the premises and objections to the licence could be made by the magistrates on grounds such as allowing drunkenness, violent or quarrelsome behaviour or serving intoxicating liquor to a drunken person. With licensing of the beerhouses bringing them under control of the local justices, many closed, were purchased by breweries, or became fully licensed public houses. Despite these measures intoxication continued to be a huge problem in Victorian England and Yoxall had its share of drunkards whose cases were heard at court and reported in the *Burton Chronicle*.

Elizabeth Astle of The Hanging Gate

The population census of 1871 enumerated Thomas Astle at Woodhouses, as a 40 year old innkeeper. In other censuses Thomas was enumerated as, in one instance, a farmer, and in others as a labourer. In the baptism entries of his first four children he appears as a labourer and the last two entries, in 1865 and 1867, as a publican. Clearly he had a dual occupation, at least between 1865 and 1871, in which he worked as a labourer, (with a few of his own cattle), although it is likely that in his absence from the premises his wife Elizabeth did the work of the beerhouse. Many editions of the *Burton Chronicle* reveal the life and unsavoury character of Thomas Astle, as he and especially Elizabeth's names regularly featured in the hearings of the Burton Police Court.

In 1866 William Cooper appeared in court for refusing to leave 'Astle's beerhouse'. The case was dismissed and no further disturbances or problems arising from the customers of the house have been discovered among the court cases published.[2]

The year 1868 seems to be Thomas's first brush with the law, when he appeared in court on the charge of a 'Highway Offence'. His four cows had strayed on the highway at Yoxall and he was fined 5s plus 9s 6d costs. The closing comment: 'Heavy penalty - defendant had been repeatedly cautioned'.[3]

In 1870 Thomas appeared in court on a far more serious charge which was reported as a 'Brutal Assault Upon a Wife'. The lengthy article states he was of the 'Gate' beerhouse. In his defence he claimed that his wife had run him into debt to the amount of £110, without his knowledge. Whether this was true is not stated, but Dr Webb, speaking in defence of Thomas, despite having seen his wife's injuries, which, according to the evidence given, were clearly not the result of a sudden loss of temper, said that he had 'borne an excellent character until lately: he was highly esteemed in his service, and lived for many years with Mr Shaw, farmer, Fradley: his parents were most respectable'. He also stated that he knew little of his wife, except that she was an 'intemperate person'. He had seen her in an intoxicated state several times. Thomas had said that he was anxious to get a separation order, and the Magistrates said they would gladly forward an application. The Chairman of the Magistrates remarked that he had most likely gone astray since keeping a beerhouse, where drink was always close at hand. In sentencing he was declared guilty of 'the most deliberate, tyrannous, and atrocious cruelty'. However, he got off with six weeks in a House of Correction, instead of the six months imprisonment they would have inflicted, but for his previous good character.[4] Had the separation of the couple gone ahead it is likely that Elizabeth may not have been the drunkard she became, as later evidence suggests.

The following year Thomas was fined 2s 6d plus costs, or 7 days imprisonment for allowing his ass to stray 'on the highway leading from Yoxall to Barton'. It was stated that he was formerly of the Hanging Gate Beerhouse, Yoxall Woodhouses. He had at some time between 1868 and this case, appeared on another 'Highway Offence' as it was noted in court that he had twice previously been convicted of a similar offence, also mentioned was his imprisonment for the brutal attack on his wife.[5]

In August of the same year began a long series of court cases concerning Elizabeth's drunkenness. On this occasion she was at Barton when charged.

She did not appear in court and was fined 5s and 10s 6d costs, or fourteen days imprisonment.[6] Undeterred, in November she was charged with being drunk at Branstone. Her name erroneously appeared as 'Ann', but it clearly was Elizabeth, as she was stated as being the wife of Thomas Astle, beerhouse keeper of Yoxall Woodhouses. If Thomas had not resided at the beerhouse in May, the month of his court case, it seemed he had soon returned. The evidence claimed that she was in a 'beastly state of drunkenness, having been found lying in the road'. She was placed on a load of grains in her donkey cart and driven to a barn in Branstone where she was detained until she became sober enough to be sent home. Her sentence was the same as in her first offence.[7]

In 1872 Elizabeth's drinking landed her in court in February, where she was discovered in Russell Street, Burton,[8] in March at Branston Road,[9] and October in New Street, Burton. The latter case appeared under the heading 'An Incorrigible Drunkard'.[10] In the April of that year her husband had again been charged, this time, with cruelty to an ass. He did not appear and was sentenced 40s and 9s 6d costs or fourteen days.[11] Cases of cruelty to horses were all too common, although many were probably due to the owner needing to work them and being unable either to fund veterinary treatment or to give them the time off to recover. Horses 'being worked in an unfit state', was a term often used by the courts, and was applied to a later case, in 1881, for which Thomas was again convicted.[12] It seems unlikely that Thomas would consider the welfare of his animals, given his carelessness regarding his cattle, (which had continued to stray onto the highway), and his brutal treatment of his wife.

Elizabeth continued to be charged with drunkenness in various places, including Burton, Barton, and on the Burton and Lichfield turnpike road. By 1881 she had on four occasions been charged 40s plus costs. Often she was in charge of a donkey and cart, and at least twice was asleep on the pile of grain in the cart, and on another occasion was discovered under a hedge. The headings varied: 'Drunk in a cart'; 'A familiar face at Court'; 'The Yoxall Drunkard again' and 'Out of Goal and in the Lock-up'. On this latter occasion she had begged for mercy but been fined 10s and 9s 4d costs, or fourteen days imprisonment.[13]

In 1881 Thomas was enumerated as a farmer of 10 acres and labourer, possibly the land had been bought with the profits from the beerhouse, as it was not mentioned in any cases after 1872. With the couple were two of their sons, Edwin a 20 year old farm servant, and James, aged 14 who assisted at home.

In 1882 Thomas was again accused of a brutal assault on his wife. In this instance Thomas's occupation was stated as a labourer. The attack included hitting her repeatedly with the teeth end of a hay rake, an act witnessed by a child. She was hospitalised on the day of the attack, 13th August, and was not released until 17th October. Her injuries included a broken leg. The magistrates considered that Thomas had had 'considerable provocation' and 'imposed a lighter term of imprisonment than they otherwise would have done'. The sentence was two months hard labour and costs of £2 8s or to go to prison for an additional month.[14]

In 1883 Elizabeth was charged with being drunk at School Green. Her summonses for drunkenness in Yoxall were infrequent, as she generally chose neighbouring villages or Burton. The report headed this case as 'Her Twenty-first Appearance'. She was sent to prison for seven days, without the option of paying a fine.[15] In 1885 Elizabeth appeared at the Lichfield Police Court charged with being drunk at Gallows Wharf near Lichfield. Sentenced to 11s 6d including cost, or seven days imprisonment. She went to prison.[16]

By 1891 Thomas and Elizabeth appear to have separated as Thomas was enumerated in one household with Ann Ward, a married 54 year old servant who was, according to the census, his housekeeper. This may have been the case, but at the time of Thomas's last arrest for attacking Elizabeth in 1882, she had accused him of being 'on too intimate terms with another woman'. Elizabeth occupied the neighbouring household, and was, at least on census night, the sole occupant, 'living on her own means'. They may have separated following her 1885 term of imprisonment as she no longer appeared on charges of drunkenness, and seems to have lived a more sober, and hopefully, a happier life.

Other Drunkards

Elizabeth Astle is exceptional in the number of times she was charged for alcohol abuse. She was a non-violent drunk who appears to have been attempting to drown her sorrows, and not without reason. The following are a few of the Yoxall cases of drunkenness and its consequences:

In 1868 Susannah Hallam of Yoxall was charged with being drunk in Station Street, Burton. She was reprimanded and discharged.[17]

In 1870 George Yeomans pleaded guilty to being drunk at Yoxall when in charge of a horse and cart drawing lime from Barton Station to the new Hall (which was in the process of being built) at Hoar Cross. He was so intoxicated that he narrowly escaped being run over. Sergeant Myatt took the horse and cart home and George's wife sobered him by giving him a liberal supply of tea. Fined 5s and costs.[18]

In 1873 Robert Deakin, a blacksmith of Yoxall was charged with being drunk and refusing to leave the Crown and the Cup when requested to do so by the respective landladies. He pleaded guilty but remarked that he was so drunk at the time that he did not know he was away from his own house. Fined 10s and costs.[19]

In 1878 the following case was reported as 'A Queer Resting Place'. John Ashmore, butcher of Morrey, was charged with being drunk while in charge of a horse and cart in Draycott. He was lying on the top of a dead horse which he was taking from Morrey to the kennels. He was fined 20s and 10s costs, or a month in prison.[20] In 1894 another case of being 'Drunk While in Charge of a Horse and Trap' was that of Edmund Pott, farmer of Yoxall. Several people had made complaints, and police constable Moyle followed him to his house and saw him get out of the trap and stagger about the place. He had previously cautioned him. Fined 5s and 8s costs.[21]

Emma Dukes, described at Elford Petty Sessions in 1879 as 'a showily attired young woman, of Yoxall, who conducted herself in a most discourteous manner to the Bench' was charged with being drunk and 'making use of bad language' at Yoxall. She was fined 20s and costs and said she would rather accept imprisonment. Her mother arranged to pay the fine.[22]

In 1894 James Berrisford Smith of Yoxall was summoned for being drunk and refusing to quit the Golden Cup Inn, kept by Ellis Wakelin. The evidence of the landlord and his wife stated that James came into the house the worse for liquor, and trying to provoke a fight with Ellis. He was ordered out, but refused to go. Ellis then went to find a police officer, but he was away at Stafford at the time. While he was absent James abused his wife, and refused to leave when requested. Two men who were in the house at the time, confirmed the statement. For the defendant, Mr. Capes said his instructions were that there had been a dispute between the two parties two or three months ago, and on James going to the Golden Cup some words again arose between them. James was fined 10s and 16s costs.[23]

Catherine Lewis, a married woman of Hadley End, was charged in 1895 with being drunk and disorderly at Yoxall. Police constable Moyle found the defendant drunk in Main Street. She was insulting the people as they were going to church. It took him an hour to get her from Yoxall to Hadley End. She had previously broken a window and assaulted a tradesman. An old offender, she was fined 10s and 8s costs, with the alternative of fourteen days.[24] The following year under the heading 'Ructions at Yoxall' a further case was reported. Catherine, was charged with being drunk and disorderly in the village. She was also charged with refusing to quit the Needwood Oak Inn at Barton and with assaulting the landlord and his wife. Catherine was subsequently locked up. She was fined 2s 6d and costs in each case, with the alternative of 7 days, the terms to run consecutively.[25]

In 1895 William Neild, a labourer of Yoxall, was described as 'A Dangerous Customer' in the report of his case. He was charged with being drunk and disorderly and assaulting police constable Moyle, while in the execution of his duty at Yoxall. The constable had been called to a disturbance in School Lane where he found William very drunk and using bad language. He refused to leave and wanted to fight and assaulted Moyle. On being told he would be brought to Burton, he promised to go home quietly, and was allowed to do so. He had a long record of previous convictions and was fined 10s and costs or 14 days and in addition sentenced to 14 days imprisonment without the option of a fine for the assault on the constable. There was a further charge against him of assaulting Sarah Birch, but on the case being called the prosecution failed to appear, and he was discharged on this indictment.[26] In 1898, reported as 'A Double Indictment', he was charged with being disorderly in, and refusing to quit, the licensed house of Samuel Lunn (the Bell and Cuckoo, Hadley End), when requested to do so. He was further charged with assaulting Hannah Lunn on the same date, but due to discrepancies as to the extent of the assault the charge was dropped and he was found guilt of disorderly conduct and fined 10s and 10s costs, or 14 days imprisonment. On hearing the alternative he said: Good day, Mrs. Lunn: 'Good day all. I'll go and do it".[27]

In 1897 Abraham Birch a labourer of Yoxall, was charged with being disorderly in, and refusing to leave, the licensed premises of Ellis Wakelin (The Golden Cup) when requested to do so. Mr. G. A. Capes prosecuted on behalf of the Burton Licensed Victuallers' Association. The landlord stated that Abraham entered his house and commenced to be abusive and became very violent. During the past 3 or 4 months he had repeatedly visited the house with the intention of causing a disturbance. He was fined 20s and 14s 6d costs, with the alternative of 14 days.[28]

In 1897 Arthur Potts a labourer of Yoxall and 'An Old Offender', was charged with being drunk and disorderly and fined 10s and 8s costs, with the alternative of 14 days.[29]

Offences under the Licensing Act

In 1875 William Claridge, landlord of the Cup Inn was summoned for permitting drunkenness in his house. After hearing the evidence, which was very conflicting, the Bench imposed a nominal penalty of 1s and costs of £1 6d.[30]

Thomas Cooper, landlord of the Crown Inn was summoned in 1880 for permitting drunkenness in his house. He said that the drink was in connection with an auction, and he was not present when it was served. He was ordered to pay costs. John Harden, labourer, Charles Potts, cooper, William Leedham, saddler and Charles Knight, coal dealer, all of Yoxall, were summoned for being drunk there on that occasion, and were each fined 2s 6d and costs.[31]

In 1891 a notice of objection to the renewal of license to James Berrisford Smith of the Shoulder of Mutton was served for offences under the Licensing Act.[32] James had many times been in court for fights, quarrels and drunkenness.

In 1899 William Fearn, landlord of the Foresters Arms, Woodlane, was summoned under the Food and Drugs Act on a charge of selling whisky diluted with water, to the extent of 16% beyond the statutory limit. He stated that he had been in the business for 20 years and had never had a complaint about his whisky before, but this particular whisky had been bought from a fresh source. Previously he had bought his whisky at proof and reduced it seventeen degrees. In this case the vendor had reduced the whisky, but that was unknown to him and the usual amount of water was added. The Bench did not consider the case to be serious but were obliged to inflict a small fine, which was 10s and £1 15s 6d costs.[33]

Plight of Wives and Children

The problems of drunken and riotous behaviour in Yoxall sometimes had extremely serious consequences. Families often had enough of a struggle to get by without what money there was coming in being spent on drink, plus the fines incurred or loss of employment due to imprisonment. The following is an example of the extreme hardship suffered by one family due to the wage earner prioritising on his own comforts above those of his wife and children:

A case was published with the headline 'Shocking Neglect of Children at Yoxall' and a sub-heading 'Starved, Ragged and Covered with Vermin'. Edward Billings, a labourer, was summoned by an inspector of the National Society for the Prevention of Cruelty to Children in 1895 for neglecting his children; Mary Susannah aged 11, John Edward, 10, and Benjamin, 6. Edward was employed by Arthur Beard, a farmer and earned 15s a week, which the court considered not a lot to keep a wife and family, but enough to keep them from want. Edward spent most of the money on drink and left his wife and family to get what they could from neighbours. An inspector who accompanied police constable Moyle to the Billings's home gave evidence that the children were 'a mass of rags and bites' and 'not in a fit state to mix with other children at school'. Miss Lucas, the head mistress said she had repeatedly fed the children, and the rector, having become aware of the situation had given orders for them to be sent to the rectory for food when they were without. Edward was sent to prison for a month's hard labour.[34]

Violence could be a threat to the wife or children of a man over fond of drinking and drunken companions:

In 1868 Thomas Hallam, a rick thatcher of Yoxall was charged with assaulting his wife who was pregnant. He had come home intoxicated and because his wife had refused to sleep with one of his drunken companions he viciously attacked her. When apprehended he showed no remorse but said he would be the death of her and would not mind hanging for it. He had been imprisoned for a month in 1862 for a similar offence, when his wife had suffered a miscarriage due to his brutal treatment. He was sent to prison for three months hard labour.[35]

Yoxall's Temperance Society and Band of Hope

The Temperance Society was formed around the 1820s, and although it did not advocate total abstinence, a more extreme form of temperance, teetotalism, was formed in the 1830s. The Band of Hope was formed in Leeds in 1847 with the aim of teaching children the importance of sobriety and teetotalism. Members had to take the pledge to abstain from all alcohol except medicine.

The first Yoxall Temperance Society was the Woodhouses Band of Hope and Temperance Society which formed in 1874. In 1878 they celebrated their fourth anniversary, parading through the village with lodges from Barton and Handsacre, and the Burton brass band, followed by a tea provided by the chapel for upwards of 200 people. In the evening the Band of Hope sang songs on the theme of abstinence, including 'We shall never be drunkards', 'The child's pleading' and 'Sign the pledge for mother's sake'. The latter 'well rendered' by Mr Wright.[36]

In 1880 a Church of England Temperance Society was formed in Yoxall. At their fete that year a large flag was carried at the head of the procession, the children mostly had small flags of various colours. This was followed by tea for 105 children in the boys' school, and play on the adjoining field. A speaker at the occasion spoke in support of total abstinence, saying that a total abstainer could do more for the Temperance cause than a partial abstainer.[37] It is likely that the two Temperance societies joined into one, which became known as the Yoxall Temperance Society. The following year a meeting was held in the girls' school room and about 60 people attended. An address was given by the Rev. Grier, vicar of Rugeley, regarding the results of intemperance, in which he argued that the only way to get rid of the results was the general disuse of alcohol, and that it was not necessary to 'health, strength, warmth, wit, intellect, happiness, convalescence, or life … its only use was for polishing mahogany and poisoning vermin'. The chairman, the curate Rev. Ding asked all present to do what they could to establish the proposed coffee room.[38] It was reported in 1883 that interest in temperance was not being lost as the gathering at the Yoxall Temperance Fete that year was one of the most successful they had held.[39]

In 1885 at the Yoxall Temperance Society Fete held in connection with the Band of Hope a new banner was presented by Mrs Bloore. It was 'large and handsome and made of blue bunting with the designs in crimson and gold on both sides'.[40] The school closed for the day on 15 June 1885 'on account of the children belonging to the Band of Hope going to Hagley Park (Entertainment)', and on 19 June 1891 'Attendance very low on Tuesday morning due to the Band of Hope picnic'.[41] In November of that year Mr Small, the retiring police constable for the district was presented with a Bible at a social gathering of the Yoxall Gospel Temperance Society for service to the society.[42]

In 1886 and 1887 the Yoxall Band of Hope annual fetes were held but in 1888 a letter to the editor of the *Burton Chronicle* stated that Yoxall Temperance

Society, established under the presidency of Rev. Lowe, had been 'inactive through declining years' and urged 'lovers of the cause in the vicinity to join'.[43]

The Band of Hope continued in Yoxall and in 1889 the children were reported to have given an excellent performance in an evening entertainment and praise was given to Mrs Rowles, (pianist), Miss Wright, Mr H. Wright, and Mr F. Lester for the pains they had taken in training the youngsters. The programme included handbell-ringing, musical drill, songs and recitations.[44] In June of that year the Band of Hope celebrated its 16th anniversary and prizes were given to the children consisting of 'good serviceable wearing apparel'.[45]

At a meeting in December 1893 Rev. Johnstone, whose appointment to the incumbency in Yoxall was reported in July of that year, explained that a society was formed in the parish in 1880 and 'for some unknown reason there did not seem to have been any meetings for some time', but he now hoped to restart the meetings in the parish. He was glad to find that a lady in the parish had continued the meetings of the Band of Hope since 1880.[46]

In 1896 the Band of Hope celebrated its 22nd anniversary when 140 members and friends assembled in Main Street and were conveyed in vehicles lent by Messrs. T. Leedham, H. Leedham, C. Perkins, G. Hall, D. Simmonds, F. Sutton, C. Bull, J. Moore, J.T. Norman, J. Hill, H. Wright, J. Sabin, J.B. Smith and D. Sharratt, to Alrewas Station to celebrate the occasion in Sutton Park. Arrangements were carried out by Mrs Wright assisted by Mr H. Wright. Subscribers included The Hon. Mrs Griffiths, Dr C.G. Armson, Mrs Sperry, and Mr J. Roobottom.[47] In 1899 a juvenile branch of the temperance society was started in the village, and in July the Misses Shipton invited members (about 70) to tea, Rev. A.A. Cory and a few friends joining them.[48]

In 1896 the People's Refreshment House Association was formed with the aim of enabling customers to get tea, coffee or light refreshments as easily as beer and spirits, and to present a respectable house of refreshment instead of a drinking bar. To encourage the landlord of public houses managed by the Association to sell non-intoxicants, there was no profit allowed on alcoholic drinks. Although these inns were few and far between the Meynell Ingram Arms at Hoar Cross was acquired by the Association in 1898.

It is not surprising that the Yoxall Temperance Movement and Band of Hope were enthusiastically supported in Yoxall, many people having seen at first hand the 'perils of drink'. The amount of cases that went to court would not be the whole story, as presumably many milder incidences received only a verbal warning from the local constable, but the amount of riotous behaviour and worse disturbing the peace no doubt led to the strong support given to its opposites of temperance and abstinence. The neglect of wives and children, seen here in the extreme, would to a lesser extent cause suffering and hunger to many families as men drank the money that should feed and clothe them.

Chapter 16

At Home and Abroad

Churchyard Cottage

In 1814 Jenny Hall sold Churchyard Cottage, inherited from her father, schoolmaster Thomas Hall, to James Coxon. With the cottage were 'two lettings in a certain pew the North side of the Parish Church of Yoxall aforesaid being the second pew behind the north door…'. The cottage was at that time in the occupation of Joseph Killingley who had married Catherine Coxon in 1781, probably the daughter of James Coxon, although no baptism has been found for her. Rhoda and Sarah Killingley, daughters of Joseph and Catherine, later held the property and the neighbouring cottage.

The properties later came into the possession of Ann Deakin, a carpenter's widow and sister to Rhoda and Sarah. In 1851 she was enumerated as a lodging house keeper whose household comprised daughter Millicent, an unmarried shoe binder, sister Mary Killingley, a deaf pauper, and lodgers John and William Brian, both single cordwainers, plus a cordwainer's apprentice and Henry Green, a 14 year old scholar. In her will of 1860, Ann bequeathed to her daughter her two cottages in Yoxall churchyard, occupied by herself and Sarah Killingley. Ann made the further provision that the house in which she lived would, after the death of her daughter, go to Edward Green provided he paid his sister Millicent Green twenty pounds. The house occupied by Sarah Killingly was to be sold, the proceeds to form part of the residue of her estate from which John Brian, who lodged with Ann, would receive ten pounds. However in the event that her daughter married and had children, the properties would go to them on the decease of their mother. In 1863 at the age 81 Ann Deakin died and in October of that year her daughter Millicent, at the age of 45 married John Brian. In 1868 John and Millicent took out a loan of £45 on the two properties, which led to them being mortgaged, also a £50 insurance policy on the life of Millicent.

A sketch shows the original elevation of Churchyard Cottage and the neighbouring cottage. Following the death of Ann the half timbered cottage was pulled down as unsightly and the land it occupied was added to the churchyard, with the exception of about 9 ft which was added to the end of Churchyard Cottage where John Brian erected a back kitchen with a shop over, extending the width of the house. The cost of building the shop was £35.

Along with the deeds of Churchyard Cottage were letters, mainly from Eliza Green. These tell of the difficulties faced by her and her husband in finding the money to pay the mortgage.

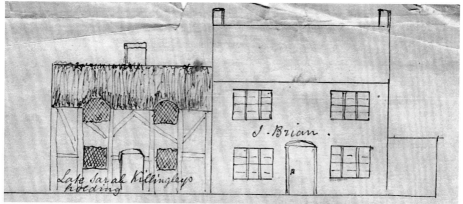

Churchyard Cottages prior to the demolition of Sarah Killingley's cottage. (Reproduced by permission of Sarah Orson).

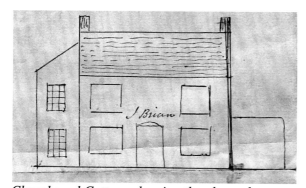

Churchyard Cottage showing the planned alterations to John Brian's cottage. (Reproduced by permission of Sarah Orson).

In 1880 Edward Green, who was to inherit Churchyard Cottage in the absence of heirs of Millicent was appointed agent to collect the rents from the properties. In 1882 Millicent died without issue and the following year a Phoenix Fire Office Policy insured the property for a maximum sum of £100, and named John Hunt Thursfield as mortgagee, Edward Green of Yoxall as mortgagor, and Isaac Small the occupier of the cottage 'situate at Churchyard or Reeve End'. Difficulties arose in keeping up the payments of the mortgage, rental arrears were the first problem and Edward's wife Eliza regularly sent letters from their home, initially in Woodhouses, to John Thursfield, asking for time or further loans and explaining the situations as they arose. A receipt signed by Edward Green for £10 received from Mr Thursfield had at the foot of the page, four pencilled loans on the property dating from July 1879 to the one receipted in January 1883, amounting to £80. In September 1884 an unsigned letter was written either by Edward or Eliza to Mr Thursfield asking for £5 for repairs which they needed to do before the County would take it. A previous letter had said that the County wanted it for a police house. Edward and Eliza had bills they could not pay, and wanted to give something on account until they could sell some farm stock, which they would do before the winter set in. They were now 'taking care' of Holly Hurst at Barton. The following day a letter was sent by Edward saying he was a gardener, now in charge of Holly Hurst. In June 1886 Eliza wrote to say that since the previous owner, Holly Hurst had been closed and her husband had done no permanent work so they had been unable to pay their half year rent. She wrote that they would not have been in 'such a fix if our cows had gone on alright but one is barren and the two Jerseys brought dead calves eight weeks before time …' If Edward did not get back to Holly Hurst the following year they would give up the land, but a few days later she wrote to say he had been taken back there. At the end of the month she wrote asking if the deeds of the cottage mentioned 'a walk from the front door into the main walk in the churchyard as there is a dispute by the Rector who wants to fence out the house and entirely stop the road out of the front and there has been a walk a yard wide for more than thirty years and can we legally take up the fence or prevent it being put down'.

In October 1893 Eliza wrote a letter from Stoney Ford, Yoxall to an unnamed recipient, regarding Churchyard Cottage's use as a police house. She felt there was little chance that the County, who rented it at £5 per annum, would give it up as it stood alone, 'so for that reason so much better for a Police Constable a Deputy comes twice a year to inspect it he was here on Friday last and gave orders for the PC to Whitewash paper & paint it throughout at the County's expense (inside) and he sent to ask us to repair the W.C. and put in a new parlour grate the one now is very old fashioned and the Brick work keeps giving way he would like it done before they begin the Whitewash'. She added 'the P.C. rents a garden in the Village at 16/- per year and we have for the last eight years found the Manure for it which we considered met him half way.' The house contained a small cell where the police officer could view a prisoner without leaving the property. Whether this feature was included with the repairs the County required before taking the cottage as the police house is uncertain.

By 1897 the couple were living at Park View, Osmaston, near Ashbourne, but still struggling with the mortgage and in February 1900 Eliza asked for a further £6 towards apprenticing their second son: 'You will be glad to hear the eldest one who you so kindly helped us with is now out of his time and is doing well so far the four children that we have out give satisfaction to their employers and make good servants which is a great comfort to us we are very anxious to give them a good start but with having other six children at home gives us little chance of saving and we shall be very grateful of your help'. On 6 December, she wrote asking for an additional loan of £20, saying there were six more payments on the cottage but they were trying to help their eldest son who had hired a bakehouse in Hanley to buy his own. They had lost a calf heifer worth £19 which would have covered the son's expenses. On 10 December she wrote saying they were going to take a small shop and do all the work themselves. They received the £20, confirmed by a letter of thanks dated 12 December.

The house remained occupied by the police into the 20th century. In 1901 Joseph Bennett, police constable was enumerated at 'The Churchyard, Yoxall'. The Greens never did complete the purchase of Churchyard Cottage and with the death of the mortgagee John Hunt Thursfield, and later his heirs, it became part of the Thursfield Trust and in 1947 was sold to Lichfield Diocesan Trust, who in turn sold it in 1960.

A Few Yoxall Immigrants

The censuses identify a few people in the parish as being born abroad, the majority of these were Irish, as they left the country of their birth in hopes of a better future, also two French governesses. However, a few came from beyond Europe and in 1851 Jane, the wife of agricultural labourer John Lester, was enumerated as born in Halifax, North America. In 1871 American born Elizabeth Hartley, a 73 year old, was an unmarried boarder in the household of 92 year old Ann Richardson at Woodhouses. Emma Jane, wife of curate John Julius Baker was enumerated in 1871, aged 26 and born in Western Australia.

In 1881 Ellen, the American wife of James Tweetland, was enumerated at the Cup and the same year Agnes, the wife of postman Daniel Sharratt was enumerated at Trent Bridge, aged 25 and born in East Indies. She was again enumerated in 1891, when her husband was a farmer at Trent Bridge. Also in 1891 enumerated as born overseas were Frederick Roe from India, a 14 year old farm servant and Australian Robert Sutcliffe Mort, both in the household of George Upton at Woodhouses. How many left Yoxall for foreign lands and how they fared is largely unknown but one exception is the Hand family, due to their connections with the Shiptons.

Hands Across the Water: The Joseph Hand Collection

In 1841 farmer Joseph Hand, his wife Sarah and their seven children, with ages ranging from 11 to 26 were enumerated at Linbrook Farm. According to the census Joseph was 59, his wife 50. By 1851 they had left and there the matter would have rested, but for a visit from a couple from America who had family connections. This led to a series of letters, during which it became apparent that there was an archive in the University of Illinois containing letters received by them from family and friends they had left behind. The 'Joseph Hand Collection Papers 1824-1906' was traced and copies of much of the archive regarding the correspondence obtained. The letters provide a rare female perspective of the harsh life of a local rural blacksmith's wife, a poor relation to the Shiptons of Bank House, Woodhouses.

With the exception of Joseph and Sarah's youngest, George, and the eldest, John, the others, Sarah, Joseph, Ann, Mary and Richard, were all baptised in Scropton, Derbyshire. Between October 1844 and February 1845 their entire farm stock, crops and household furniture at Linbrook was auctioned and the family set sail for America. Joseph's wife Sarah was born a Shipton, the families of Scropton and Woodhouses were related and Shiptons at Woodhouses held land in Scropton. The will of William Shipton of Woodhouses, gent, made in 1804 left bequests to nephews and nieces which included Shiptons, Joseph, John, Richard, Robert and Sarah, the minors amongst them to inherit on reaching the age of 21 years. Sarah may have been the future wife of Joseph Hand. The will of John Shipton of Woodhouses, farmer, in 1826 included a bequest of interest of money to his sister 'Sarah Hand wife of Joseph Hand'.

The 1851 census lists Richard Shipton, a farmer of 100 acres at Woodhouses, and in the same household Joseph Shipton, both were unmarried and born in Scropton. In 1853 the will of Richard bequeathed £100 to Ann Wilson daughter of his late sister, Sarah Hand, wife of Joseph. Richard, having like his brother Joseph, been born in Scropton, it follows that Sarah Shipton/Hand was probably also born there.

There is uncertainty regarding the date and place of birth of Joseph Hand but likely that he too, was born in Scropton. On 4 July 1775 Joseph, son of Joseph and Ann Hand was baptised in St Paul's Church, Scropton. If this is correct it puts his age to 66, not 59 as in the 1841 census of Yoxall. However this may be one of the many errors of age given in the census, or a deliberate attempt to put his age back on formal documents if he was already thinking of emigrating. A descendent has received information that when Joseph died in 1860 he was 84 years old which ties in with the Scropton baptism. A widowed Ann Hand made her will and died in Yoxall in 1826, and if the mother of Joseph, the family may have lived in Yoxall from at least the 1820s.

It would appear that as a farmer of 100 acres with a wife who had received bequests from her wealthy family, one of which was interest of money for life, that the family were in a good financial position. However, the couple had seven children and the early letters, prior to their departure, suggest the farm income could not maintain them all as they grew to adulthood.

Some of the early correspondence, prior to the Hands' departure, concerns the employment of their daughter Sarah, who was in service. In 1843 a letter was sent from Coton Hall, asking Sarah Hand to go into service there on 15 March. Coton, was Coton-in-the-Clay, within the parish of Hanbury, close to Tutbury and Scropton. It was the home of John Bott and his wife Susanna Maria, youngest daughter of Major Arden, of the 3rd King's Own Light Dragoons of Longcroft Hall. On 26 July of that year Sarah senior wrote to her daughter saying she did not know why the 'task masters' should burden Sarah without more wages. In February 1844 Jane Geary, a servant at Byrkley Lodge wrote to Sarah, addressing the envelope to Doxey's High Street, Burton. John Docksey was a 'Tea Dealer and Family Grocer'. It appears that Sarah had left Coton Hall and was employed at the shop. This was followed in June by a letter also sent to the shop from Emma Bentley, a servant at Coton Hall, saying she was pleased that Sarah was 'comfortably settled' and a further, undated letter, from Emma Brown, also a servant at Coton Hall, doubting that Elizabeth, who appears to have been Sarah's replacement at the Hall, would stop a year as she 'is almost as sick of the place' as Sarah was. A letter to Sarah from Mary Green in August refers to Sarah and herself having been at Byrkley Lodge.

196

Whether Sarah worked there before Coton Hall or for a very short time afterwards is uncertain. What is clear was the need for Sarah to work, even if the situation was not always a happy one and she was not the only daughter who was in need of a situation. In January 1845 Joseph had tried to gain employment for Mary on a farm at Dunstall, a letter survives from the farmer, Edward Watkin to Joseph saying that they never took on a girl aged more than 12 or 13, and there was a lot of 'nasty work' that he would not want Mary doing. He also added that he thought a girl as young as Mary would be wrong to 'take herself from under the protection of her parents'. According to her age in the census, Mary would have been about 23 in 1845, so strange words, given the age of the girls he was employing. At the time the Hand family were nearing the date of their departure, and perhaps Joseph was anxious to raise as much money as possible, to help pay the passage for his family and their new start in life.

There is little doubt that there was discontent amongst the farmers in the area at this time. In February 1845 Edward Price, the incumbent of Christ Church, Newchurch, in a letter to Joseph wishing him well wrote a tirade against the situation in England and his belief that the family were going to a better place: 'On England you have turned your back, and therefore <u>hope</u> lies before you'. He continued his theme regarding the situation in England when in January 1848 he wrote to Joseph telling him of the death of 'Mr Gisborne', (the Rev. Thomas, who died in March 1846). The letters of Edward Price were the only letters which were received transcribed, so either the year of 1848 is incorrect or it took Price almost two years to inform the Hand family of the reverend's demise.

Sixteen members of the Hand family travelled from Liverpool to New Orleans on the ship Walpole. The ages given for Joseph's children are incorrect so whether John and Joseph were his children or members of the extended family is uncertain. Between them all there were only a few boxes of possessions and 3 casks.

Only fifteen Hands disembarked, Joseph's wife Sarah having died during the passage. The family had already been fragmented as at least one member, daughter Ann had remained behind. In 1843, as a dressmaker aged 22 she had married William Wilson, a blacksmith of Newborough. The couple had married at the Parish Church of Hanbury. The majority of the letters in the collection are from her to the family she so sorely missed.

It is believed that the family made their way north on the Mississippi River to St Louis and from there to a small town called Bunker Hill in the State of Illinois. At the time of their arrival and establishing farms and homes, a short distance north, in Springfield, Abraham Lincoln was beginning the career which eventually lead him to the Presidency of the United States in 1860.

Things had not improved in England, when in September 1848 William Elkin of London wrote to Joseph regarding an estate of which they were both executives, and a letter he had received from Abraham Hardy of Yoxall the previous week, which he quoted from in his letter to Joseph: 'He and most of the Farmers are grumbling about free trade, reducing the price of their produce, they dare not lay it to the real cause, namely high rents, tithes, game laws, army & navy and many other aristocracy made laws, that injures themselves and others. Being carried out by Parson Magistrates in the country localities. A person has just published a book wherein he proves that our Protestant clergy receive about ten million sterling annually'.

In April 1846 Ann Wilson wrote to her family in Madison County, Illinois, apologising for not writing before. She asks her father to let her know how they like the country, which she states none of the family have done. She writes that times in England are bad, and she thinks will get worse.

In March 1847 Ann wrote to the family telling them that although the potatoes were a good crop, they were rotten by the time of harvesting them and she 'is turned farmer' keeping four cows. She also sends them news that they are expecting a railway through Newborough, 'just above the church it will be settled sune weather it comes or not'. She asks her father that when he writes to Mr Harding, (the land agent for the Meynell Ingram family), that he recommend her for the work as she has heard they are not satisfied with the man they have as he is a drunkard. It seems unlikely that she is trying to take a man's work, especially as Samuel Harding lived at Willoughbridge Wells, in the Staffordshire parish of Ashley. It seems more likely that she meant for him to arrange to have blacksmith work done by her husband, presumably for the Meynell Ingrams. She apologises for not writing sooner and says she has three small children and her husband is very busy as he has not had a man working for him for a month. She also apologises for her bad writing and mistakes, the letters often state she is in a hurry. She expresses wishes to see her family again, a recurrent theme of her letters.

Ann's next surviving letter to America was in October 1850. She had given birth to another girl that July. They had bought a cow from Joseph Leedham for £8, which was 'going on very well and very quiet'. They had previously bought one they believed to be three years old from John Swindell, which they discovered was four and was 'such a rank kicker we could do no good at all with her'. They had paid £10 10s and Swindell bought the cow back paying them only £6 10s. Ann states 'we was swindled pretty well'. Ann updates her family with the local news that Mr Price (the incumbent of Christ Church, Newchurch) has left Newchurch and is living amongst his friends and a man by the name of 'Weasy' a stranger, is 'doing duty' at the church. Things were not improving for the farmers as there were 'strange grumblings' amongst them the previous Christmas, the same is expected as 'corn selling is very bad'.

Ann did not have an easy life, the family struggled financially, and childbirth and the worry she had raising her children undermined her health. In 1854 she wrote to Ann Hollis, a servant of the Shiptons at Bank House, telling her she had given birth to twins and was very weak, (she had borne three other children prior to the twins), and that Ann, one of the older children, had 'bad' eyes and she was afraid she would lose one of them. She asked if Mrs Hollis (presumably Ann's mother) could take one of her little girls. She also refers to a funeral but does not say whose, only that she could not have gone had not George Shipton of Woodhouses supplied a black dress for her. This was probably the funeral of her uncle Richard Shipton of Woodhouses, who died the previous year and bequeathed her £100 which she would not have received before the funeral. Richard left his estate to his brother Joseph for his lifetime, which included land he had inherited from his brother, Robert of Scropton who died in 1852. Land at Yoxall included 'a field of land held jointly by myself and my said brother Joseph called Luce Pool'. This consisted of nine acres, which he had bought from Hugo Charles Meynell in 1840. Following the decease of Joseph, the land was to go to, amongst others, his nephews, William Shipton of Yoxall, farmer and Thomas Shipton of Orgreave (Hall).

In a further letter in 1854 Ann wrote to her family telling them that her husband, William, had been ill with nervous fever and had not left the house for two months, though he was now better. Ann wishes that some of her children were in America with her family, as she cannot bring them up as she would wish to. Ann's struggle to cope with her children is highlighted when she writes that her last child was a boy, saying 'we must have no more'.

The next letter of Anne's appears to be written in 1855, and again her husband has been ill, this time with Rheumatic Fever. She had been to Woodhouses in June and seen her Uncle Joseph. Ann and Mary Hollis were keeping house for him and she believed that they are 'dowing very well for themselves, they are very selfish and want all they can get and are jealous of her Uncle George's housekeeper', who Ann thinks is very nice.

In 1856, despite Ann's letter of 1854 stating that they must have no more children, she has another boy, the total now being three boys and six girls, the oldest girl, aged twelve, wants to go into service but Ann wants her to remain at school for longer. The children often say they would like to go to America to their grandfather and aunt. She is again very critical of Ann and Mary Hollis, although she has not been to Woodhouses for 'a long time'.

In her letter of 1856 it is clear that Ann and William had borrowed money from the family in America, as William is very glad they will wait a bit longer for it as they are very short of money. William is very busy but does not have a man working for him and she regrets that none of their sons are working for him, as the journeymen want high wages and provisions are dear. She refers to her father knowing what it is like to be short of money, which perhaps refers to hard times in England and the need to send his children into service work prior to their emigration.

In 1857 she writes to her father asking the year of her birth, as several people have asked her and she does not know it and later in the year she received £25 from Mr Rushton (solicitor), which presumably was sent by her father. Ann and William had borrowed £10 from her Uncle George and had now been able to repay him. There had been a large flood in Newborough, the worst that could be remembered. This happened in August, with a dreadful thunderstorm, and she writes that not many houses did not have water in them. All the children are at home, but things appear to have improved for William as he has 'a great deal of work, and is pleased with his men'.

Occasionally Ann's letters reveal that there had been hopes that some of the family may have visited England, but the proposed visits never materialised. This was not only disappointing for Ann, but also for those of her children who had wanted to go to America when the visiting family returned there.

In September 1859 Ann wrote to say that if George (her brother) could have come she would have sent her daughter Betsy back with him, as she had a 'hard place where she now lives' (in service). Another daughter, Ann, was more fortunate and was living at the home of John Leedham, 'she has a very nice place'. The Leedhams, who had a daughter living at home, had either employed Ann recently, or had allowed her to go to help her mother, as Ann senior had another child, a boy, in May and had been very ill since and Ann had been a help to her. She had been to her Uncle George at Scropton for three weeks 'for a change of air', and would have written to her father had she not been so ill. Her Uncle Joseph of Woodhouses, who was finishing the harvest, had sold her a cow for £6. The family had not had one in the summer as she could not look after it, but had felt the loss of not having butter and cheese.

Ann's next two letters are uncertain regarding the year, but the first appears to be written in January 1860. Ann is very concerned about her daughter Mary who has been very ill for more than a year and she is afraid that she is consumptive. She fears for her life, as she writes 'She will be twenty if she lives till the 2nd September'. She and William have eight surviving children out of a total of thirteen. Of the children, she makes no further mention of the girls, except to say there are four of them, but the four boys are all at home and William is learning his father's trade but George seems unwilling to become a blacksmith, and his father wants him to become a shoeing smith. The following letter which appears to be 1861, written on the 27th March, acknowledges the receipt of her family's letter to her, received on the 23rd March. It is unusual for Ann to reply so soon to their letters, given she so often apologies for her delay, citing the fact that she is always so busy. However, it is likely that at this time Ann feels the need for contact with the family who are so far away. Not only has her daughter Jane died the previous August, aged 11, but since her last letter, her father Joseph, has died in America, which she describes as a double grief. Ann wishes she could see her sister and as she has things to tell her that she cannot write. In November 1861 Ann again writes, having had a better summer and a good harvest. She was glad to hear that her sister was not near the [Civil] war, and hopes that it would soon be over. Ann still hopes that her sister will visit, as does her daughter Bessy, who was very disappointed when she previously failed to come over, as she had made up her mind to return with her. This was the last letter written by Ann Wilson to her family in the collection.

A letter in June 1866, from Mary Hand at Audleyville County to her sister (name not stated), informs that 'they' are living on the Plains six miles from where they were the previous year, and the land is good. She has 40 acres of wheat planted. She refers to Willie, who is ploughing corn and the baby being six months old. In December she wrote to say the baby had died.

Joseph Hand died on 19 August 1860 and was buried at Bunker Hill, Macoupin County, Illinois. Joseph's daughter, Sarah separated land from a corner of the farm provided to her by her father's will as a cemetery for the family. This became known as the Hand Cemetery, with a requirement that some percentage of those buried there must be the descendants of Joseph Hand. Sarah remained unmarried and was buried in the Hand Cemetery, her monument is inscribed 'Sarah Hand born in Scropton Derbyshire Eng. May 24 1819 Died Dec. 12. 1906'. Bunker Hill was settled by pioneers in 1830, and at that time was known as Wolf Ridge, due to the presence of wolves in the vicinity. The Hand family prospered in the area. Another of Joseph Hand's children, Mary, married William Cruickshank, born in Scotland, his trade was a tailor and he migrated to America prior to the Mexican War. William was recruited to the army and was one of the escorts of General Winfield Scott. Following the Mexican War he went to Colorado and made his fortune mining over four years. From there he went to Illinois where he married Mary Hand. The couple had eight children, one of whom, Josie, married Thomas Mize in 1890. It is this line which continues to live in the home of Joseph Hand. The Mize Cemetery, despite the name change, is still known to be that of the Hand family who came before them.

Mary Stretton Blood

According to an article on the Family Search site Mary was born in Yoxall the daughter of Thomas Stretton and Elizabeth Deakin on 25 July 1811. In fact her baptism took place at St Peter's on 11 August of that year, her parents named as Thomas and Elizabeth Stretton. The article adds she was 'a great cook; she learned this from her father, who was the baker'. No documentary evidence has been found to substantiate this, at the time of her baptism the occupation of fathers were not included in the entries.

Most of the following information is taken from the article:

Mary, described as about 5'6" with light hair, blue eyes and a clear complexion, was employed as a dairymaid at Hare Hill Farm near Sudbury Derbyshire where she met her husband, William Blood, who was employed there as a farm foreman and the couple married in February 1836. The couple lived at Barton, William was a plate layer on the railway and Mary kept a shop and bakery. The census for 1841 enumerated the couple, as both aged 30, and William as an agricultural labourer. No occupation was given for Mary, but in 1841 usually only the occupation of the head was given. The couple had 2 children, Ann aged 4 and William 1. However, while the Barton baptism register entry for their son William, baptised in 1839, gives William senior's occupation as labourer, that of their daughter Mary in 1842 states he was a baker of Barton.

Mary Stretton Blood. (Reproduced by permission of Canon Jim Dean).

At what point the couple became Mormon converts is uncertain, but in January 1844, with three children, they sailed to America, and arrived in New Orleans in March, of that year. They then travelled by steamboat up the Mississippi river, to Nauvoo, Illinois, where on their arrival in April they were met by the prophet Joseph Smith who greeted the new Saints. Shortly after they arrived William was stricken with fever, and within 3 weeks of arriving he was dead, leaving Mary and their children among strangers in a strange country. Worse was to come, in May Mary gave birth to a girl she called Emma but in June the child died and was buried next to her father.

Mary was present when Brigham Young, a leader and 2nd president of the Church of Jesus Christ and the Latter Day Saints addressed his people. Among his nicknames is 'Mormon Moses', as he led his people through a desert to what they saw as a promised land. Like many Mormons at that time, he was a polygamist. He is said to have stated on learning that plural marriage was part of Mormonism 'It was the first time in my life that I desired the grave'. The sentiment appears to have been short lived as he accumulated 55 wives.

In September 1844 Mary purchased 10 acres of land at Big Mound, 9 miles north of Nauvoo and began building a house. Henry Woolley, also from Staffordshire had travelled with the Bloods and applied for work on Mary's house and in March 1845 the couple married. A membership record to the Latter Day Saints records that the couple married in March or May 1845. The article states that the couple had 3 children, and due to persecution they left Nauvoo and built a home on Center Street three blocks west of Main Street in Kaysville, Davis County, Utah, where they spent the rest of their lives. Mary claimed to be the first dairywoman in Davis County, making butter and cheese and selling them at the market in Salt Lake City. Having raised her children in the faith she had converted to, she died in March 1891. Her son William, baptised in Barton was baptised a Mormon in 1849 and in 1887 was sentenced to 6 months imprisonment for taking a plural wife. He became a president, and later senior president of a 'quorum of Seventy'.

The True Story of 'Major' Mort

Mort's Charity is included in the chapter 'Poverty, Charity and the Poorhouse' and still benefits people in Yoxall, long after the true memory of the man who bequeathed it to the village has faded into obscurity. The story has passed down through time of 'Major' Mort, a merry, elderly gentleman who lived at Rookery Cottage, and who is most remembered for his habit, on returning from his weekly journey to Burton, of galloping his pony and cart down Town Hill and as he neared the bottom throwing down the reins and shouting to his pony 'Left!' if he wanted to go home 'Right' if he wanted the pub. Whether there is any more truth in this story than his age and status is uncertain.

Little is known about the man himself, but his family were well known in Australia, and their memory lives on the name Mortdale, named after Robert's father, Thomas Sutcliffe Mort. It is through the history of Thomas that a little can be understood about the life of Robert.

Thomas Mort and his wife Mary, parents of Robert Sutcliffe Mort. (Reproduced by permission of the State Library of NSW).

Thomas was born in Bolton, Lancashire, in 1816, a son of Jonathan Mort and his wife Mary, nèe Sutcliffe. The family moved to Manchester where Thomas was privately educated. However Jonathan was not successful in Manchester, and when he died in 1834 his estate was insufficient to give his sons a good start in life. Thomas became a clerk, but seeing no prospects, took up the offer of a position in Sydney, Australia, and arrived at Port Jackson in 1838. Beginning as a clerk he moved into auctioneering and by 1850 was the premier auctioneer in Australia. He became a very successful entrepreneur and through the creation of the Bodella Estate, a pioneer of Australian dairying, and was responsible for improving refrigeration. In 1841 he married

Theresa Shepheard, daughter of James Laidley, and the couple had eight children, the second being Robert Sutcliffe, born in 1853.

Greenoakes, Darling Point, home of the Mort family. (Reproduced by permission of the State Library of NSW).

Thomas visited England in 1857-1859, bringing his family including Robert, and in 1857 attended the July-August 29 day sale of 4000 lots, the entire contents of Alton Towers. There he purchased Elizabethan armour, old English coats of mail, and a cabinet that had belonged to Marie Antoinette, along with antique oak furniture and about 120 pictures. On his return home to Greenoakes, Darling Point, he had his Gothic styled house extended and included an art gallery, which with his gardens, were opened to the public.

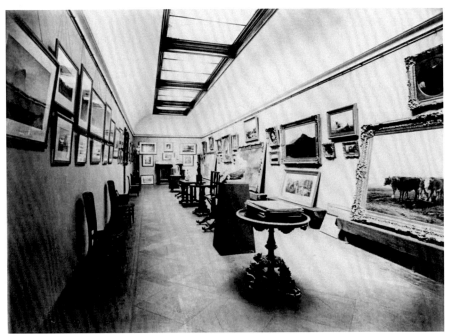

Art Gallery at Greenoakes, built to display pictures Thomas Mort bought at the Alton Towers Auction. (Reproduced by permission of the State Library of NSW).

Whether Robert grew up surrounded by these artefacts from England is uncertain, as at some unknown time he came to England. It is possible that his father left him after the 1857-1859 visit to be educated in England. What is certain is that in 1871, at the age of 18, he was a pupil at Abbey Hill School, in Kenilworth, Warwickshire. In 1878 Robert was back in Australia and was amongst those appointed to form the Public School Board for Bodella[1] and in 1882 was appointed a magistrate of the Colony of New South Wales.[2] In 1885 he was in England and a witness at the marriage of his younger sister, Annie Catherine Mort, his parents eldest daughter, who was married at Paddington to widower Bishop John Selwyn, (curate at All Saints Alrewas 1869-1870), the son of George Selwyn, the first Anglican Bishop of New Zealand, who returned to England in 1868 and became Bishop of Lichfield until his death in 1878.

Rookery Cottage, once the home of Robert Sutcliffe Mort, he is pictured in white on the back row.

If Robert knew his brother in law prior to his marriage to Annie he may have visited Yoxall during John's incumbency in Alrewas, or possibly on a later visit, but the link with John Selwyn does suggest how Robert may have come to live in Yoxall. It is also uncertain when he moved to Yoxall, possibly following his sister's wedding, but by 1888 he was at Rookery Cottage, evidenced by his account at Norman's store, from which it became apparent he moved to Holly Bank, Woodhouses in 1890. He proved to be a sociable and generous man. He frequently gave entertainment, and mixed not only with people of his own social status, but also entertained the elderly and poor of Yoxall. In 1888 he treated about seventy old women of the village to tea at the Crown Inn, and by 1890 included the aged poor, both men and women, of the village, numbering about ninety. That year he gave tea to the children from the Church Schools of

Yoxall, who were entertained in a tent at the Upton's farm. In 1891 he was enumerated as an unmarried visitor, living on his own means in the household of John Upton, a farmer of Holly Bank Farm, Woodhouses, who with his wife Frances was also involved in the social life of Yoxall. Amongst other occasions the couple hosted St Peter's choir's annual dinner.

Holly Bank Farm, Woodhouses. (Photo by author).

Perhaps Robert preferred life in England to Australia, but the loss of both parents may have had some bearing on his decision to stay. Following the death of his wife, Thomas was widowed and remarried in 1874 and the couple had two sons. Thomas was at the time of his death in 1878 considered the greatest benefactor of the working man in Australia. The working men of Sydney resolved to show their esteem for him with a sculptured statue which stands in Macquarie Place and was unveiled in 1883.

Robert died of tuberculosis on 2 February 1892 aged 38. His bequests included his share in the Bodella Estate, an adjoining farm and shares in Morts Dock and Engineering Company Ltd. The majority of his estate was bequeathed to his female relations, which he directed was to be for their own use. Just days before his death, on 30 January, he added a codicil to his will in which he made monetary bequests to the Upton family and his horse and trap to Frances Upton, also the bequest which was to become Mort's Charity.

Chapter 17

Through Fire and Flood

Part of the house known as Rookery Cottage in Main Street was burnt down and the adjoining Georgian house known as The Hollies was built as a replacement. Fire damage is evident on timbers inside both properties where the houses are joined.

The Hollies and Rookery Cottage. Rookery Cottage, formerly a farm is believed to have once housed the tape factory and The Hollies the factory owner. (Photo by author).

Fire Insurance Plaques

Royal Exchange Insurance Plaque, one of two examples in Main Street. (Photo by author).

Two cottages in Main Street display fire insurance metal wall plaques. These were erected by insurance companies to signify the property was insured against fire. The two plaques have the emblem of the Royal Exchange, who were granted a royal charter in 1720. The design featured on the cottage's plaques was issued between 1820 and 1890. A similar design issued by the company was pear shaped, the wider part showing more of the building, which represented the Royal Exchange building. This was possibly an earlier design, once displayed on a Yoxall inn. Although the name of the inn was not stated, a surviving insurance document[1] would suggest it to be the Crown, as the insured person was Thomas Waltho of Yoxall, 'innholder', who was listed there in 1818 as the victualler.[2]

The sum insured is itemised as follows:

Dwelling House & Brewhouse adjoining with chambers over the same	£250
On furniture, appliances & plate books therein	£140
On brewing & trade in the same	£60
On a house adjoining, Northside thereof in the occupation of John Marsh Sadler & Collar maker	£50
On two Stables adjoining each other on Northside with Lofts over said stables	£100
Sum Insured	£600

Fire at Bond End Malthouse

In 1865 an 'Alarming Fire at Yoxall' broke out in the stockyard of John Brown of Bond End. It was discovered in the morning in an outhouse adjoining the rickyard and malthouse, and quickly spread to the stackyard and two thatched cottages, a waggon hovel and other shedding, which became a mass of flames. Three large haystacks and two cottages were completely destroyed along with the outhouses, part of the malthouse, and drying kilns, carriages and other items.[3] The Western Insurance Company promptly settled John Brown's claim and in addition paid a 'liberal sum' towards the expenses incurred.[4]

In 1870 a second fire broke out at John Brown's premises. A messenger was sent to Burton for the fire engines, and the brigades of Allsop & Sons and Bass & Co. and the town firemen set out, but by the time they reached Barton Turns they were met by John Brown's son William who told them the fire had been extinguished. Fortunately there had been plenty of help at the scene and the fire was put out before it reached adjoining thatched buildings, and so not much damage was done. The cause was believed to have been overheating flues in the carriage house.[5] Had help not been speedily available the situation would have been far worse as the messenger would have had to travel ten miles to Burton to alert the fire brigades, which would then have to travel the same distance to Yoxall.

Fire in a Rickyard

In 1881 Hannah Pott, a servant of farmer Arthur Beard discovered a rick on fire in his rickyard. She immediately raised the alarm and a message was sent to Burton for the fire brigade. The engines of Bass & Co., Allsops & Sons and the Corporation arrived but were unable to extinguish the fire before two ricks of clover and two of hay had been destroyed. The damage was estimated at between £220 and £250 and the ricks were not insured. While it was not certain as to the cause of the fire, a boy aged about six had been seen running from the direction of the rickyard at the time the fire was discovered. He was afterwards 'lost' for several hours and eventually found concealed in a field of wheat.[6] What followed on the discovery of the child was not reported. Within days an appeal had been made through the *Burton Chronicle* by a committee formed in Yoxall for the purpose of raising money to compensate Arthur Beard for his loss. The letter, written by the curate Ding, stated that Arthur was 'well known in and around Burton as a straightforward hard-working farmer, and respected by all who know him'. His loss was almost the entire produce of 45 acres. The other fifteen members of the 'Beard Relief Fund' included the rector J.B. Lowe, the Catholic priest H. McCarten, Dr C.G. Armson, and farmers, including G.H. Shipton, S. Archer, and J. Upton.[7] The following week the appeal was repeated, stating that the loss was estimated at £250 at the lowest estimate, and that the fact that the farm was not insured had left some people less sympathetic than they might otherwise have been. They had not raised a quarter of the amount of the damage estimated. They had a promise of £10 from one gentleman and hoped that if nine others offered the same they would have a substantial start and hope of success.[8] This also failed to raise sufficient funds as the appeal was again repeated.

Fire Engine for Hoar Cross Hall

In 1893 a trial of a steam fire engine made by Shand, Mason and Co. of London, for the protection of Hoar Cross Hall and estate was witnessed by the Hon. Mrs Meynell Ingram and 'a distinguished company'. The engine arrived at noon and at 2.30 Mr Elliot, representing the makers received instructions to get the engine to work. In 6 ½ minutes the engine was working and 100 lbs of steam produced and 2 jets were thrown over the hall. Then from 80 ft of hose laid to the church, jets 165 ft high were thrown. Other experiments were made, 1,000 ft of hose being laid up a hill, the engine pumping copious steam. The trial was reported to have ended satisfactorily.[9]

Fire was a particular hazard for children, with open fires in the home and often easy access to matches. In 1878 an inquest was held at Hadley End on the body of 4 year old John Law who had been left in the house with 3 other children while their mother went to a neighbour's house about 50 yards away. During her absence a younger brother lit a piece of paper and John's clothes caught fire and he died the following morning.[10] He was not alone in suffering so terrible a fate, in 1892 Louisa Emily Dukes, aged 3, the daughter of Lucy Dukes of Yoxall, was sent with her brother Thomas to their grandmother's because their father was ill. The children were put to bed but got up early on the Saturday morning and went downstairs taking a box of matches with them. Their grandmother heard screams and found Louisa with her nightdress on fire. The fire was put out and the child taken to hospital where she died the following Monday. An inquest held at the Crown found that she had died from shock.[11]

Water was perhaps as much a threat to children as fire, the drowning of a young member of the Arden family in the moat was not the only case of a child drowning. In 1886 Richard Bird, aged 2, of Hadley End, who had been playing in the morning near his house was missing. A search began and he was discovered dead in a nearby pit of water. An inquest at the Bell and Cuckoo returned a verdict of 'accidentally drowned'.[12]

Like Burton and Branston, Yoxall has had more than its share of floods and where the following were not floods reported in Yoxall, they affected people from Yoxall.

The Sough

In 1848 a 'Fearful Storm at King's Bromley and Hamstall Ridware' was reported. The storm began in Kings Bromley and took place in the afternoon, leaving in its course 'many awful remains of the desolating ravages'. The article describes terrific thunder which resembled 'the continuous rolling of heavy artillery', lightning which flashed without intermission and torrential rain. Trees were stripped of their branches and many blown down, and four 'patriarchal' oaks were uprooted. After twenty minutes the storm crossed the Trent and headed to Hamstall Ridware, where it continued to wreak havoc, including displacing lead from the church, and breaking down a parapet wall. No storm like it had been seen in living memory.[13] There is no mention of Yoxall in the account, but it seems unlikely that the village and its surroundings did not suffer. So heavy a storm is unlikely to have been confined to Kings Bromley and Hamstall Ridware, and with so much water having fallen during the storm rivers are likely to have flowed in torrents, taking with them whatever debris they collected on their way, before breaking their banks and flooding low lying areas.

There is perhaps a clue that the water level rose to a considerable height in Yoxall as there is carving on a stone in the wall which curves into the main entrance of St Peter's, which clearly bears the inscription 'SOUGH' and below two lines of faded inscription which appear to read '4- FEET DEEP' '1848' with a possible day and month before the year, now eroded. A sough, from the Old English suggests a boggy place or drain, and the wall may have been the highest point that the water rose to.

A wall was in situ at the time of the storm, as in 1830 £70 was paid towards the repairs of the church and churchyard walls.[14] It seems likely that the force of water and its accompanying debris damaged the wall and if so it may have been rebuilt and the stone carved to mark the incident, and placed at the appropriate height.

By the turn of the 20th century the walls are pictured with wrought iron joining the walls to two pillars from which hung the gates, also in wrought iron. This may have been done at the time of the flood to replace what was there prior to any damage, or as part of the restoration of the church, completed in 1868. It seems likely that with all the work on the restoration an imposing main entrance to the church and churchyard would be included. The stone is set low in the wall, although it would probably have originally been set at a height 4 ft above ground level, as a further indicator of the flood, as is seen in Burton flood stones. However there is also the possibility that the stone was reused from a previous site when building or repairing the present wall. Prior to the 1848 storm, in May of that year a payment of £15 was paid by the Town Lands 'towards soughing Church Yard'.[15] This can only suggest work on drainage and it may be in part due to a block in the drainage that the presumed flooding took place. It seems unlikely that a stone would have been carved with a date if only to record the depth of a drain.

Edwin Leedham and the Great Flood of Burton

In October 1875 torrential rain caused what was reported as 'The Great Flood of Burton'. There was no mention in the report of the weather causing damage at Yoxall but of the two people who lost their lives, one was Yoxall born Edwin Leedham, son of plumber and glazier, Stephen Leedham, and his wife Ann. Edwin was enumerated in 1861, aged 20, as a plumber in his father's household. In 1875 he was living in Guild Street, Burton with a wife and one child and employed as a painter by a Mr Perkins of Burton. Like many other people who left Yoxall, Edwin would not have been included in this history but for the fateful day that led to his return to the village. The *Burton Chronicle* detailed the last hours of his life. On the Thursday of the flood he had worked tirelessly trying to help his employer and employer's son to deal with removing goods from the path of the flood. He also fetched a pony for his employer which he stabled at the Star Inn and headed for home about 9.30 that evening, having seen Thomas Perkins, his employer's son who later confirmed that Edwin had not eaten since that morning and was 'perfectly sober'. Edwin was not seen alive again. An eye witness stated that on the Thursday night the water in Guild Street was about 4 ft deep. On the Sunday morning the water had receded to approximately 3 ft and the witness had waded up Guild Street and discovered Edwin's body, tragically 300 to 400 yds from his home.[16]

Identified by his father Stephen, Edwin was brought back to Yoxall where he was buried. The entry in the burial register states 'Drowned in the Great Flood of Burton'. Edwin's wife, Harriet died in 1877 at Yoxall, aged 34. The *Burton Chronicle* lists her in the obituaries as 'the widow of Edwin Leedham of Guild Street'. Harriet was buried at Yoxall, probably with her husband. There are no surviving monuments.

George Brierley

In November 1890 storms had swollen the Trent and flooded the adjoining meadows. George Brierley, a 62 year old farmer of Whitewood, Yoxall, was concerned for the safety of his cattle on a portion of his farm and drove out to make an inspection. He was accompanied by a youth in his service who witnessed the accident and stated that his master was backing the pony when in close proximity of a deep culvert. The stream was exceptionally strong and the horse was released by the breaking of the shafts. George was swept away by the current. The boy raised the alarm immediately and a search was made. The body was later found three or four hundred yards from where the trap overturned. A correspondent wrote 'a gloom has been cast over the parish, as the deceased was an eminent agriculturalist and widely respected, not only in his own parish but by all who knew him. He has been churchwarden for many years, and one of the managers of the school. Much sympathy is felt for his family in their sudden bereavement'.[17] He shares a grave at St Peter's with his son, William who died aged 31. The stone is appropriately inscribed with the phrase: 'In the midst of life we are in death'.

More Heavy Weather

When in 1861 the Yoxall mail cart was unable to reach Branstone (Branston) post office due to severe flooding, the driver left his cart and carried the mailbags along the canal towpath, but unfortunately arrived too late for the despatch of letters that morning.[18]

In 1876 a heavy thunderstorm passed over the village. The lightning was reported as very vivid, and besides demolishing and damaging several trees, killed a cow belonging to Mr Astle of Woodhouses.[19]

In 1894 a gale caused 'a considerable amount of damage' in the village and neighbourhood. Trees were uprooted and a wall blown down, chimney pots and ridge tiles flew in all directions. Mr Sabin's hay barn was carried a distance of 30 yards and some thatched cottages were partly unroofed. The end of a cottage belonging to a Mr Large at Woodhouses was blown in while he was in bed, but fortunately he was unhurt.[20] The following month it was reported that the recent severe floods on the Trent brought many wildfowl to the meadows and flights of widgeon and teal were still there, which the report stated probably meant bad weather was to come.[21]

In 1898 a thunder storm 'of unusual severity' with heavy rain and large hailstones passed over the village. A valuable horse belonging to Mr Roobottom of Rowley Farm was killed and the gable end of a barn at Holly Bank Farm was struck, stripping about 2 ft width of tiles off the ridge of the eaves.[22] Fortunately no one was reported as injured but the following week it was reported that during the storm in Burton an 8 year old girl had been struck by lightning and died the following day.[23]

In 1901 it was reported that a storm in Yoxall was worse than any witnessed in many years. The Swarbourn overflowed its banks inundating many houses and in one shed cows were standing in 2 ft of water. The following day was an anxious time for getting horses, cattle and sheep from the Trent meadows, 'which was a complete sea'. No losses were reported.[24]

Chapter 18

Death Do Us Part

The Gospel Oak

The Gospel Oak, described in 1886 as 'a remarkably antique oak' stood at the road side, halfway between Hoar Cross and Yoxall. Prior to there being a church at Hoar Cross the deceased were taken to Yoxall for interment. It was at this oak tree that the funeral procession halted and put down the body.[1] While the bearers were likely to have been glad of a rest on the journey, the name of the tree and the tradition of stopping beside it may suggest that also a small service was held beneath its boughs.

Carved in Stone

The oldest surviving headstone in St Peter's churchyard is that of Hugh Pott who died in 1723, his wife Margery, their son John who died in 1734 and his wife Elizabeth who died in 1732. The inscription was in poor condition when recorded in 1988 by Hilda White and the author and has since deteriorated.

George Raworth was the only known monumental mason in Yoxall. It is likely that he left the village to learn his craft, but by 1851 he was living at the Saw Yard with his brother John, a sawyer. By 1861 George, who was by then both an engraver and registrar of marriage, had his own household, a wife and two of the couple's eventual six children. George's surviving memorial inscriptions include one headstone at St Francis of Sales, Woodlane, and at least eighteen at St Peter's Churchyard, including that of Elizabeth, first wife of Joseph Wait, founder of Woodmill Methodist Chapel, but for George Raworth there is no surviving monument.

Monumental inscriptions are a rich source of information, and those surviving the elements at Yoxall are no exception. Many of the stones carrying a religious message or verse express acceptance of what was believed to be the will of God, such as 'Thy will be done' and record a belief that the deceased is blessed in death, often including hopes to meet again on 'the immortal shore'. In the last quarter of the 19th century, some struggled with that acceptance. The stone of Thomas Green and his wife records the death of their two infant sons, concluding 'Not my will O Lord, but thine be done', and a stone next to it records the death of Mary Haddock, who died in 1886 aged 23, 'In love she lived, in peace she died. Her life was asked, but God denied'.

The uncertainty of life is a recurrent theme both in wills and on monumental inscriptions. The stone of Joseph Baldwin, who died in 1874 aged 47, bears the inscription 'In the midst of life we are in death'. The grim fact highlighted by the recording of two daughters who both died in January 1870, one aged 3 years, the other 7 weeks. Other Yoxall examples warn the reader of their impending fate, such as the stone of Lydia Thompson, who died in 1828, aged 31:

Reader stay, and shed a tear
Over the dust that sleepeth here:
Consider well this state of mine;
Which will another day be thine.

The stone of Sarah Lester, who died in 1836 aged 35, suggests death to be a form of punishment:

Weep not for me, my dearest friends,
 But make your peace with God.
 We cannot tell who next may fall
 Beneath his chastening rod.

Another recurrent theme is that of suffering. One of several examples is the stone of Elizabeth Cox who died in 1853 aged 40:

Afflictions sore long time I bore,
Physicians were in vain;
Till God did hear my fervent prayer,
And eased me from my pain.

Some inscriptions are more unusual than others. In 1807 Robert and Elizabeth Tarlington of Woodhouses died, Elizabeth in March, followed by her brother in July. The inscription states that they 'for Seventy three Years lived affectionately together in a State of Celibacy'.

A stone dated 1843 records: 'Designed to protect from interruption the mortal remains of George Harvey'. The fear of body snatchers, euphemistically called 'Resurrection Men' had abated following the Anatomy Act of 1832, which allowed anatomists to use unclaimed corpses, in particular of those who had died in prison or a workhouse. This ended the fear of being disinterred by resurrectionists who dug up newly buried corpses and sold them to unquestioning anatomists.

A few record those whose service in life was much appreciated, among them is the stone of Isaac Tooth who died in 1794 aged 76, and his wife, in 1807, aged 82. Their stone was erected at the request of the late Rev. John Arden 'in grateful remembrance of their Long and Faithful Service to him and his Family'. At what age, or if, they had retired from that service is unknown, but they were not forgotten.

French born Apoline de Soycourt died in 1853 aged 77 and was interred at Woodlane with a stone bearing the inscription 'Having been long a beloved inmate of the family of Hugo [Charles] Meynell Ingram Esq… Created by the above named Gentleman'. By 1851 Apoline had become a British subject and was residing at Hoar Cross Hall with the Meynell Ingrams, where she was enumerated as a governess. However, although the family were in residence at the time, there were no children in the household. In the role of governess it is likely that her charges spent far more time with her than with their parents, and it seems that at least one had retained an affection for her into adulthood, welcoming her to stay with the family she had served. Another servant was Mary Preston who died of typhus and pneumonia in 1860 and although only 15 years old she had made sufficient an impression on her employer to warrant a headstone proclaiming 'much regretted by her late Mistress Dorothy Brown'.

One stone records a particularly unusual burial arrangement. Ellen Dukes who died in October 1861 shares a plot, not with her husband Edward, but with his brother Thomas who died in February of that year.

There are two almost identical headstones for 28 year old Elizabeth Smith. The difference being the inscriptions. One stone records her as the wife of John Smith and daughter of Elias and Elizabeth Pyecroft, and granddaughter of Hugh and Ellen Pott. The same verse appears on both stones, but the first line of the above quoted stone reads 'Grieve not dear Husband ...'. The second stone records her as the daughter of Elias and Elizabeth Pycroft, with no reference to her name of Smith and the verse beginning: 'Grieve not dear Parents...'. Her parents seem unable to have accepted her marriage or agree with her husband on an inscription for one stone, and each born the expense of providing their own, but which she rests beneath will, no doubt remain a mystery. The burial register records the burial of Elizabeth Smith on either 10 or 16 August 1790, presumably a mistake in the register, the date of death on both headstones being 29 August. Her burial was followed on 1 September by that of Elizabeth Smith 'daughter of the above'. This suggests that the Elizabeth commemorated on the headstones died due to complications in childbirth. Although the child is not included on either headstone, perhaps she rests alongside her mother.

Many stones are a testimony of the high mortality rate of the nineteenth century. Some men left a widow to support a large family, including Henry Green who died in 1847 aged 52, 'Leaving a Widow and six children to deplore their irreparable loss', and the instruction to his widow 'My dearest Wife weep not for me, On God through Christ depend, For He'll thy needful wants supply, And be my Children's friend'. The stone of James Winter who died in 1839 aged 47 also bore an inscription regarding the leaving of a disconsolate widow and large family but concluded with 'Also two of his Children died young...' (aged 3 years and 12 months).

For families to lose any children to an untimely death was bad enough, but for some the bereavements kept on coming, many dying in infancy but others having safely reached maturity predeceased their parents. Ann, wife of James Dawson, died aged 72, her husband died aged 92. During their lifetime they had lost 5 of their sons. Their headstone records '4 died infants the other aged 26'. A daughter, who survived to the age of 51 also predeceased them.

Fearn Family

Amongst those whose children grew to adulthood before being struck down in what should have been the prime of their lives is the Fearn family, for whom three neighbouring headstones stand in St Peter's churchyard. William and Elizabeth had six children, and of these three daughters are commemorated on one headstone. The first is Lavinia, who died in 1881, aged 24, followed by Francis who died in 1886 aged 18, while the family were living in Alrewas at the Royal Oak. The third was Annie Eliza who died in 1891 aged 27. A second headstone records son Charles, a bricklayer, who died in 1898 aged 42.

In January 1901, having outlived four of their six children, Elizabeth died aged 69. Later that year William junior, who like his father had been a publican and bricklayer died aged 46. In his will he appointed his father and son, also William, as his executors. To his son he bequeathed all his scaffolding materials, ladders, tools and implements of his trade as a bricklayer, along with his watch, chain and bicycle. No headstone survives to commemorate him. In 1911 at the age of 82, William senior also died, he and his wife occupy the grave under the third headstone. Their daughter Mary, the sole survivor of their children was the wife of James Berrisford Smith, and was joint executor of her father's will with his granddaughter Lavinia, son of the late William junior and wife of George Hill.

Enoch Fleming

Enoch Fleming, a carrier between Burton and Yoxall for 30 years, pictured on his retirement in his 75th year. Burton Observer, 1 May, 1920. (Reproduced by permission of The Magic Attic).

When a man with a family lost his wife, unless other family members could take over the care of his children, it often became necessary for him to remarry, and many wasted little time in doing so regardless of whether they had children to care for. An example of this is Yoxall carrier, Enoch Fleming. In 1867 Enoch, aged 22, a labourer of Hadley End, married Mary Valentine, a widow of 'full age', and in 1871 the couple were enumerated with 3 children from Mary's marriage to John Valentine. Ten years later the couple were enumerated with only one of Enoch's step-children in the household. In July 1890 Mary died aged 55 and in December of that year Enoch married Hannah Taylor, who was enumerated in 1891 as aged 35. Between 1892 and 1898 the couple had three daughters and in the baptism register Enoch's occupation is a carrier. In 1898, the youngest daughter, Phoebe died aged 1 year. In January 1900 Enoch's wife Hannah was buried aged 44 and in August of the same year he again married, this time to 29 year old Anne Brown, Enoch was 55 years old. He was a carrier between Yoxall and Burton for 30 years and retired in 1920 in his 75th year.

A widow with young children could find herself struggling or unable to find the means to support her family. Police Sergeant Myatt was 55 years old and the oldest sergeant in the county when he died at his home in Yoxall. A newspaper report stated 'he leaves a widow and ten young children to mourn his loss, seven of the children being now entirely dependant upon the exertions of the mother and charity of friends… there is no question but that this is a case where the benevolent might wisely and liberally lend their aid'.[2]

Infant Mortality from St Peter's Burial Registers

Prior to April 1795 the age of the deceased was not entered in the burial registers. The period 1700-1749 included the following: between 1700 and 1717 there were 16 entries of 'infant' but none between 1719-1749, and between 1705 and 1731 a total of 30 'children' were entered. Also between 1700 and 1749 there were 120 entries of 'son of' and 127 'daughter of' who were presumably children, but could have included young adolescents.

For the period 1750-1799 'infants', of which there were 11, only appeared from 1764. From 1795 there were 20 age stated children of which 2 were under the age of 1 year; 11 aged 1-4 years; 4 aged 5-10 years and 3 aged 11-14 years with an additional 10 entered as 'child'. Listing of ages was inconsistent during the period and until 1814, many entries did not include an age or clue regarding it.

From 1814 to 1849 there were a total of 908 burials of which 147 were 'infants' and 125 age stated up to 15 years, of which 18 were recorded under 1 year old and 69 aged 1 to 5 years (inclusive), making a total of 234 children classed as infants and up to 5 years old from a total of 272 children, just over a quarter of all burials being children aged 5 years or less.

From 1850 to 1899 there were a total of 1016 burials of which 36 were 'infants', a category not named after 1879, and 212 age stated up to 15 years, of which 116 were under 1 year old and 75 aged 1 to 5 years. The infants and those aged up to and including 5 years being 227 out of 248 children, just under a quarter of all burials being children aged 5 years or less.

One of the most common causes of death amongst women of child bearing age was likely to be childbirth. There are close entries in the burial record of some women of child bearing years and newborns of the same name which suggest childbirth to be a cause of death of the woman. This would only account for some of the number as in many cases the infants may have survived, also the registers have their limitations as not all children were baptised, and of those that were not all were in infancy, although the majority appear to have been, evidenced by their ages in the census years.

The following are extracted from burials of presumed mother and infant who were either buried together or within at most a few months of each other, between 1876 and 1891. When Joseph Patrick and Ann Biddulph married on 26

January 1816, they could have no idea of how short that marriage was to be. Ann was pregnant and the baby, also Ann, baptised on 8 February of that year, died 6 days later and was buried on the 16th. Her mother Ann aged 19 was buried 6 days later. The marriage of Samuel Jennings to Hannah Sharratt in November 1874 lasted for eighteen months. Baby Samuel was born and baptised privately on 2 May 1876, aged 9 hours, which suggests that the infant was not expected to live long enough for the arrangement of a later baptism. Both mother and child were buried on 6 May, Hannah was 27 years old. Ann Patrick and Hannah Jennings both died after giving birth to first born infants, if no marriage has been found in St Peter's registers it is uncertain as to how long a couple were married before the fatality, and if no earlier baptisms of their children were registered, there is no clue as to how many, if any, were born before.

On 17 June 1891 Mary Jane Dainty aged 33 was buried with John aged 2 days. No baptism was registered for John.

Sarah Ann Riddell, wife of Edward had a daughter Stella who was baptised in January 1864 and another daughter, Sarah Jane baptised in November of that year who was buried in June 1865. In June 1866 Sarah Ann was buried and her infant son Lewis, baptised in April, was buried the following month.

Six months were to elapse between the burials of Sarah Ann Dean, wife of Charles, buried in June 1871 and daughter Alice, born and baptised in May and buried in November. Sarah left two children.

The possibility cannot be ruled out that other causes of death of both mother and child were possible, as they would both be less likely to survive infectious diseases than older children and women who had not recently been weakened by childbirth.

A Word on Baptisms

Date of birth was rarely included in the baptism register before 1867 and continued until 1885, when only the first 3 baptisms included the date of birth, and with the exception of a few entries was never resumed consistently. Earlier inclusions of date of birth in the registers tended to be where baptisms of several children of the same family had taken place. In 1837 4 children of Thomas Sedgewick, clockmaker of Yoxall were baptised on the same day with dates of birth ranging from 1830 to 2 months before baptism, and in 1846 children of John and Sarah Preston were baptised together, aged 12 and 14 years. From 1867 where birth dates were included baptism generally took place within a few months of birth, although there were some exceptions including 3 children of Mary Hudson, a widow of Morrey, who were born between 1859 and 1865 and baptised on the same day in 1869.

Occasionally the baptism registers give evidence to the fragility of infant life, in 1904 the baptism of John Lawrence was registered as 'Emergency F.G. Armson surgeon'. It seems his skills saved the child as his name did not subsequently appear in the burial register. Less fortunate was Thomas, son of Charles and Caroline Leedham who was baptised in 1908 'in extreme danger by Elizabeth Leitch District Nurse'. He was buried the following day having lived only 6 hours.

Perhaps the most unusual name to appear in St Peter's baptism register is that of the son of Thomas and Ann Dunn, Horatio Nelson, baptised in 1805, clearly named after the Viscount and English naval commander who died in battle in October of that year. Throughout the long reign of Victoria her name was conspicuous by its absence, appearing only once, in 1894, and then only as a second name.

Tailor Samuel Lindsey of Hoar Cross may hold the record for the number of children he fathered, or at least of those for whom the number fathered in wedlock is known. Between 1830 and 1846 baptisms have been found for 8 children, the first and last at Yoxall the rest at Christchurch, Newchurch. Of these one died in 1836 and the last born, Zilla, was baptised privately in January and at St Peter's in February, suggesting she was initially considered unlikely to survive long. Her mother Mary was buried three days before Zilla's private baptism, and Zilla followed her to the grave in July of that year. In 1851 Samuel remarried and had a further 11 children. The total of 19 places him as 2 ahead of the children of Rev. John and Margaret Arden.

Occasional References

Little information was given regarding the deceased and rarely any clue to the cause of death, but among the few exceptions was Joseph Ballad in 1796, whose age was not stated but that he was 'killed in digging a well', and in 1798 Joseph Taylor was entered as 'a chimney sweep boy'. Again no age was stated but the information regarding his occupation may suggest it was the cause of his death. In 1799 between 7 March and 19 April 5 victims of smallpox were entered, all under age 23 and 3 of them aged 2-3 years. In 1804 William Nutt aged 56 met 'A most sudden death' and Edward Lightwood aged 47 met 'A very sudden death'. In 1800 John Prince aged 64 was 'found dead in bed about two hours after his wife had left him'. William Tipper aged 53 was buried on 4 September 1807 with the additional information 'a suicide the Coroner's verdict Lunacy'.

An Older Generation

Of the 71 people buried in their 80s in the period 1814-1849 the highest incidence of burials was in January with 13, a dip in February to 5, followed by 8 in both March and April, rising to 12 in May. Between June and November the figures range from 1 to 4 burials until rising in December to 9.

From 1850 to 1899 a total of 108 people in their 80s were buried, with again the highest number in January, but this was followed by 14 in February before evening out at between 7 and 10 until August when the number ranged between 3 and 6, until December when it rose to 12. Throughout the whole period there was virtually no difference between the number of male and female burials.

The burials for those in their 90s show no indication of being more prone to death during the winter months. From the first recorded burial in 1816 to 1849, of the 12 burials, 6 females and 6 males, only 4 were recorded between January and March and none between August and December. Between 1850 and 1899 the 22 burials included a total of 10 spread evenly over the winter months of January to February and November to December, but here there was a difference in the gender, being 15 females to 7 males. The oldest person, aged 99 and two 97 year olds were all female. According to Dr Plot a Mrs Swynbourn was 'upwards of an hundred' at the time he was living in Yoxall. He fails to give a date of his residency but it would have been prior to 1686.[3] Instances of couples dying within a short time of each other include Mary Coxon aged 78 who was buried in September 1856 followed by Stephen aged 79 in the November, and George Moore who died in April 1893 aged 94 and was followed to the grave by his wife Ann aged 92 in May of that year.

Inquests

It was a requirement for Coroner's Inquests to be held not only in public, but specifically in public houses, a tradition began during the reign of Edward I (1272-1307). In later times the press were regularly in attendance and in some cases a jury was present. Such inquests were not considered acceptable to some people and most notable amongst the opponents to the system was Charles Dickens, who graphically described the proceedings at their most undignified in his novel Bleak House. Neither was this arrangement popular with some publicans. In 1889 a publican in Totnes refused to take the body of a drowned man and the coroner supported him saying that where there was not a mortuary the body could be left at the churchwarden's house, and advised the police to adopt that course in future.[4]

Yoxall was one of the many places where public houses continued to be the place to take bodies and hold inquests. During the 19th century the *Burton Chronicle* reported inquests at the following: The Crown 5, Bell & Cuckoo at Hadley End 3, Forresters Arms 2, Needwood Oak at Hadley End 1, Golden Cup 1, and unnamed public houses: Morrey 1, Needwood 1, Hadley End 1. The first inquest naming a public house in Yoxall reported in the *Burton Chronicle* took place at the Crown and concerned an accident in which 17 year old James Ball, a waggoner who had been riding on horse shafts, fell between them and under the horse. Despite the prompt attention of Dr Snoad, the surgeon, James Ball died and the jury reached a verdict of accidental death.[5] The same verdict was returned, also at the Crown, in 1876 on the death of 81 year old Edward Heathcote who died in hospital following a fall from the shaft of a waggon.[6]

Another conclusion of accidental death was reached in 1886 at the Foresters Arms on the body of 16 year old William Mosedale, who was fatally injured when a young man ran a grain fork into his face, near his eye.[7]

In 1879 the *Lichfield Mercury* reported a 'Strange Fatal Accident' in which 2 men had left their homes in Burton and walked to Hadley End, where they were seen drinking at the Bell and Cuckoo and later at the Crown where they remained until 10 o'clock in the evening after which they returned to Hadley End, where they entered a stable at a butcher's shop belonging to Mr Potts. Mewis had a gun which he had divided into 2 parts, concealed in a pocket inside his coat. Once inside, it was conjectured, that Mewis unfastened his coat and the barrel of the gun, which was loaded with cartridges fell on the stable floor. The cap caught something which caused it to explode and the whole contents of the gun were discharged into Mewis's thigh and he sank to the ground where he bled to death. Birch went for assistance and Mewis was taken to a public house and a doctor sent for. The matter was reported to the coroner and Birch was taken into custody at Burton lock up on a charge of being in a stable for an unlawful purpose.[8] The slightly early publication of the *Burton Chronicle* was further advanced with the case of the 'Extraordinary Shooting Fatality' in reporting that an inquest was held on the body at the Bell and Cuckoo and the jury returned a verdict of accidental death. Birch was taken before Major Arden and was discharged.[9]

In 1878 an inquest was held at the Needwood Oak beerhouse in Hadley End on the body of 63 year old wheelwright William Cooper whose body was discovered in the forest pit, opposite a blacksmith's shop. For a number of years he had been of intemperate habits and had been in hospital a fortnight previously. He had not lived with his wife for 5 years and for a time had stayed in Cannock but latterly had no fixed place of residence but had wandered about the neighbourhood 'in a desponding and friendless condition'. On the night before his death he was seen, apparently sober, on a road leading from Hadley End and was discovered in the pit the following morning. The jury failed to agree on his state of mind and a verdict of 'found drowned' was returned.[10]

The following year the *Burton Chronicle* reported an inquest held at the Bell and Cuckoo on a 'Revolting Case of Suicide'. It concerned 57 year old Ann Cooper, who had been unwell for about a fortnight and had sometimes showed signs of insanity. She had for a few days prior to her death been nursed by her niece as Dr Snoad, who was in attendance, had advised that she should be constantly watched. However on the day of her death the niece had left the room but returned within minutes to hear a strange sound, she turned back the covers to discover that her aunt had disembowelled herself with a knife. Dr Snoad was immediately sent for but despite replacing the bowel and stitching the wound he was unable to save her. At the inquest he stated that she had been suffering from pains in the head, which he attributed to a troubled mind. The jury returned a verdict of suicide while in a state of temporary insanity.[11] William and Ann Cooper were husband and wife, and between 1851 and 1871 had been enumerated at Hadley End with a total of 10 children. It can only be surmised that William's drinking had led to a break up of the relationship, but for some reason he had returned to Hadley End, possibly even with the hope of returning to his wife. Whatever the truth was will probably never be known, but possibly the news of his death troubled his wife so much that she was ultimately unable to come to terms with it.

In 1880 an inquest at an unnamed public house in Hadley End was reported. Catherine Barnes, aged 58, had been found dead in a pit at the back of her house. She had been married for between 4 and 5 years to Thomas Barnes, a bricklayer and beerhouse keeper. Business had been indifferent and there had been frequent quarrels. The couple were said to have lived unhappily together owing to his 'disuse of her and his idle and dissipated conduct'. Catherine had been previously married and was the mother of 12 children, one of whom she had told that she had a bill she did not know how to pay and during the morning a man named Ashmore had been to the house and mentioned a bill of sale. This had led to a quarrel between her and her husband and that afternoon she was found in the pit. While her friends were getting her body out of the water her husband came and inquired what had happened, and on being told walked away, apparently unconcerned. Although she had no marks of violence she had a week previously been assaulted by her husband and the jury, who gave a verdict of suicide while in an unsound mind, strongly condemned the conduct of her husband, who at their request was severely censured by the coroner.[12]

In 1895 an inquest was held at the Golden Cup on the body of Mary Woolley, a tramp who was described as being of weak intellect, who had been wandering about the district, calling at several houses where she obtained relief but was found dying on the road at Hadley End. The jury returned a verdict of death caused by exposure to the cold.[13] The burial register records her as being aged about 64 and of no fixed abode.

Last Wishes

Of prime concern to many male testators was that their worldly goods would not go to a future spouse of their widow, and the wills regularly reflect this. A typical example is the will of John Bradbury, a farmer of Hoar Cross who in 1724 stipulated that his bequest to his wife was relevant only 'during the terme of her natural life keeping my name & her widowhood'. If she married again the bequest was to be equally divided between his children. Tape weaver John Snape in his will of 1829 not only limited the interest received on his estate to his wife Dorothy's widowhood, but also her guardianship of his children. That Dorothy was their mother is evidenced by a baptism register. It was not only wives who had restrictions placed on their inheritance. In 1723 yeoman John Hudson bequeathed £100 to granddaughter Sarah Sadler at the age of 21 with the proviso that if she marry anyone without the consent of his executors and her grandmother she would only receive £50. Another granddaughter, Ann

Sadler was to receive the same, but if she married Thomas Scragge, or any other person without the consent of his executors and her grandmother she would receive £50. Two other unmarried Saddler granddaughters were to receive £100 each without the same restrictions. Ann did not marry Thomas Scragge, in 1733 she married Edward Thompson, who was perhaps more acceptable to her grandmother and her grandfather's executors.

When making the wills that were to provide for their loved ones, some men considered the fact that they may have unborn heirs to consider. Edward Biddulph, a yeoman of Morrey Hall in his will of 1715 instructed that 'if the Childe my wife now goeth with be borne alive and live' it was to receive twenty pounds at the age of twenty one. Many testators whose bequests included future generations would specify that these children were to be born legitimate if they were to inherit. It was rare for a testator to provide for an illegitimate heir. The few that did include cooper James Graham who bequeathed the residue of his estate equally between his children, but stated that if his daughter Sarah died, Anna Louisa, her natural child would inherit her share. In 1863 John Round of Hadley End made bequests to his 'natural son Joseph Douce commonly called Joseph Round' who was at that time residing with his father. Included in the bequests to him was his freehold garden by the road side leading from Hadley End to Morrey. With regard to the home they lived in he added 'as far as my humble desires and wishes can extend but with the permission of my respected landlord Captain Butler I trust that my said son John Round may have the privilege of the possession and occupation of the house and land I now hold under that Gentleman'. Also farmer Joseph Mason in his will of 1809 bequeathed to his sister Mary Ann Summers £50 to be paid her in twelve months after his decease, but if she should die then the £50 to be paid to her two illegitimate children in equal shares.

Rarer still was a will that requested the testator's family live in harmony, but in 1675 the will of joiner Thomas Salloway, whose bequests included timber, working tools and clothes urged all relatives who received a bequest to 'put away from amongst them all bitterness & wrath & anger & clamour & evil speaking & all malice & that they may be kind one to another, tender hearted, forgiving one another'. William Terry, a labourer of Woodhouses, in his will of 1750 showed concern regarding the relationship between his sons: 'I do desire and recommend to my sons that they live quietly and peaceably together and be ready and willing to assist each other'.

In 1807 Susannah Poyser made a will in which she chose to be buried at Kings Bromley, at the discretion of her husband. The couple had previously lived, married and had their children baptised there. It will never be known whether she changed her mind with regard to her place of burial between the making of her will and her death in 1816, but she shares a grave in St Peter's churchyard with her husband Michael who died in 1838. Although her name is 'Susannah' in all known documents, the headstone records her as 'Susan' and her inscription is below that of her husband, suggesting that prior to his decease she may not have had a memorial. It was not until 1839, the year after the grant of probate on her husband's will that probate was granted on Susannah's, due to the fact that a married woman had nothing to bequeath as everything she may have considered hers belonged to her husband prior to the Married Women's Property Act of 1882. This gave wives the right to retain ownership of property received as a gift from a parent, and the 1893 Act of the same name completed the process, giving married women full legal control of all property they owned before, or acquired after marriage, either by inheritance or their own earnings. Susannah was clearly aware of this as she bequeathed her houses and lands at Kings Bromley to her son, 'as soon as it is free from my husband Michael Poyser'. She also left bequests to her daughter, including her clothes, but unless her husband had given them to Dorothy, she would have had to wait for probate of her father's will to receive them. In 1837 Thomas Jackson, bequeathed his worldly estate to his wife Sarah Jackson including 'all her Clothes and Wearing Apparel for her own use and benefit'.

Several wills contain bequests of wives clothing to daughters years after the decease of their mothers and other testators bequeathed the clothing to other family members or servants. In 1726 Thomas Ady, yeoman of Hadley End, (husbandman in his inventory), bequeathed to Catherine Insley his servant, the bed that she lies on, the blankets and one pair of sheets, also a Mantua petticoat and riding hood that was his wife's, and to Ann wife of Thomas Mason of Fradley a 'half silk gown', presumably also his late wife's. In 1725 Edward Lane gent, of Hoar Cross Hall, bequeathed to his sister in law his late wife's best silk gown and petticoat. To his cousin her callico gown & petticoat with a suit of pinners and one muslin apron. These items he had kept despite having remarried as he also left a bequest to his wife of £10 'to buy her mourning'.

Edward Lane was one of the testators who provided for his servants after his decease. To his servant Thomas Clerke he left £20 and his best coat and waistcoat and leather breeches, also a hat, grey waistcoat and breeches 'as I now ware'. His maid servant was to receive half a year's wages above what she may be owed. Farmer John Jackson in 1852 bequeathed to his housekeeper Elizabeth Harvey £100 free of legacy duty provided she was living in his service at the time of his death. Earlier examples include Richard Agard who in 1562 bequeathed to his brother Charles 'my bay trotting gelding best doublet and cut jerkin' and a bequest to his servants at the day of his death, the amount they were to receive was not stated.[14] Also George Turner, a yeoman of Woodhouses, who in 1602 bequeathed to his man servant a pair of stockings and a pair of hose, also a ewe and lamb.

In 1839 George Hollis, servant to the Rev. Thomas Gisborne of Yoxall Lodge, foresaw his untimely end as he bequeathed to John Fox, 'now my fellow servant at Yoxall Lodge' £150, the interest of 2s a week to be paid to his mother Margaret Hollis who was living at Hoar Cross, and annually pay any accrued interest to her. After her death the £150 to be paid to his wife Hannah.

In his will of 1818 Benjamin Bond left bequests to his wife and children, adding that daughter Dorothy Bond would also get household furniture and items, the list of which covers most of the space of the will, 'in consideration of her Grandmother having forgot her in her will'.

For some their burial and memorial were of sufficient importance for them to leave instructions regarding them. John Arden in his will of 1704 requested to be buried in a decent manner according to his birth and quality. Henry Shipton the elder, gent, requested in his will of 1715 'a Christian Buryal as becometh one of my estate and degree, desiring to have my Grave covered with a large hansom Gravestone neare to my wife in a convenient place where it may not be broaken up, and also another large hansom Gravestone to be layd upon her Grave'.

It was also important to some that the mourners be appropriately attired for the occasion. In 1709 when weaver Robert Coxon made his will his concern was that his family be appropriately turned out, leaving his daughter and son each one shilling to buy gloves, his daughter in law twenty shillings to buy her a mantle, and his neighbour, who was also his executor, half a crown to buy gloves. Nathaniel Brown, yeoman, requested in his will of 1799 to be buried at Barton if he died there, or at Yoxall if it was his place of death. He wished to have four strong men to carry him to his funeral, these bearers to have gloves and hatbands. Also four named relations to follow the corpse. These were his grandsons William and John Brown, his son in law William Pott and his son Hugh Pott.

For those with the means to do so, funerals were an occasion to display their wealth and status and follow strict rules of funeral etiquette. The more lavish the funeral, the higher the status of the deceased and mourners. Those who could not afford the extravagant funerals of the rich, made the best effort they could. Undertakers or 'funeral furnishers' supplied everything, from coffin and carriage down to gloves and hatbands which could be hired for the occasion.

In Yoxall both the Wright and Twamley families were coffin makers, one Twamley entered in his diary 'From August 1851 to December 1906 I have made 561 coffins'. In Burton Yoxall born William Pott was amongst those who supplied funerary requirements. In 1878 he married Sarah, the only surviving daughter of William Wardle of Burton, a boot and shoemaker. By 1879 William was trading from 3 addresses as Potts & Broughton Funeral Furnishers and Undertakers and in 1881 was enumerated as an undertaker, sub postmaster and shoe dealer possibly having taken on his late father in law's business. By 1882 he was trading alone at 103 High Street as W. Potts The Burton Complete Funeral Furnishers.

IMPORTANT NOTICE.

W. POTTS,
THE BURTON COMPLETE FUNERAL FURNISHER.

IF you want Cheap and Well-conducted FUNERALS, go to W. POTTS, 103 HIGH ST., BURTON.

FUNERALS COMPLETELY FURNISHED FROM £1 5s. 6D.

FUNERAL CARRIAGES separate, if required.   COFFINS supplied from 7s. 6d.   HATBANDS and GLOVES on HIRE; warranted best materials.

ANY DESCRIPTION OF COFFIN AT A FEW HOURS NOTICE

Advertisement in Burton Chronicle on 23rd March 1882, one of several advertising the business of Yoxall born William Potts. (Reproduced by permission of The Magic Attic).

Chapter 19

Legends and Other Stories

A Blacksmith's Apprentice

When suicide was a crime those who resorted to it while considered to be of sound mind were not allowed burial in consecrated ground, typically being buried at night at a crossroads with no clergy present and often with a stake through the heart, traditions which ceased with The Burial of Suicide Act of 1823. According to legend a blacksmith's apprentice in Yoxall was so ill treated by his master that he took his own life and in the absence of a crossroads, two places have been suggested as possible sites for his burial, one being at the end of Savey Lane where it meets Main Street, the other Victoria Street where it meets King Street, both sites being near St Peter's. It was said that no horse would pass his burial site. One version of the story is that he was buried with a stake through his heart and in another version he was buried in a tumulus, suggesting a different site to those above, which when unearthed revealed the skeleton of a boy who had been speared to death.

A St Peter's burial register records the burial of 16 year old Daniel Worthington in 1804, having 'hanged himself in Mr Fletcher's Cart Hovel, with whom he lived Servant The Coroner's verdict, lunacy'. This verdict is seen in several inquests and was possibly chosen in some instances as a means of allowing burial in consecrated ground. Suicide was decriminalised in England and Wales by The Suicide Act of 1961.

There is also a story regarding a fatal accident to a member of the Meynell Hunt at the bottom of Savey Lane, and again no horse would pass the point, but no details have been traced.

The Mystery of Mince Pie Piece

By a footpath in Morrey there is a stile over which is a triangular piece of land (Plot 460 on the Tithe map) which the accompanying apportionment names as Mince Pie Piece. A trawl of the Survey of the Manor of Yoxall in 1742 has not uncovered the name amongst land in Morrey, some of which was owned by the Wood family. The link with mince pies as Christmas food is unlikely. More likely it was a pie made of mince meat, the shape of the plot suggesting a triangular portion which may have been eaten by men working the land there, which could suggest how it got its name.

A legend attached to it has two versions, one is that a young woman fell in love with a man and for a while all went well, but she was eventually jilted. Why is not known, perhaps he preferred another, but she baked a poisoned pie and took it to the men working on the plot, knowing her faithless lover was amongst them. The story has it that the other men were ill but her 'loved one' died. Dr

Gerald Armson offered another version in which a man poisoned his lover. He wrote of a haunted lane with a stile into a field called Mince Pie Piece, 'so called because many years ago a lover poisoned his sweetheart who was expecting his baby, by giving her a poisoned mince pie to eat whilst she sat on the stile.' Dr Armson added that he exercised horses and several dogs before it was light and about mid December he 'used to run into difficulty at this point. The dogs who usually ran ahead would crouch amongst my horse's hooves and whimper, and the horses would stick their toes in and refuse to budge. Whatever I did was of no avail but presently a curious light would flit up the hedge, the dogs would gaily go on their way and the horses strode on as if nothing had occurred. I do not try to explain this but it happened. I think that animals sense things that are beyond our ken'.[1] Occasionally people have recorded strange lights and shadows in the area. Whether there is any element of truth in either story will never be known, but in 1798 Jane Wood was buried at St Peter's and although her age was not recorded, the word 'poisoned' was. Is it coincidence that her death fell between the 1742 survey and the 1839 Tithe Map? No inquest has been traced so it may never be known whether she could have been the victim of a poisoned piece of mince pie and therefore the basis of a legend.

Longcroft Hall

Longcroft Hall outbuildings. (Ref: C/P/65/2/1/59/59.
Reproduced courtesy of Staffordshire Record Office)

Longcroft Hall had an outbuilding large enough to house two carriages. It featured a middle archway with iron gates through which the carriages passed. In later years the archway had laths going across it which became dilapidated.

A barn owl bred there and because it flew low at night got the reputation among the children of being 'Arden's Ghost'.

Dr Armson wrote of the ghost of a lady that walked along the landing and down the stairs, stating that he remembered hearing her tapping her stick as she went. After the house was sold the new owners shied away from the topic, but the doctor felt that they also had the same experience. He added that although the house was been pulled down and several houses built on the site he had heard that there were still some 'unexplained manifestations'.[2] Another version of the ghost of the lady is that she was the mother of the boy who drowned in the moat, therefore Margaret Elizabeth, wife and widow of Rev. John Arden. The story is that many years later a disused cupboard was opened which revealed a ladies costume of a time long gone and a stick.

Other Hauntings

Dr Armson also mentioned a 'very large and ancient house near here'. From where he was likely to be writing, Moat House, the nearest property of age would have been Little Manor House, but that is not large. Perhaps the old rectory or Old Hall was the ancient house referred to. He described a long passage leading from the library to the gun room, which after dark it was impossible to get a dog along, something he had witnessed on several occasions. On the subject of the supernatural Dr Armson also noted that his father went 'on an evening visit to an old lady who lived in a hamlet about half a mile away. It was dusk and as he arrived he was horrified to see his patient, dressed only in her night attire, come out of the door and hurry round the corner of the house. Full of righteous indignation he strode through the front door, but before he could speak the husband turned and said, 'She's just died Sir'.[3]

According to local lore a 'blue lady' haunted part of the old rectory, and it is said that when the Girl Guides held their meetings there the girls would not go into one of the rooms alone.

Fact and Fiction

Billy Meikle's 'Ghost at the Golden Cup'

Billy Meikle wrote retrospectively that he came to Yoxall in 1874, at the time the 'Hoar Cross Murder' had taken place, and he stayed the night at the Golden Cup. He recalled his experience there under the above title. Before going to the inn he had heard all about the murder and had seen the spot that it had taken place. He went to a shop in Yoxall to buy something to read and was told that the landlord of the Golden Cup had been drinking because his wife had left him. He also had a gun which he had borrowed from 'Master Nutt' and she did not know why he had it but guessed for no good purpose and advised Billy to go to the Crown as the Golden Cup was not safe.

Billy did not heed her warning and went to the Golden Cup where the tap room was full and 'the talk about the murder, and murders for a hundred years had been talked up'. It was the day of the inquest on the murder of Mary Kidd, and unable to read in his small room by the light of a candle he 'could do nothing else but listen to the gruesome accounts of different murders'. The tension was broken by Ned Dukes standing on his head on the table and singing 'When the World was Upside Down', and 'finished up by doing a step dance on the ceiling'. Billy failed to report the quantity of alcohol he had consumed by this time!

Billy then went to the church for evensong and arriving before anyone else, he looked at the tombs. He noted that on the tomb of Humphrey and Mary, which he erroneously wrote as 'Margery' Welles, the inscription for Humphrey included 'yielded up his soule to God' and that 'Margery's' inscription merely stated that she died. He remarked that 'Humphrey condescended to die inasmuch as he yielded up his soul but Margery died a common or garden natural death with no condescension about it whatever'.

Watercolour of The Club Room at the Golden Cup by Billy Meikle, the scene of his troubled night. (Meikle Collection: Middle of the Midlands 63/1. Reproduced by permission of Walsall Local History Centre).

After the church service he returned to the Cup to find that things had not improved as the landlord was seeing things that did not exist and he seriously considered going to the Crown. However things calmed down and at ten o'clock 'when everyone in a Public House becomes a gentleman: At least the Landlord says "Time Gentlemen Please!" and the customers all went home full of drink and murder'.

After a supper of soup, bread and cheese taken with the landlord and his daughter, Billy went up an old oak staircase with Queen Anne balustrades, into a long club room and passed pedestals with Odd Fellows' devices painted on them. His room for the night was at the far end of the club room and partitioned off from it. The partition could be taken down on occasions when more space was needed.

Billy locked his door, his thoughts on the borrowed gun, and went to sleep. He was awoken by 'a fearful crash' and wondered if he had been shot. Realising he had not, he 'ventured to look from under the bedclothes, there sure enough 30 feet away stood the landlord with a candle in one hand and the borrowed gun in the other'. The cause of the disturbance was discovered to be the partition that had fallen and Billy went back to bed in a room '6 times as large as it was two hours before'.[4] So no ghost in Billy's story, despite the title, but for him the experience was possibly equally frightening as seeing one would have been.

Charles Hancock was innkeeper of the Golden Cup in 1874 and unless his wife left him, and later returned, as the couple were together in the 1881 census, then the above story suggests that Billy's visit to Yoxall was later. This is evidenced from a court case reported in the *Burton Chronicle* in 1879. Rebecca, wife of John Richards, who was at the time the landlord, was sued by her son in law John Twigg. It was stated that John's wife had left him 'some time ago' and returned her wedding ring. The couple had been living at the Golden Cup which had been transferred to John Richards and he had returned to collect some things which he said belonged to him. Rebecca refused to let him take them and he refused to leave and in the scuffle that followed she bit his arm. She was fined 5s and costs for the assault, and the case against John Twigg, who the couple had charged with refusing to leave the premises, was dismissed.[5]

Five years elapsed from the time of the murder of Mary Kidd in November 1874 and the above court case. Due to the flights of fantasy which tend to be woven into Billy Meikle's stories of his travels, it remains uncertain as to whether the story of the landlord's wife having left him was fabrication, or whether he based it on the above account. If the latter, he would have visited Yoxall in 1879, at the time John Twigg's wife had left him. He would also have known about the murder as it was well publicised and may have given a false date of his visit in order to place himself in Yoxall just after the murder, in order to write his fictitious account of the case.

Billy Meikle at The Crown Inn

Billy Meikle claimed he revisited Yoxall a year after the murder of Mary Kidd and discovering the Cup closed he stayed at The Crown, and later wrote about his experience there.[6] Billy described the landlord, Thomas Cooper and his wife Jane as 'a splendid old Staffordshire couple', though according to the census of 1881 Thomas was born in Ticknall Derbyshire and both were in their 40s. Billy described the Crown as 'a Tudor Building but the front has been altered and spoiled, but the interior is unaltered and very quaint'. He told of how after tea he had read in the *Birmingham Post* accounts of the Arctic expedition led by

Nares and Markham [1875-86] which, having been given up as lost, had unexpectedly arrived in Scotland. Billy went to the tap room where all were eager to hear the news and a reader was appointed to relate it to the farmers there.

Billy then wrote of Nellie the daughter, and only child of the 'old folk'. Nellie was in fact born in 1875 to Jane, then Upton who was single, and was registered and baptised as Ellen, although in the censuses she was Nellie. Her parents married soon after her birth and Nellie was enumerated with her grandmother, Anna Upton in 1881 but with her parents at the Crown in 1891. Clearly Billy is wrong with his calculation of the year of his visit, evidenced by both the age of Nellie at the time of his visit and the fact that the expedition referred to had been presumed lost. Nellie came into the bar asking for a candle to go to bed, which her mother refused. Billy stated that there was a 'Mr Brierly' [George Brierley of White Wood Farm] in the bar who was a big farmer and cattle dealer who knew how to 'pull Mrs Cooper's leg and knew how to nag her', which he did about Nellie wanting a candle which he said was outrageous. Mrs Cooper replied "Mind they own business Master Brierly if Candles were a quid each I could buy 10 times as many candles as the could Master Brierly and pee for them in gold Master Brierly which the couldna do".

Billy described his bedroom as having a concrete floor and no carpets and very little furniture, and it was exceptionally cold as winter had started early, at the end of October, 'and to cap it all when I got into bed the sheets were linens'. He jumped out of bed and shouted "Mrs Cooper I've found it; I've found it!' She came to the door and asked what he had found to which he replied the North Pole. She took the candle from him and told him he would go to bed without one, like Nellie had to. Billy concluded his story with mentioning that Mrs Brierly drowned when taking a short cut home from Alrewas when the Trent was in flood. Again this last 'fact' is inaccurate as it was George Brierley who drowned in the Trent in November 1890.

The Swarbourn

Billy was not alone in mixing fact and fiction. The fact that when the Swarbourn broke its banks it ran through the houses, across the road and visited the Crown is indisputable, but that trout were caught in the bar, cooked and served there is more likely a fisherman's tale.

Old Bones

More convincing perhaps is a story remembered by a former resident who was told during the 1940s that large old bones were found in or immediately outside the churchyard. These were discovered early in the 20th century and were believed to be tall people from the forest. Rev. Cory is said to have buried them but there is no record of this in the burial register. If the details are accurate the events would have taken place prior to his death in 1922.

232

Another Side to Thomas Gisborne

The following story was not included with the discussion of Thomas Gisborne, the author and abolitionist, in chapter 8. If true it shows a different side of his character to the one generally portrayed:

Sir James Fitzjames Stephen married Wilberforce's sister Sarah, who was the widow of Rev. D. Clarke of Hull. She is said to have been a rather eccentric but very vigorous woman who spent almost all of her income, which was between £300 and £400 per year on charity, saving only £10 for her clothes. She was often seen parading Clapham in rags and tatters and Thomas Gisborne, described as a leading light of the Clapham set, once tore her skirt from top to bottom at Yoxall Lodge, saying "Now Mrs Stephen, you must buy a new dress". Her response was to calmly stitch it together and appear wearing it the following day.[7] Her husband's response was not recorded.

John Brown's Jug

Maltster John Brown died in 1853 and amongst the effects not listed in his will was a white porcelain jug, painted with hops and barley and inscribed in gilt 'John Brown, Yoxall, 1811'. It is currently in the possession of Stoke Museums. To accompany the jug is the information that John Brown had his horse stolen in September 1822 and advertised in the Staffordshire Advertiser for its recovery with a reward offered of 5 guineas, the same amount also being offered by the Yoxall Association for the Prosecution of Felons but had no response.

The following spring John Brown had two men arrested who were riding through Yoxall on suspicion that their horses were stolen. The men were two professional thieves who, over a period of two years, had stolen around 200 horses in Staffordshire, Derbyshire, Bristol and London, including John's own mare which was safely returned to him. The thieves were tried in London and John gave evidence against them and they received the death sentence.

John was again the victim of crime in 1823 when silver and money were taken from his house. He offered a reward of 40 guineas but the outcome is not known.[8]

It is likely that Brown's Lane, otherwise known as Doctors Lane due to the fact that it ran alongside Brook House surgery, may have been named after John Brown who owned and occupied land in the village as well as a malthouse.

Chapter 20

Leisure and Celebration

Reading Room and Library

In 1864 a concert, held in aid of the funds of the Yoxall Reading room and Library, was given in the boys' school room. Mr Thomas Brandon of Gloucester Cathedral, once a well known inhabitant of Yoxall, and Mr Bedsmore, the accomplished organist of Lichfield Cathedral, provided the entertainment.[1] In 1885 Yoxall Amateur Choral Society held a concert from which the proceeds were given for the benefit of the village reading room. The amount raised was not stated. The room, open from 10 am to 10 pm was supplied with 'a good number of useful and instructive books, as well as two daily papers and weekly illustrated and other periodicals'.[2] It seem that this closed at some time as in 1891 it was announced that a reading room was opened in Yoxall. No mention is made of books but 'a liberal supply of papers and games' were available to members. Described as a 'long-felt want', the attendance on the first night was good.[3] The Parish Magazine of July 1897 announced that the library had been increased by more than 20 volumes given by Mr Norman, besides several travel books given during the year by Mr Arden. The reading room was well attended, 'and supplies the young men with much-needed evening resort. We should like to see a greater demand for books other than novels'. At a meeting of the Parish Council it was agreed that £1 a year should be paid to the rector for the use of the library as a meeting room for the Parish Council.[4] The parish magazine of January 1899 included a reminder that the library was open on Tuesday afternoons between 3 and 4 o'clock and Thursday evenings between 7.30 and 8. Quarterly submissions were one penny each.

Musical entertainments were held for other fundraising purposes. In 1886 £3 17s 6d was raised towards new uniforms for the Yoxall band and to obtain additional ropes for the hand bell ringers.[5]

Parish Magazine

The first surviving copy was published in December 1896, entitled *St Peter's Church, Yoxall, Parish Magazine*. It does not appear to be the first issue as there is no mention of its introduction. The magazine comprised three printed sides and was initially produced quarterly. The first issue included a mention of the first quarterly meeting of the Mothers' Union and the hope that 'the MU will become really useful in this parish'. New lamps at the church had been in use for some weeks. 'Visitors to Yoxall all congratulate us on the beauty of the design and the pleasant lights'.

The magazine served more than the purpose of updating people on events in the parish, it was also a means of publicising occasions when funds were needed.

In July 1897 it was reported that the churchwardens had found considerable repairs to the church necessary, and asked for assistance in funding them as they were more than could be met by the income of the church. Ladies of the congregation proposed to hold a sale of work in August to meet the churchwardens needs and repay the debt of the Choir Fund. Should sufficient funds be raised a scheme had been suggested to re-heat the church, so that it 'may be warm without being stifling, and air fresh without drafts'. The cost of the scheme was believed to be about £200, which was admitted to be ambitious, with the new schools having just been paid for. By 1900 the magazine had extended to five sides.

Penny Readings

Penny readings, consisting of readings and other performances, for which a penny was charged, became popular from the mid 19th century. In February 1868 Yoxall held the fourth of a series of readings, in the girls' school room. It was presided over by Mr G. Shipton and the attendance was as numerous as on the first occasions.[6] In March the last of the series was so well attended that standing room was uncomfortably pressed. The programme opened with an overture played by Miss Ellis and Mrs Smelt, (music teachers), and a duet was included, on the pianoforte, by Master Smelt and Miss Riddell, which was 'admirably performed considering the ages of the performers' who were about twelve years old.[7] In 1869 the audience of a Penny Reading was estimated as at least 300 people.[8]

Sport

Alfred 'Pop' Lester, 'England's oldest cricketer'. (Reproduced by permission of The Magic Attic).

In 1868 members of Yoxall Cricket Club included T. and C. Hancock, W. Riddell, C. Upton, E. and M. Snoad, F. Riddell and T. Leedham.[9] In December 1880 a dinner was held at Holly Hurst, residence of Captain Willoughby Wood, who was president, to celebrate the amalgamation of Yoxall football and cricket clubs. During the event Mr Bagot announced that he and Captain Wood each intended giving a silver cup of equal value for the best batting and bowling averages during the season of 1881.[10] By 1886 Yoxall Rangers Football Club had been formed.

There was also a Hoar Cross cricket club from at least 1889 when it held an account at Norman's store, and in 1891 the club held a ball which was attended by over 100 people, despite heavy rain, and dancing continued until 5 am.[11] One keen cricketer of note was blacksmith, wheelwright, craft and tradesman, Alfred 'Pop' Lester. He played into his 80s and became, unofficially, Britain's oldest cricketer. During the 1950s a reporter interviewing him asked why his sons did not play for Yoxall. Pop, then aged 84, replied that they were much too old for such activities and had long since retired.[12] Pop, who won both cups in 1900, and E. Roberts were 'useful all-rounders' and Dr Charles Armson, a prolific batsman. During the inter war years the Twamley family dominated, four of them have their names on the trophies.[13]

Yoxall also had a tennis club by 1894,[14] and in 1896 a Private Lawn Tennis Club held a tournament arranged by Miss Arden and Mrs Boden. Miss Clark, the matron of the hospital gave tea on the ground.[15]

Horticulture

The Yoxall and Hamstall Horticultural Society exhibited at each place in alternative years. In 1880 it was the turn of Yoxall, where the exhibition was held in a 'monster' marquee in a field adjoining the Cup Inn. The principal exhibits were arranged on a table stretching almost the length of the marquee, which also housed exhibits on 3 smaller tables. This was despite the fact that about 3 weeks before the event Yoxall was visited by 'a terrific and destructive hailstorm. Hailstones as large as marbles fell thickly and cut off a large quantity of garden produce, especially lettuce, cabbage and similar vegetables'.

Yoxall Flower Show, 1913. (Reproduced by permission of the Magic Attic).

Class I, the 'chief class', comprised garden and wild flowers, bouquets, greenhouse plants, fruit and vegetables. The principal Yoxall prize winners in this class included Major Arden and Mrs Shipton. Class II was open to cottagers and included baskets of flowers, berries, potatoes and window plants. Children were entered in class III, where they exhibited wild flowers, and prizes were awarded for design or garland, bouquet, and collections of different grasses. Class IV was for model flowers, Class V was open to honorary members only and Class VI was for the best dish of fruit. There was also a prize for the best cottage and garden, which for Yoxall was won by W. Bostyn and the best stocked and cultivated flowers, for which W. Hutchinson took 1st prize.[16]

Teas and Dances

Clubs, societies and individuals held teas and dances, one such being the 24th anniversary of the Ladies Club in 1898. Tea was provided for about 200 by victuallers the Wakelins in a large tent at the Cup Inn, after which the tent was cleared for dancing. Among those present were Rev. Cory, Dr Frank and Mrs Armson, Misses Brown, Miss Loverock and Mrs John Upton. They were entertained by Mr Weir of Burton and his display of electric light.[17] The same year the annual Christmas tea and dance took place in the new school, organised by Miss Brown of Bond End House. Dancing continued until the early hours, to music supplied by Mr G. Heathcote. Proceeds from the evening were to go to the school fund.[18] The following year it was reported that dancing had continued at the Old Ladies Club until 10 pm.[19]

One person who stands out for the amount of entertainment he offered was Robert Sutcliffe Mort. In March 1889 a report of a fancy dress ball at the Crown was the 4th invitation ball he had given during the past season. Dancing commenced at 8 pm and continued until 4 am. Amongst the most conspicuous characters represented were Buffalo Bill, a brigand, Spanish bull fighters, court dress, etc.[20]

Brides, Bracelets and Triumphal Arches: Two Nineteenth Century Shipton Weddings

In 1877 Yoxall celebrated the wedding of Sarah Elizabeth, the 32 year old eldest daughter of George Harvey Shipton and his wife Elizabeth, of Bank House, Yoxall. Sarah married widower Herbert Russell, a solicitor of Lichfield.

Reported in the *Burton Chronicle*, the article states '…the village was given to rejoicing and decoration. Nearly every house had flags and banners exhibited, while from the tower of the church floated the Union Jack, and on the road from the house of the bride to the church eight triumphal arches were erected, each bearing a motto suitable to the occasion.' This 'testified to the great esteem in which the bride and her family were held'. The bride was attended by four bridesmaids who were her unnamed sisters. There is no description of what the bride or bridesmaids wore. After the wedding breakfast at Bank House the bride and groom left for Burton Station bound for their honeymoon in Scotland.[21]

The second daughter, 34 year old Helen, married in 1880. The *Burton Chronicle* account of Helen's wedding is far longer than that of her sister. The bridegroom, also a widower, was James Samble of Burton, a timber merchant for Charles Perks and Sons. The number of triumphal arches is not stated but they are described as 'spanning the roadway from the bride's residence to the church, and in the other direction from Bank House to midway between Yoxall and Barton.' The bride wore a 'cream satin dress, trimmed with limerick lace, gracefully adorned with a bridal veil and wreath of orange blossoms'. The bridesmaids, Helen's sisters, Louisa Harvey, Mary and Kate Emmeline and Miss F Dingle, were 'each attired in cream satin dresses and wore handsome bracelets, the gift of the bridegroom'.

The wedding presents, described as 'numerous and valuable and arranged on a trio of tables at the bride's residence' included 'a pair of crystal flower stands supported by gilt figures', and 'a watercolour landscape in a massive gilt frame', also silver cutlery and cruets, two sets of silver bracelets, various crystal items and a china candelabra. Amongst the silver items was a cream jug and bowl from 'the tenants and friends on the estate', and a 'biscuit barrel etc. from the children attending the Yoxall National School'.

The wedding breakfast for about 40 friends, was served in a marquee on the lawn in front of Bank House, after which the bride and groom left under a shower of rice and old shoes for their honeymoon on the Continent, via London. Tea was provided for the school children in a marquee. Although the sun had shone during the wedding by the time the children assembled it was raining, but despite the heavy rainfall and the subsequent cancellation of outdoor amusements the children marched through the village, headed by the brass band. In the evening the bell ringers and friends dined at the Cup Inn.[22]

Few Yoxall weddings would have been so spectacular. Many brides of the time would not have had a wedding dress but worn the best dress they had. If Yoxall residents looked forward to the wedding celebrations of George Harvey Shipton's other three daughters they were to be disappointed as none of them married. Some readers will remember the youngest, Kate Emmeline, who later lived at Yew Tree House and died in 1960, aged 95.

Marriage of the Prince of Wales

In 1863 the marriage of the Prince of Wales was celebrated in Yoxall. Prior to the occasion a meeting was held by the inhabitants who unanimously agreed that the day should be a general holiday, and that the shops would close at 11.30. A procession of children and the Yoxall clubs was to be followed by tea for the children and refreshments for the labourers and their wives, also a firework display.[23] A report of the day states that 'garland after garland was erected over the streets, each trying to outdo his neighbour in devise, colour, and appearance'. At one o'clock the procession of 700 people formed, including the Yoxall band, friendly societies with their banners, and other inhabitants including the poor men and women. 'At the School Green, from its open space, the scene was grand and imposing. Upwards of 300 men partook of the national fare - roast beef, plum pudding, and ale. The school children were regaled with buns and tea, and afterwards the women, 550 in number, had tea etc, in the school. Fireworks by Mr Wilder of Birmingham, succeeded. Altogether the managing committee so far carried out their plans that the village could not be said to be second to any place in the kingdom of its size'. The rector, the Rev. Henry Sullivan, attended at Windsor Castle, and was presented at the Royal wedding.[24]

Queen Victoria's Jubilees

In 1887 the Golden Jubilee of Queen Victoria was celebrated throughout the nation. Not since the troubled reign of George III had a monarch reigned for fifty years. Yoxall enthusiastically joined the celebrations on Saturday 18th June, when the monarch was 'right worthily honoured'. The village was decorated with flags, mottos, garlands of flowers and evergreens. The day began at 6 am. Mr and Mrs Shipton presented a new flag, which was hoisted on the church tower, a *feu de joie* (a salute fired by musketry), and bell ringing followed. A thanksgiving service, conducted by the Rev. T. Lewis (curate), was held at St Peter's at 12 o'clock. This was followed by a traditional feast of roast beef which was combined with dishes 'of a more recent introduction'. The *Burton Chronicle*, does not elaborate on what these dishes were. However it does quantify the amount of alcohol served as being 'three thirty six gallons'. (Possibly to avoid confusion as barrels and casks are often confused. Cask is the overall term, a barrel contains 36 gallons). The alcohol was provided by Mr A. Crossman of Longcroft Hall, a partner in the brewery Mann, Crossman & Co. Teetotallers were catered for with lemonade and ginger-beer. This earlier meal was for the estimated 150 men, for whom the women waited at table. The roles were reversed at 4 pm when about the same number of women sat down to a 'substantial meat tea', following this about 200 children were served meals. The tent, was decorated with festoons, also garlands and vases of flowers, all of which had been the work of most of the ladies of the village. The band played music during the dinner, and afterwards for dancing. Left over food was distributed to invalids and others unable to attend. George Fearns of the Golden Cup had been granted an extension of two hours beyond the usual licensing hours for the celebration of the Jubilee.[25]

In 1897 the sum of £100 was collected to celebrate Victoria's Diamond Jubilee. Again the day began at 6 am with the hoisting of a new flag and a volley of twenty-one shots fired from the church tower, followed by bell ringing. A service was held at 10.45, followed at 12.30 by a dinner of roast beef, mutton, veal, with plum puddings etc., and a meat tea for the women and children at 4.30. A supper was also provided at 8.30. During the afternoon and evening various sports were enjoyed and the evening concluded with a bonfire.[26]

End of the Boer War Celebrations

The Boer War broke out in 1899 and in February 1900 the relief of Ladysmith was a significant victory, and when the 1901 census was taken farmer Stephen Knight at Hoar Cross was enumerated at 'Ladysmith Farm (formerly The Gullets)'. News of the relief of Mafeking was brought into Yoxall village by the mail driver, and the place was quickly decorated with flags. In the evening the village band played, a bonfire was lit in the Hall orchard, and several guns were fired. 'Afterwards Dr Armson regaled the rejoicing crowd with tea, coffee, etc.'.[27]

The surrender of Pretoria followed quickly and Yoxall celebrated the news of the surrender of Pretoria rather more dramatically. The church bells were rung, flags and banners appeared and during the afternoon repeated volleys of 21 guns were fired from the church tower. In the evening Joseph Roobottom drove a pair of horses and dray loaded with children round the village. This was followed by a procession, headed by the Yoxall brass band, and a conveyance carrying an effigy of a well guarded Mr Kruger, followed by the Field Marshall on a white trooper, Mr Wakelin's carriage and a crowd bringing up the rear. After parading the village Oom Paul was publicly hung and placed in a large heap of thorns put together for the occasion in Mr Hall's Lea field. Dr Armson proposed cheers for Lord Roberts, Badon-Powell, and the generals, officers, and men of both army and navy. Then came the last act of the drama, the setting fire to the sticks and burning the President of the South African Republic. During the process volley firing went on amid renewed cheering, and the whole concluded with "God save the Queen".[28]

Opening of the Parish Hall

Lady Noreen Bass laid the foundation stone of Yoxall Parish Hall in 1904.
(Reproduced by permission of The Magic Attic).

240

In October 1904 contractor John Wright of Yoxall commenced the building of the parish hall, and Lady Noreen Bass laid the foundation stone that November. The building was opened in August 1905 by Lady Burton. The building, with furnishing cost between £700 and £800 and was opened free of debt. Apart from the initial £200 given by John Siward Arden in 1897 to raise funds for the hall, to which he added a further £100, other subscribers were: Mr L. Arden of Barton, £100; Lord Burton, £75; Mr W. A. H. Bass, £75; Mr Franklyn of Longcroft, £25; Sir Gerald Hardy, £10; Mr C. J. Clay, £5; Major Ratcliff, MP, £5; and Lord Leigh £3. Members of the parish council raised £15, the cost of installing the lighting system, which was by lamps. The interior was described as a good sized vestibule giving access to the main room of 50 ft by 25 ft and behind it ante rooms, one being 18 ft by 12, the other 7 ft by 10, and at the rear of the building a covered in outbuilding. The interior walls were colour washed, the lower part being painted and varnished in dark brown.

Lady Burton opened Yoxall Parish Hall in 1905. (Reproduced by permission of The Magic Attic).

For the opening ceremony both interior and exterior parts of the building were decorated with flags, streamers and bunting. The approaches to the roadway in front of the building were spanned by arches with inscriptions in red and blue letters, on backgrounds of white material, edged with ivy and other greenery. There was a very large attendance at the opening ceremony, at which Dr F. G. Armson, chairman of the parish council presided. Lady Burton was accompanied by Lord Burton and Miss Thornewill. Among those who were then present, or at the bazaar which followed were Countess Crawford, Lady Mary Meynell, members of the Franklyn family and Rev. and Mrs Cory. The bazaar was held to raise funds for the repair of the church tower and the replacement of the clock, also a thorough cleaning of the organ. The parish had raised £100 and it was hoped that the bazaar would raise the rest of the money required which was at least £80. Stalls displayed needlework, fancy work and goods, photographs, china, flowers and rummage. Amongst the names of those assisting on the stalls were ladies from the families of Arden, Armson, Cory, Franklyn, Loverock, Shipton, Upton, Wright and Wibberley.[29]

Yoxall Parish Hall.

Opening of Yoxall Dairy

Opening of Yoxall Dairy in 1906. (Reproduced by permission of The Magic Attic).

At a meeting of the Dairy Farm Association held at the Crown in 1898, a letter was read from the county secretary suggesting a co-operative factory in the district.[30] It was to be some time later before a dairy factory was built at Yoxall, but in 1906 Lady Burton opened the newly formed Yoxall and District Co-operative Dairy Society Limited.

Again the village was festooned with flags, banners and flowers. After the opening, which was well attended, Lord Burton read a portion of a letter from Lord Lichfield, who trusted that the company would be a success and that the farmers would obtain a better price for their milk. He was not a believer in a great number of these factories, but 'under the exceptional circumstances in which Yoxall was placed he believed it was necessary'. He was prepared to give £100 in preference shares on condition that the factory was conducted on the lines laid down by the committee of the Farmers Association, and stated the importance of keeping cows cleanly, for the success of the business.[31] The premises included separating, cheese making and drying rooms on the ground floor, and a room for storing and drying cheese above. A cold storage and freezing plant was connected to the building, with a bacteria bed, to deal with any sewage remnants found in various processes of the manufacture. The machinery was capable of dealing with the product of 700 cows daily. The audience at the opening ceremony was reminded that the Yoxall company was the first of its kind established in Staffordshire.[32]

Work stopped for a photo at Yoxall Dairy. Date unknown. (Reproduced by permission of Audrey Jackson).

Moving Forward and a Backward Glance

Yoxall has seen both continuity and change. A returning Georgian would recognise parts of the village, with many of its older houses having a façade created during that period.

King Street, showing from left to right, wall of Flixton Cottage, the thatched building was later demolished, Fearnlea, St Peter's School, Yoxall Parish Hall and a house now demolished. Date unknown.

(Reproduced by permission of The Magic Attic).

Bond End showing Yew Tree House and The Hollies, prior to infill building. Date unknown. (Reproduced by permission of The Magic Attic).

The Great War took its toll on the sons of Yoxall and the majority are commemorated on a memorial plaque in St Peter's, which names thirty, but they are another story.

In 1960 three cottages facing St Peter's were demolished and replaced by a house. The decade saw not only the demolition of Old Hall, but the building of a housing estate between Savey Lane and Bondfield Lane from the end of the decade and into the 1970s, which also saw the building of Gisborne Close off Victoria Street. Houses were built at Weaverslake in the late 1990s and Alexandra Drive in 2001, and most recently St Peter's Walk has been built on land late of Leafields farm, between the A515 and Hadley Street.

Rental of pews to families or individuals continued in churches until the early to mid 20th century. In 1934 the Yoxall Parish Magazine began to advertise on the cover the fact that all seats were free. The cemetery, which belongs to Yoxall Parish Council, was opened in the 1950s. The churchyard surrounding St Peter's was closed by Order of the Council in 1980 as there was no space left for burials.

Not everyone welcomed the 20th century, or even the 19th as an auction sale which took place in 2013 at Hanson's Auctioneers at Etwall, Derby revealed. Publicised as 'A Passion for the 17th Century The Complete and Valuable Oak and Country Contents of a Staffordshire Estate' the contents of a large cottage were sold, the majority of furniture from the 17th and occasionally the 18th century.

Described as a 17th century 'time capsule' by Charles Hanson. Furniture in situ at the hamlet home. Another bed was alleged to have been slept in by James I. The jewel in the crown of the sale was an oil painting of two boys, in the manner of Sir Peter Lely, which fetched £62,000. (Photo copyright Paul Tonge for Hansons Auctioneers).

NOTES

CHAPTER 1

1   Horovitz, *Place Names of Staffordshire,* p.598.
2   Ibid., p.397.
3   Ibid., p.134.
4   Ibid., p.318.
5   Erdswick, *A Survey of Staffordshire*, p.209.
6   Horovitz, *Place Names of Staffordshire,* p.472.
7   Ibid., p.499.
8   Kettle, *List of Families, SHC,* [4th ser.], 8, (1976), pp.172-4.
9   Hislop, 'Reeve End Cottage', *SSAHCT,* XXVII, (1987), p.52.
10 Shaw, *Staffordshire,* I, p.331.
11 *VCH, Staffordshire,* I, (1908, reprinted 1968), p.185.
12 LRO, B/A/15/752.
13 SCC, *Historic Environment Charter Assessment: East Staffordshire,* (2013), p.76.
14 Shaw, *Staffordshire,* I, p.99.
15 Palliser, 'Staffordshire Castles a Provisional List', *Staffordshire Archaeology*, I, (1972), p.8.
16 Hislop, 'Two Medieval Houses in East Staffordshire', *SSAHST,* XXXVIII, (1999), p.35.
17 *Burton Mail*, 15 July, 2004; *Lichfield Mercury*, 22 July, 2004.
18 Stuart, *Yoxall: a walk through history,* p.7.
19 Ibid., p.12.
20 All references to the Court Baron are SRO, D (W) 1522/20-27.
21 Stuart, *Yoxall: a walk through history,* p.5.
22 *VCH, Staffordshire,* X, (2007), p.287.
23 Macfarlane, *120 Years a Village Doctor,* p.25.
24 *VCH, Staffordshire,* X, (2007), p.288.
25 Shaw, *Staffordshire,* I, p.99.
26 Macfarlane, *120 Years a Village Doctor,* p.28.
27 *SHC*, [1st ser.], VII, (1886), p.48.
28 *SHC*, 1911, p.249.
29 Shaw, *Staffordshire,* I, p.95.
30 Ibid.
31 *VCH, Staffordshire,* X, (2007), p.288.
32 *SHC*, [1st ser.], XI, (1890), p.279.
33 SRO, D603/K/5/19.
34 *VCH, Staffordshire,* X, (2007), p.288.
35 *SHC*, 1938, pp.65-6.
36 *Burton Chronicle*, 10 October, 1867.
37 *SHC*, 1911, p.250.
38 Pitt, *Staffordshire,* p.54.
39 *VCH*, II, (1967 reprinted 1984), p.349, n.18.
40 Armson, *The History of Yoxall,* unpublished.
41 Johnson & Vaisey, *Staffordshire and the Great Rebellion*, undated, p.26.
42 SRO, Q/SR. M.1654, f.46; Johnson & Vaisey, *Ibid.* p.66.
43 Ibid., Q/SR. E.1659, ff43 sqq.; Johnson & Vaisey, *Ibid.* p.67.
44 Palliser, *Staffordshire Landscape*, p.71.
45 *SHC*, [new ser.], X, (I), 1907, pp.88-92.

46 Beresford, *Diocesan Histories*, p.168-9.
47 *VCH*, X, (2007), p.294.
48 Ibid., pp.302-3.
49 *SHC*, 1912, p.296.
50 SRO, D (W) 1522/20-27.
51 Stuart, *Yoxall: a walk through history*, p.18.
52 Armson, *The History of Yoxall*, unpublished.
53 *SHC*, 1934, p.25.
54 Jervoise, *Ancient Bridges*, p.3-4.
55 *SHC*, 1934, p.87.
56 *Burton Chronicle*, 16 April, 1874.

CHAPTER 2

1   Wesley, *Burton upon Trent*, p.150.
2   *VCH*, X, (2007), p.289.
3   Ibid., pp.289-90.
4   Field, *English Field Names*, p.270.
5   LRO, B/A/15.
6   Kelly's *Dir. Staffordshire*, 1851, p.612.
7   Ibid., 1896, p.524.
8   White, *Dir. Staffordshire*, 1834, p.470.
9   *VCH*, X, (2007), p.290.
10 White, *Dir. Staffordshire*, 1834, p.470.
11 Harrod, *Dir. Staffordshire*, 1870, p.1151.
12 Kelly's, *Dir. Staffordshire*, 1872, p.860.
13 Ibid., 1860, p.747.
14 Ibid., 1872, p.860.
15 Ibid., 1924, p.632.
16 Ibid., 1936, p.636.
17 Ibid., 1880, p.156.
18 Ibid., 1896, p.195.
19 Armson, *The History of Yoxall*, unpublished.
20 Kelly's, *Dir. Staffordshire*, 1896, p.524.
21 *St. Peter's Church & Village Magazine*, January 2000.
22 Kettle, 'List of Families', *SHC*, [4th ser.], 8, (1976), pp.172-4; LRO: B/A/27ii.
23 Stuart, *Social History of Yoxall*, p.14.
24 Shaw, *Staffordshire*, I, p.99.
25 Morris, *Journeys of Celia Fiennes 1685-c.1712*, (1995), p.149.
26 *VCH, Staffordshire*, I, (1908 reprinted in 1968), p.323.
27 *Burton Chronicle*, 17 November, 1870.
28 *Burton Mail*, 11 September, 2006.
29 Tringham, *Study of the Barton Census for 1881*, p.8.
30 Ibid., p.10.
31 Stuart, *Abbots Bromley*, p.18.
32 *Burton Chronicle*, 1 November, 1894.
33 Ibid., 28 November, 1895.
34 Ibid., 20 August, 1896.
35 Ibid., 26 August, 1897.
36 Ibid., 25 March, 1897.
37 Ibid., 13 March, 1898.
38 Ibid., 20 April, 1899.

39   Ibid., 26 October, 1899.

40   Ibid., 26 April, 1900.

41   Ibid., 2 April, 1914.

42   Stuart, *Yoxall: a walk through history*, p.9.

43   Ibid., *The Yoxall Bridge-Ashbourne Turnpike Road*, p.13.

44   Stuart, *Yoxall: a walk through history*, p.4.

45   Housecroft, *Olde Yoxall*, p.8.

46   SRO, D730/7/1, Parish Charities 1798-1874.

47   *Burton Chronicle*, 19 July, 1877.

48   Ibid., 27 February, 1890.

49   *VCH*, II, (1967), p.324.

50   Yates, *South Staffordshire Railway,* I, (2010), p.70-71.

CHAPTER 3

1   Shaw, *Staffordshire*, I, p.99.

2   Pitt, *Staffordshire,* p.59.

3   Shaw, *Staffordshire,* I, p.104.

4   Jansen & Jordan, *Welles Anthology,* p.3.

5   Ibid., pp.5-7.

6   Shaw, *Staffordshire,* I, p.100.

7   Chetwynd-Stapleton, *Chetwynds of Ingestre*, p.188.

8   Landed families of Britain and Ireland, Nick Kingsley,
     http://landedfamilies.blogspot.co.uk.170-arden-of-park-hall-and-longcroft.html.
     This source has provided much information regarding the Arden family, in
     conjunction with Burke's Landed Gentry 1969 and other sources.

9   Shaw, *Staffordshire,* I, p.102.

10   *VCH*, X, (2007), p.288.

11   *SHC*, [new ser.], IX, (1906), p.26.

12   *SHC*, XIII, (1892), p.296.

13   Shaw, *Staffordshire,* I, p.102.

14   Stuart, *Social History of Yoxall*, p.117.

15   *Burke's Landed Gentry*, (1969), p.16.

16   Australian Dictionary of Biography, online edition:
     http://adbonline.anu.edu.au.biogs/A010027b.htm.

17   *Leeds Times,* 21 February, 1846, p.4.

18   Shaw, *Staffordshire,* I, p.332.

19   Pitt, *Staffordshire,* p.59.

20   Armson, *The History of Yoxall*, unpublished.

21   *VCH*, X, (2007), p.303.

22   *SHC*, 1912, p.148.

23   Ibid., [1ˢᵗ ser.], XII, (1), 1891, p.212.

24   Shaw, *Staffordshire,* I, p.101.

CHAPTER 4

1   Stuart, *Social History of Yoxall*, p.68.

2   Pevsner, *Buildings of England: Staffordshire*, p.330.

3   Shaw, *Staffordshire,* I, p.100.

4   *SHC*, [new ser.], X, (2), (1907), pp.137-8.

5   Ibid., 1916, p.191.

6   Ibid., 1911, p.253 & 255.

7   Ibid., [1st ser.], I, (1880), p.284, n.20.

8   Ibid., p.286, n.18.

9   *VCH, Staffordshire,* X, 2007, p.299.

10   Ibid., p.293.

11   *SHC*, 1915, p.357.

12   Jennings, *History of Staffordshire Bells*, p.30.

13   *VCH, Staffordshire,* X, p.298.

14   *SHC*, 1915, p.357-8.

15   Ibid., p.358-9.

16   Stuart, *Social History of Yoxall*, p.53.

17   Ibid., p.54.

18   *SHC*, 1929, p.132.

19   *VCH, Staffordshire,* II, p.357.

20   Shaw, *Staffordshire,* I, p.332.

21   *VHC, Staffordshire,* X, (2007), p.300.

22   LRO, A/VI/2d.

23   *SHC*, [4th ser.], X, (1980), pp.134-5.

24   Shaw, *Staffordshire,* I, p.102.

25   Ibid., p.101.

26   *SHC*, 1923, p.309.

27   Ibid., 1915, p.358.

28   Ibid.

29   *Burton Chronicle*, 29 June, 1865.

30   Macfarlane, *120 Years a Village Doctor*, p.166.

31   *Burton Chronicle*, 22 November, 1866.

32   Ibid., 29 November, 1866.

33   Ibid., 26 September, 1867.

34   Ibid., 1 July, 1886.

35   Ibid., 17 December, 1896.

36   Ibid., 15 April, 1880.

37   Ibid., 28 September, 1893.

38   Ibid., 17 May, 1894.

39   *Lichfield Mercury*, 27 October, 1922.

40   *SHC*, 1929, p.148-9.

41   Shaw, *Staffordshire,* I, p.101.

42   Robinson, D.B. 'Staffordshire Clergy in 1830', *Transactions for the Staffordshire Archaeological and Historical Society,* 24, (1984 for 1982-3), pp.84-98, p.93.

43   Ibid., p.94.

44   Kelly's, *Dir. Staffordshire,* (1860), p.747.

45   *Burton Chronicle,* 12 November, 1863.

46   Kelly's, *Dir. Staffordshire,* (1880), p.414.

47   *Lichfield Mercury,* 28 May, 1880.

48   *Burton Chronicle*, 1 January, 1880.

49   Ibid., 6 August, 1884.

50   Ibid., 2 October, 1884.

51   Sowerby & Farman, *Burton upon Trent Looking Back,* p. 26.

52   *Burton Chronicle*, 12 November, 1891.

CHAPTER 5

1   *SHC*, 1915, p. 381-2.
2   *VCH, Staffordshire,* X, (2007), p.299.
3   *SHC*, 1915, p.357.
4   Greenslade, *Catholic Staffordshire,* p.93.
5   Stuart, *Social History of Yoxall,* p.67.
6   Greenslade, *Catholic Staffordshire,* p.161.
7   Ibid., p.179.
8   Ibid., p.166.
9   Ibid., p.181.
10 Thorpe, *Woodlane*, p.6.
11 *VCH, Staffordshire,* IX, (2003), p.130.
12 Thorpe, *Woodlane,* p.10.
13 Ibid., p.12.
14 *VCH, Staffordshire,* IX, (2003), p.131.
15 *Burton Chronicle*, 26 October, 1876.
16 Thorpe, *Woodlane*, p.12.
17 Ibid., p.13.
18 *SHC*, [4th ser.], III, (1960), p.135.
19 Ibid., p.9.
20 Ibid., p.54.
21 Ibid., p.72.
22 Ibid., p.93.
23 *Burton Chronicle*, 17 June, 1869.
24 *Ibid.,* 30 June, 1870.
25 Armson, *The History of Yoxall,* unpublished.
26 *Burton Chronicle*, 11 August, 1870.
27 Ibid., 20 April, 1871.
28 Ibid., 5 May, 1881.

CHAPTER 6

1   *SHC*, [new ser.], IV, (1901), pp.240-1.
2   Ibid., [1st ser.], XV, (1894), p.212.
3   Ibid., 1935, p.298.
4   National Archives, WO 25/307.
5   Ibid., WO 25/294.
6   Ibid., WO 25/334.
7   Ibid., WO 25/321.
8   Ibid., WO 25/411.
9   Ibid., WO 100/10.
10 Ibid., WO 97. Chelsea Pensioners British Army Service Records 1760-1913.
11 SRO, L13-/3/2. Overseers Accounts Book, 1809-1828.
12 Harris, *Black Country Vc's,* p.31.
13 National Archives, WO 97/1575.
14 Ibid., WO 22/26.
15 Ibid., WO 23/49.
16 *Burton Chronicle,* 30 November, 1865.
17 Ibid., 20 May, 1869.
18 Ibid., 12 May, 1871.
19 Ibid., 15 September, 1870.

CHAPTER 7

1 *SHC*, [4th ser.], VI, (1970), p.1.
2 Ibid., 1923, pp.170-173.
3 Ibid., 1957, p.90.
4 Shaw, *Staffordshire*, I, p.66.
5 Fisher, *The Arithmeticke Project*, 'The Yoxall Report', unpublished, 2001.
  The final results of the project were published in *Family and Community History,*
  Journal of the Family and Community Historical Research Society,
  Vol. 6, No. 1, May 2003, pp.5-17.
6 Shaw, *Staffordshire,* I, p.99.
7 Ibid.
8 Armson, *The History of Yoxall*, unpublished.
9 *Burton Chronicle*, 15 July, 1880.
10 *VCH, Staffordshire*, X, (2007), p.297.
11 Lynam, *Church Bells of the County of Stafford*, p.593.
12 *VCH, Staffordshire*, X, (2007), p.297.
13 *Burton Chronicle*, 28 July, 1870.
14 *VCH, Staffordshire,* X, (2007), p.297.

CHAPTER 8

1   Whitten, *Nollekens and his Times*, I, p.214.
2   Myer, *Obstinate Heart: Jane Austen,* p.15.
3   Armson, *The History of Yoxall*, unpublished.
4   Kirby, *Kirby's Wonderful and Eccentric Museum,* 4, (2013), pp.344-5.
5   Brabourne edition of Jane Austen's letters, 1799, XVII.
6   Honan, *Jane Austen: Her Life*, p.227.
7   Tomalin, *Jane Austen: A Life*, p.202.
8   Myer, *Obstinate Heart: Jane Austen,* p.137.
9   Halperin, *Jane Austen: Bicentenary Essays*, p.276.
10 Honan, *Jane Austen: A Life,* p.161.
11 Harman, *Jane's Fame: How Jane Austen Conquered the World*, p.56-7.
12 Gisborne, T. *An Enquiry into the Duties of the Female Sex,* [4th edition], (1799),
    p.183.
13 Ibid., p.184.
14 Gisborne, J. *A Brief Memoir of the Life of John Gisborne*, p.211-2.
15 Stott, *Wilberforce Family and Friends*, p.16-17.
16 Lean, *God's Politician: William Wilberforce's Struggle,* p.12.
17 *VCH, Staffordshire,* X, (2007), p.62.
18 Sheppard & Whyte, *Rothley and the Abolition of the Slave Trade,* p.7.
19 Stott, *Wilberforce Family and Friends,* p.61.
20 Lean, *God's Politician: William Wilberforce's Struggle,* p.143.
21 Stott, *Wilberforce Family and Friends,* p.66.
22 Ibid., p.45-6.
23 Gisborne, T. *An Enquiry into the Duties of the Female Sex,* [4th edition], (1799),
    p.62.
24 Ibid., p.59.
25 Ibid., p.60.
26 Gisborne, T. *Walks in a Forest,* [8th edition], (1813), p.99.
27 Ibid., p.333-4.

28 Chitham, *A Life of Anne Brontë,* p.92.

29 Ibid., p.116.

30 Barker, *The Brontës,* p.457.

31 Ibid., pp.333-4.

32 Ibid., p.469.

33 Ibid., p.470.

34 Ibid., p.927, n.97.

35 Jay, (ed.), Gaskell, *The Life of Charlotte Brontë*, p.212.

36 Barker, *The Brontës,* p.492.

37 Jay, (ed.), Gaskell, *The Life of Charlotte Brontë*, p.214.

38 Barker, *The Brontës,* p.551.

39 Jay, (ed.), Gaskell, *The Life of Charlotte Brontë*, p.204-5.

40 Dinsdale, *The Brontës at Haworth*, p.145.

41 *Report of North Staffordshire Naturalists Field Club, 1929-30,* LXIV, p.180.

CHAPTER 9

1 Armson, *The History of Yoxall,* unpublished.

2 Shipman, *A History of Abbots Bromley*, pp.58-9.

3 *Burton Chronicle*, 30 November, 1899.

4 Ibid., 6 December, 1900.

5 Ibid., 24 January, 1901.

6 Carter, 'Notes on Staffordshire Families', *SHC,* 1910, p.283-4.

7 SRO, D730/7/1.

8 Ibid., D1/A/PZ/2.

9 Ibid., D730/3/5.

10 Ibid., D730/3/8.

11 Ibid., D730/3/6.

12 Ibid., D730/3/22.

13 Ibid., D730/3/21.

14 Ibid., D730/3/24.

15 Ibid., D730/3/25.

16 Ibid., L13-/3/2. Overseers Accounts Book 1809-28.

17 Ibid., D730/3/3. Overseers Account Book 1829-1848.

18 Ibid., D730/3/9.

19 Ibid., D730/3/116.

20 Ibid., D730/3/117.

21 Ibid., D730/3/119.

22 Ibid., D730/3/118.

23 Ibid., D730/3/120.

24 *Burton Chronicle*, 20 August, 1896.

25 Ibid., 30 November, 1899.

26 Ibid., 6 December, 1900.

27 *VCH, Staffordshire,* X, (2007), p.296.

28 *Burton Chronicle*, 27 January, 1887.

29 Ibid., 22 March, 1888.

30 Ibid., 23 January, 1890.

31 Ibid., 27 December, 1894.

32 Ibid., 1 January, 1885.

33 Ibid., 4 March, 1897.

34 Ibid., 12 November, 1896.

35   Ibid., 3 December, 1896.
36   Ibid., 24 January, 1901.

CHAPTER 10

1   *VCH, Staffordshire,* X, 2007, p.293.
2   Parson & Bradshaw, *Dir. Staffordshire,* (1818), p.47.
3   SRO, D730/8/6.
4   Ibid., D1/A/PZ/1.
5   Ibid., D730/8/12.
6   LRO, B/C/5/1832/12-14; *Lichfield Mercury,* 4 July, 1823.
7   *Lichfield Mercury,* 1 July, 1831.
8   LRO, B/C/5/1832/12-14.
9   *VCH, Staffordshire,* X, 2007, p.294.
10 SRO, D1/A/PZ/26.
11 *VCH, Staffordshire,* X, (2007), p.294.
12 SRO, D730/3/8.
13 WI, *Staffordshire Within Living Memory,* p. 246.
14 *Burton Chronicle,* 8 September, 1881.
15 Ibid., 24 March, 1887.
16 SRO, D730/8/1.
17 *Burton Chronicle*, 8 October, 1896.
18 Ibid., 22 October, 1896.
19 SRO, D730/8/1.
20 Ibid.
21 Kelly's, *Dir. Staffordshire,* (1924), p.632.
22 WLHC, Meikle Collection: *Middle of the Midlands*, 63/1.
23 Kelly's, *Dir. Staffordshire,* (1916), p.230.
24 Ibid., 1872, p.636.
25 *VCH, Staffordshire,* X, (2007), p.311.
26 Kelly's, *Dir. Staffordshire,* (1880), p.156.
27 Evans, *Hoar Cross Hall: Portrait of a Victorian Country House,* p.70.
28 *Burton Chronicle*, 5 October, 1893.
29 Ibid., 21 November, 1895.
30 *VCH, Staffordshire,* X, (2007), p.311.
31 *Burton Chronicle,* 5 June, 1890.
32 Ibid., 6 August, 1891.
33 White, *Dir. Staffordshire,* (1834), p.472.
34 Pigot, *Dir. Staffordshire,* (1835), p.392.
35 *Burton Chronicle*, 21 September, 1876.
36 Ibid., 17 July, 1879.
37 Kelly's, *Dir. Staffordshire,* (1896), p.524.
38 *Derby Mercury,* 20 April, 1859

CHAPTER 11

1   Parson & Bradshaw, *Dir. Staffordshire,* (1818), pp.46-7.
2   White, *Dir. Staffordshire,* (1834), pp.472-3.
3   Kain & Prince, *Tithe Surveys for Historians,* p.111.
4   Kelly's, *Dir. Staffordshire,* (1896), p.534.
5   *SHC,* (1950/51), Appendix.

6   Kelly's, *Dir. Staffordshire,* (1872), p.860.
7   *Burton Chronicle*, 1 February, 1877.
8   Ibid., 25 August, 1892.
9   Ibid., 14 December, 1865.
10   Ibid., 8 March, 1866.
11   Ibid., 15 March, 1866.
12   Ibid., 17 April, 1881.
13   Ibid., 22 December, 1881.
14   Ibid., 7 September, 1882.
15   Ibid., 19 October, 1882.
16   Butcher & Kings Bromley Historians, *Snippets of the History of Kings Bromley,* p.16.
17   *Burton Chronicle*, 12 July, 1894.
18   Ibid., 15 October, 1896.
19   Ibid., 4 March, 1901.
20   Private collection.
21   Butcher & Kings Bromley Historians, *Snippets of the History of Kings Bromley,* p.16.
22   *Burton Chronicle*, 9 October, 1880.
23   Ibid., 6 October, 1887.
24   Ibid., 9 October, 1890.
25   Ibid., 7 October, 1897.
26   Ibid., 30 June, 1887.
27   Ibid., 3 April, 1890.
28   Kelly's, *Dir. Staffordshire,* (1860), p.747.
29   *Burton Chronicle*, 4 February, 1869.
30   Ibid., 6 January, 1876.
31   Ibid., 19 January, 1893.
32   *The London Gazette*, 6 September, 1892.
33   *Burton Chronicle*, 4 December, 1879.
34   *VCH, Staffordshire*, X, (2007), p.290.
35   Ibid.
36   Job, *Staffordshire Windmills,* p.48.
37   Horne, 'Historical Notes on Staffordshire Windmills', *Staffordshire Life,* Vol.6, No.1, (1954), p.23.
38   Job, *Staffordshire Windmills,* p.49.
39   Smith, *My Life as a Country Child in and around Yoxall,* p.14.
40   LRO, B/A/15/752.
41   Ibid., B/A/15.
42   Raven, *Staffordshire and the Black Country*, p.400.
43   Sherlock, *Industrial Archaeology of Staffordshire*, p.69.
44   Stuart, *Yoxall: a walk through history,* p.5.
45   Sherlock, *Industrial Archaeology of Staffordshire*, pp.67-8.
46   SRO, 653.
47   VCH, X, p.291.
48   White, *Dir. Staffordshire,* (1834), p.472.
49   Ibid., (1851), p.614.
50   Harrod, *Dir. Staffordshire,* (1870), p.1151.
51   Kelly's, *Dir. Staffordshire,* (1880), p.41.
52   Ibid., (1896), p.524.
53   Stuart, *Yoxall: walk through history,* p.5.

54 White, *Dir. Staffordshire,* (1851), p.614.
55 Kelly's, *Dir. Staffordshire,* (1880), p.414.
56 Randall, *History of the Meynell Hounds and Country, 1780-1901*, Vol.1, p.26.
57 Ibid., p.88.
58 Armson, *The History of Yoxall*, unpublished.
59 Randall, *History of the Meynell Hounds and Country, 1780-1901*, Vol.1, p.179.
60 Ibid., p.303.
61 Ibid.
62 Ibid., p.306.
63 Ibid., Vol.2, p.179.
64 Parson & Bradshaw, *Dir. Staffordshire,* p.47.

CHAPTER 12

1   White, *Dir. Staffordshire,* (1851), p.614.
2   SRO, D730/7/1.
3   *Burton Chronicle*, 30 August, 1883.
4   Ibid., 3 September, 1891.
5   Macfarlane, *120 Years a Village Doctor,* p.116.
6   *Burton Chronicle*, 24 November, 1892.
7   Pigot, *Dir. Staffordshire,* (1835), p.392.
8   White, *Dir. Staffordshire,* (1834).
9   Private collection.
10 Ibid.
11 *VCH, Staffordshire,* 11, (1967), p.221.
12 Shaw, *Staffordshire,* I, p.101.
13 Pitt, *Staffordshire,* (1817), p.59.
14 Raven, *Staffordshire and the Black Country*, (1988), p.399.
15 *VCH, Staffordshire,* X, (2007), p.191.
16 Ridware History Society, *The Ridwares: A Brief History for the Millennium*, p.14.
17 Parson & Bradshaw, *Dir. Staffordshire,* (1818), p.46.
18 SRO, 6944/1/1-2.
19 White, *Dir. Staffordshire,* (1834), p.472.
20 Stuart, *Yoxall: a walk through history,* p.7.
21 Fisher, *A Measure of Migrants*, unpublished Open University Project, (1995).
22 White, *Dir. Staffordshire,* (1851), p.737.
23 *Burton Chronicle*, 18 May, 1871.
24 White, *Dir. Staffordshire,* (1834), p.472.
25 Ibid., p.473.
26 Kelly's, *Dir. Staffordshire,* (1860), p.747.
27 Harrod, *Dir. Staffordshire,* (1870), p.1151.
28 Kelly's, *Dir. Staffordshire,* (1896), p.524, also (1900), p.546.
29 Ibid., (1908), p.593.
30 Ibid., (1912), p.605.
31 Ibid., (1924), p.633.
32 Ibid., (1896), p.524.
33 *Burton Chronicle,* 3 June, 1875.
34 Ibid., 9 October, 1890.
35 Ibid., 6 October, 1892.
36 Ibid., 5 October, 1893.

37   Ibid., 5 January, 1871.
38   Ibid., 11 January, 1871.
39   Stuart, *Yoxall: a walk through history,* p.17.

CHAPTER 13

1   Smith, *Wild Strawberries*, p.32.
2   Stuart, *Social History of Yoxall*, p.16.
3   Stephen, (ed.), *National Dictionary of Biography*, III, (1885), p.9.
4   SRO, Paget Papers: D603/K/16/31.
5   Shaw, *Staffordshire,* I, p.99.
6   *Burton Chronicle*, 6 February, 1862.
7   Ibid., 4 and 25 July, 1861.
8   Ibid., 6 November, 1879.
9   Macfarlane, *120 Years a Village Doctor,* p.171.
10   Ibid., pp.171-2.
11   Burton on Trent Management Committee, *Meynell-Ingram Cottage Hospital Yoxall*, p.1.
12   Stuart, *Yoxall: a walk through history,* p.10.
13   Burton on Trent Management Committee, *Meynell-Ingram Cottage Hospital Yoxall*, p.4.
14   *Burton Chronicle*, 24 June, 1886.
15   Ibid., 8 April, 1897.
16   Ibid., 6 May, 1897.
17   *Burton Mail*, 3 February, 1959.

CHAPTER 14

1   *SHC*, [1st ser.], XIII, (1892), p.107.
2   Ibid., [1st ser.], XVII, (1896), p.11-12.
3   Ibid., p.17.
4   Ibid., VI, (1), (1903), p.133.
5   Ibid., (1927), p.137.
6   Ibid., (1935), p.323-4.
7   Ibid., (1935), p.418.
8   Ibid., (1947), p.93.
9   WLHC, Meikle Collection, *Middle of the Midlands*, 63/1.
10   *Burton Chronicle*, 26 November, 1874.
11   WLHC, Meikle Collection, *Middle of the Midlands*, 63/1.
12   *Burton Chronicle*, 31 December, 1874.
13   Ibid., 31 October, 1872.
14   Ibid., 13 August, 1885.
15   Ibid., 2 June, 1881.
16   Ibid., 2 January, 1896.
17   Ibid., 6 May, 1875.
18   Ibid., 15 July, 1879.
19   Ibid., 14 January, 1886.
20   Ibid., 15 July, 1886.
21   Ibid., 20 June, 1889.
22   Ibid., 27 June, 1889.
23   Ibid., 14 April, 1892.

24   Ibid., 13 July, 1893.
25   Ibid., 20 July, 1893.
26   Ibid., 28 December, 1893.
27   Ibid., 20 April, 1899.
28   Ibid., 8 March, 1900.
29   Ibid., 11 July, 1901.
30   Ibid., 15 July, 1886.
31   Ibid., 19 December, 1895.
32   Ibid., 13 February, 1896.
33   SRO, D730/8/1.
34   *Burton Chronicle*, 22 September, 1898.
35   Ibid., 4 November, 1869.
36   Ibid., 11 November, 1869.
37   Ibid., 23 March, 1871; *Staffordshire Advertiser*, 25 March and 8 April, 1871.
38   Ibid., 24 September, 1863.
39   Ibid., 10 January, 1884.
40   Ibid., 10 June, 1886.
41   Ibid., 14 November, 1867.
42   Ibid., 21 November, 1867.
43   Ibid., 3 June, 1869.
44   Ibid., 1 July, 1869.
45   Ibid., 9 December, 1869.
46   Ibid., 17 June, 1879.
47   Ibid., 27 August, 1879.
48   Ibid., 27 September, 1866.
49   Ibid., 29 May, 1890.
50   Ibid., 20 October, 1870.
51   Ibid., 11 February, 1872.
52   Ibid., 31 May, 1877.
53   Ibid., 2 August, 1877.
54   Ibid., 10 August, 1882.
55   Ibid., 23 August, 1888.
56   SRO, 6944/1-2.

CHAPTER 15

1   White, *Dir. Staffordshire,* (1834), p.472.
2   *Burton Chronicle*, 25 October, 1866.
3   Ibid., 11 June, 1868.
4   Ibid., 17 February, 1870.
5   Ibid., 25 May, 1871.
6   Ibid., 17 August, 1871.
7   Ibid., 9 November, 1871.
8   Ibid., 20 February, 1872.
9   Ibid., 24 March, 1872.
10   Ibid., 10 October, 1872.
11   Ibid., 25 October, 1872.
12   Ibid., 21 April, 1881.
13   Ibid., 8 September, 1881.
14   Ibid., 2 November, 1882.
15   Ibid., 9 August, 1883.

16   Ibid., 20 August, 1885.
17   Ibid., 26 November, 1868.
18   Ibid., 1 September, 1870.
19   Ibid., 11 December, 1873.
20   Ibid., 6 June, 1878.
21   Ibid., 5 July, 1894.
22   Ibid., 5 June, 1879.
23   Ibid., 16 August, 1894.
24   Ibid., 25 April, 1895.
25   Ibid., 16 July, 1896.
26   Ibid., 4 July, 1895.
27   Ibid., 17 November, 1898.
28   Ibid., 25 March, 1897.
29   Ibid., 22 April, 1897.
30   Ibid., 11 November, 1875.
31   Ibid., 4 March, 1880.
32   Ibid., 3 September, 1891.
33   Ibid., 19 October, 1899.
34   Ibid., 24 October, 1895.
35   Ibid., 28 January, 1868.
36   Ibid., 6 June, 1878.
37   Ibid., 3 June, 1880.
38   Ibid., 5 May, 1881.
39   Ibid., 7 June, 1883.
40   Ibid., 4 June, 1885.
41   SRO, D730/3/8, Diary or Log Book Yoxall Church of England School.
42   *Burton Chronicle*, 5 November, 1885.
43   Ibid., 19 January, 1888.
44   Ibid., 23 May, 1889.
45   Ibid., 20 June, 1889.
46   Ibid., 7 December, 1893.
47   Ibid., 4 June, 1896.
48   Ibid., 6 July, 1899.

CHAPTER 16

1   *Government Gazette*, 6 July, 1878, p.3.
2   *Police Gazette of South Wales*, 1854-1930, p.221-2.

CHAPTER 17

1   Information on the insurance document thanks to Ian Galloway.
2   Parson & Bradshaw, *Dir. Staffordshire,* (1818), p.47.
3   *Burton Chronicle*, 29 June, 1865.
4   Ibid., 24 August, 1865.
5   Ibid., 29 December, 1870.
6   Ibid., 4 August, 1881.
7   Ibid., 11 August, 1881.
8   Ibid., 18 August, 1881.
9   Ibid., 31 August, 1893.
10   Ibid., 21 February, 1878.

11 Ibid., 4 January, 1892.
12 Ibid., 18 May, 1886.
13 *Staffordshire Advertiser*, 30 September, 1848.
14 SRO, D730/7/1.
15 SRO, *Ibid.*
16 *Burton Chronicle,* 28 October, 1875.
17 Ibid., 13 November, 1890.
18 Sowerby & Farman, *Burton upon Trent Looking Back,* pp.26-7.
19 *Burton Chronicle*, 29 June, 1876.
20 Ibid., 15 February, 1894.
21 Ibid., 1 March, 1894.
22 Ibid., 26 May, 1898.
23 Ibid., 2 June, 1898.
24 Ibid., 3 January, 1901.

CHAPTER 18

1 Redfern, *Uttoxeter*, p.47.
2 *Burton Chronicle*, 27 April, 1871.
3 Plot, *Staffordshire*, 1686, (1973), p.319.
4 *Burton Chronicle*, 26 September, 1889.
5 Ibid., 15 August, 1867.
6 Ibid., 13 July, 1876.
7 Ibid., 22 July, 1886.
8 *Lichfield Mercury*, 11 April, 1879.
9 *Burton Chronicle*, 10 April, 1879.
10 *Lichfield Mercury*, 28 June, 1878; *Burton Chronicle*, 4 July, 1878.
11 *Burton Chronicle*, 29 May, 1879.
12 Ibid., 24 June, 1880.
13 Ibid., 31 October, 1895.
14 Not among LRO wills and inventories but quoted by Carter, 'Notes on Staffs. Families', *S.H.C.* (1910) p.283-4.

CHAPTER 19

1 Macfarlane, *120 Years a Village Doctor*, p.118.
2 Ibid., p.118-9.
3 Ibid., p.118.
4 WLHC, Meikle Collection, *Middle of the Midlands*, 63/1.
5 *Burton Chronicle*, 6 November, 1879.
6 WLHC, Meikle Collection, *Middle of the Midlands*, 63/1.
7 Stephen, *The Life of Sir James Fitzjames Stephen, Bart.,* p.18.
8 http//www.stokemuseums.org.uk/blog/potted-histories-john-brown-1783-1853/.

CHAPTER 20

1 *Burton Chronicle*, 4 May, 1864.
2 Ibid., 23 April, 1885.
3 Ibid., 12 November, 1891.
4 Ibid., 12 November, 1896.
5 Ibid., 2 December, 1886.

6   Ibid., 6 February, 1868.
7   Ibid., 12 March, 1868.
8   Ibid., 28 January, 1869.
9   Ibid., 27 August, 1868.
10   Ibid., 30 December, 1880.
11   Ibid., 5 February, 1891.
12   'When 'Pop' Lester was Yoxall's Oldest Active Cricketer', *The Bugle*, June 1994.
13   *St Peter's Church and Village Magazine*, January, 2000.
14   *Burton Chronicle*, 30 August, 1894.
15   Ibid., 27 August, 1896.
16   Ibid., 5 August, 1880.
17   Ibid., 30 June, 1898.
18   Ibid., 29 December, 1898.
19   Ibid., 13 July, 1899.
20   Ibid., 7 March, 1889.
21   Ibid., 7 June, 1877.
22   Ibid., 16 September, 1880.
23   Ibid., 5 March, 1863.
24   Ibid., 19 March, 1863.
25   Ibid., 23 June, 1887.
26   Ibid., 24 June, 1897.
27   Ibid., 24 May, 1900.
28   Ibid., 9 June, 1900.
29   Ibid., 3 August, 1905.
30   Ibid., 3 February, 1898.
31   Ibid., 9 April, 1906.
32   National Library of New Zealand, *Marlborough Express*, Vol.XXXIX, Issue 146, 25 June, 1906.

Bibliography

Armson, F.G.A., *The History of Yoxall,* unpublished.

Austen-Leigh, J.E., *A Memoir of Jane Austen,* publisher unknown, 1870.

Australian Dictionary of Biography, [online] available at:
http://adbonline.anu.edu.au/biogs/A010027b.htm

Barker, J., 2nd ed., *The Brontës,* London: Weidenfeld & Nicolson, 1998.

Beresford, W., *Diocesan Histories,* Society for the Promotion of Christian Knowledge, n.d.

Blore, G., *Dicky Blood's War,* Dreamstar Books, 2003.

Brabourn edition, *Letters of Jane Austen,* 1799, XVII [online] available at:
http://www.pemberley.com/janeinfo/brablets.html pp.1-8 [Accessed 14/01/2016]

Burton Chronicle, dates as cited in chapters and notes.

Burton Mail, dates as cited in chapters and notes.

Burton Observer, dates as cited in chapters and notes.

Butcher, I., and the Kings Bromley Historians, *Snippets of the History of Kings Bromley,* Lichfield: The Lichfield Press, 2001.

Carter, W.F., 'Notes on Staffs. Families', *SHC* 1910.

Chetwynd-Stapleton, H.E., *The Chetwynds of Ingestre,* London: Longmans Green, 1892.

Chitham, E., *A Life of Anne Brontë,* Oxford: Blackwell, 1991.

Dinsdale, A., *The Brontës at Haworth,* London: Frances Lincoln, 2006.

Erdswick, S., *A Survey of Staffordshire,* London: J.B. Nichols & Son, 1820.

Evans, G., *Hoar Cross Hall Staffordshire: Portrait of a Victorian Country House,* Stafford: Stowefields, 1994.

Field, J., 2nd ed., *English Field Names: A Dictionary,* Newton Abbot: David & Charles, 1982.

Fisher, S., *A Measure of Migrants,* unpublished Open University Project, 1995.

Fisher, S., *The Arithmeticke Project,* unpublished FACHRS Project, 2001.

Gaskell, E., *The Life of Charlotte Brontë,* 1857, reprinted Jay, E., ed., London: Penguin Books, 1997.

Gisborne, J., *A Brief Memoir of the Life of John Gisborne, to Which Are Added Extracts From His Diary,* 1852, reprinted in the United States of America, n.d.

Gisborne, T., 4th ed., *An Enquiry Into the Duties of the Female Sex,* London, 1799, Reproduction of the British Library, Eighteenth Century Collections Online, print edition, n.d.

Government Gazette, 6 July, 1878. [online] Available at:
http://trove.nla.gov.au/ndp/del/article/28394228?search Term=robert Sutcliffe mort&seachLimits= [Accessed 30/01/2014]

Greenslade, M., *Catholic Staffordshire 1500-1850,* Leominster: Gracewing, 2006.

Halperin, J., ed., *Jane Austen: Bicentenary Essays,* Cambridge: Cambridge University Press, 1975. Harman, C., *Jane's Fame: How Jane Austen Conquered the World,* Edinburgh: Canongate Books, 2009.

Harris, B., *'Black Country Vcs',* Black Country Society, 1985.

Harrod, J.G. & Co., *Postal and Commercial Directory of Staffordshire,* Norwich: J.G. Harrod & Co., 1870.

Hislop, M., 'Reeve End Cottage, Yoxall: A Medieval Aisled Timber-Framed Cottage', *South Staffordshire Archaeological and Historical Society Transactions for 1985-1986,* Vol.XXVII. Walsall, 1987, pp.48-52.

Hislop, M., 'Two Medieval Houses in East Staffordshire', *South Staffordshire Archaeological and Historical Soc. Trans.*, Vol.XXXVIII. Walsall, 1999, pp.32-48.

Honan, P., *Jane Austen: Her Life,* London: Max Press, 2007.

Horne, J.S., 'Historical Notes on Staffordshire Windmills', *Staffordshire Life and County Pictorial,* 6, I, Spring 1954.

Horovitz, D., *The Place-Names of Staffordshire,* Brewood: David Horovitz, 2005.

Housecroft, B., *Olde Yoxall,* unpublished, n.d.

Jansen, S.L. and Jordan, K.H., *The Welles Anthology: MS. Rawlinson C. 183,* New York: Medieval & Renaissance Texts and Studies, 1991.

Jennings, T.S., *A History of Staffordshire Bells,* London: publisher unknown, 1968.

Jervoise, E., *Ancient Bridges of Mid and Eastern England,* written on behalf of The Society for the Protection of Ancient Buildings. London: The Architectural Press, 1932.

Job, B., *Staffordshire Windmills,* Midland Wind and Water Group, Birmingham, 1985.

Johnson, D.A. and Vaisey, D.G. eds., *Staffordshire and the Great Rebellion,* Staffordshire County Council, Council Records Committee, 1964?

Kain, R.J.P. & Prince, H.C., *Tithe Surveys for Historians,* Chichester: Phillimore, 2000.

Kelly's Directories of Staffordshire, 1860, 1872, 1880 and 1896 Part 1.

Kettle, A., ed., 'A List of Families in the Archdeaconry of Stafford, 1532-3', *SHC,* 4th ser. VIII. Staffordshire Record Society, 1976, pp.172-4.

Kingsley, N., *Landed Families of Britain and Ireland,* 2015, [online] available at: http;//landedfamilies.blogspot.co.uk.170-arden-of-park-hall-and-longcroft.html. [Accessed 28/10/2015]

Kirby, R.S., *Kirby's Wonderful and Eccentric Museum; Or Magazine of Remarkable Characters,* 4, 1820, reprinted 2013. London: Forgotten Books.

Lean, G., *God's Politician: William Wilberforce's Struggle,* London: Darton, Longford & Todd, 2007.

Lichfield Mercury, dates as cited in chapters and notes.

London Gazettee, dates as cited in chapters and notes.

Lynam, C., *Church Bells of the County of Stafford,* publisher unknown, 1889.

Macfarlane, E., *120 Years a Village Doctor: memoirs of Dr Gerald Armson,* Blurb, 2013.

Marlborough Express XXXIX, Issue 146, 25 June, 1906, National Library of New Zealand.

Meynell-Ingram Cottage Hospital Yoxall 1873-1973, Burton on Trent Management Committee, 1973.

Miller, B., *Potted Histories: John Brown 1783-1853,* [online] available at: http://www.stokemuseums.org.uk/blog/potted-histories-john-brown-1783-1853/ [Accessed 21/11/2016]

Morris, C., ed., 2nd ed., *The Illustrated Journeys of Celia Fiennes 1685-c.1712,* London, Alan Sutton, 1995.

Myer, V.G., *Obstinate Heart: Jane Austen, A Biography*, London: Michael O'Mara Books, 1997.

Marlborough Express XXXIX, 146, 25 June, 1906. National Library of New Zealand.

New South Wales Police Gazette, 1854-1930. 11 October, 1882, [online] available at: http://interactive.ancesterylibrary.com/Print/1942/31842_216741-00275? [Accessed 14/10/2013]

Palliser, D.M., 'Staffordshire Castles: A Provisional List', *Staffordshire Archaeology,* 1. 1972.

Palliser, D.M., *The Staffordshire Landscape,* London: Hodder and Stoughton, 1976.

Parson W. and Bradshaw, T., *Staffordshire General and Commercial Directory for 1818,* Manchester, 1818.

Pevsner, N., 2nd ed. *The Buildings of England: Staffordshire,* Handsworth: Penguin, 1975.

Pigot & Co., *Historical and Occupational Trade Directory of Staffordshire,* publisher unknown, 1835.

Plot, R., *The Natural History of Staffordshire,* Oxford, 1686. Reprinted Manchester: E.J. Morton, 1973.

Pitt, W., *A Topographical History of Staffordshire,* Newcastle under Lyme, publisher unknown, 1817.

Randall, J.L., *History of the Meynell Hounds and Country, 1780-1901*, I & II. London: S. Low Marston & Co., 1901.

Raven, M., *Staffordshire and the Black Country,* Stafford: Michael Raven, 1988.

Redfern, F., *History and antiquities of the town and neighbourhood of Uttoxeter,* London: Simpkin, Marshall, & Co., 1886.

The Bugle, June, 1994.

The Ridwares: A Brief History for the Millennium, Ridware History Society, 2000.

Robinson, D.B., 'Staffordshire Clergy in 1830', *Transactions for the Staffordshire Archaeological and Historical Society,* 24, 1984 for 1982-3, pp.84-98

Shaw, S., *The History and Antiquities of Staffordshire,* I. London, 1798; reprinted with additions, Wakefield: E.P. Publishing, 1976.

Sheppard, T. and Whyte, I., *Rothley and the Abolition of the Slave Trade,* Leicester: Rothley Heritage Trust, 2007.

Sherlock, R., *Industrial Archaeology of Staffordshire,* Newton Abbot: David & Charles, 1976.

Shipman, E.R., *A History of Abbots Bromley,* Abbots Bromley Council, 1996.

Smith, D., *Wild Strawberries,* Dartford: publisher unknown, 2011.

Smith, J., *My Life as a Country Child in and around Yoxall, Staffordshire,* Burton on Trent: publisher unknown, 2007.

Smith, T., 2nd ed., *Nollekens and His Times,* London: Henry Colburn, 1829.

Sowerby G. and Farman, R., *East Staffordshire Needwood Forest to the Weaver Hills,* Stroud: Chalford, 1995.

Sowerby, G. and Farman, R., *Images of England: Burton upon Trent Looking Back,* Stroud: Tempus, 1995.

Staffordshire County Council, *Historic Environment Charter Assessment*: *East Staffordshire*, August 2013.

Staffordshire Historical Collections, publications of the William Salt Archaeological Society, and later Staffordshire Record Office.

Stephen, L., ed., *Dictionary of National Biography*, III, London: Smith, Elder & Co., 1885.

Stephen, L., *The Life of Sir James Fitzjames Stephen, Bart., K.C.S.I: A Judge of the High Court of Justice,* publisher unknown, 1906.

Stott, A., *Wilberforce Family and Friends,* Oxford: Oxford University Press, 2012.

Stuart, D., ed., *The Yoxall Bridge-Ashbourne Turnpike Road 1766-1889,* Keele: University of Keele, 1979.

Stuart, D., ed., *Yoxall: a walk through history,* Keele: Dept. of Adult Education, University of Keele, 1979.

Stuart, D., *Abbots Bromley: A Glimpse into the Past,* Keele: University of Keele, 1981.

Stuart, D., ed., *A Social History of Yoxall in the Sixteenth and Seventeenth Centuries,* Keele: University of Keele, 1990.

Thompson, ed., *Report of the Staffordshire Naturalists Field Club, 1929-1930*, LXIV. Stafford: Alison & Bowen, 1930.

Thorpe, R. and B., eds., *A History of the Chapel of St Francis of Sales, Woodlane, Yoxall 1704-1994,* unpublished, 1994.

Townsend, P., ed., *Burke's Landed Gentry,* London: Burke's Peerage, 1969, pp.15-17.

Tomalin, C., *Jane Austen: A Life,* London: Penguin Books, 1998.

Tringham, N.J., ed., *Barton-under-Needwood in 1881: A Study of the Barton Census for 1881,* Barton local residents, 1983.

The Victoria History of the Counties of England, Staffordshire volumes as indicated in notes.

White, W., *History, Gazetteer, and Directory of Staffordshire,* Sheffield, publisher unknown, 1834 and 1851.

Wesley, W., *A History and Description of the Town and Borough of Burton upon Trent, with notices of surrounding villages,* publisher unknown, n.d.

Whitten, W., ed., *Nollekens and his Times*, I, publisher unknown, 1920.

Williams, A. and Mallett, W.H., *Staffordshire Towns and Villages,* publisher unknown, n.d.

Staffordshire Federation of Women's Institutes, *Staffordshire Within Living Memory,* Newbury: Countryside Books, and the SFWI, Stafford, 1992.

Yates, B., *The South Staffordshire Railway,* I, Usk: publisher unknown, 2010.